Management and Industrial Relations Series

4

Industrial relations and management strategy

Management and Industrial Relations Series

Edited for the Social Science Research Council by

DOROTHY WEDDERBURN
Principal of Bedford College, London

MICHAEL BROMWICH
Professor of Finance and Accounting, University of Reading

and

DOUGLAS BROOKS
Director, Walker Brooks and Partners

Social science research has much to contribute to the better understanding and solution of problems in the field of management and industrial relations. The difficulty, however, is that there is frequently a gap between the researcher and the practitioner who wants to use the research results. This new series is designed to make available to practitioners in the relevant fields the results of the best research which the Social Science Research Council (SSRC) has supported in the fields of management and industrial relations. The subjects covered and the style adopted will appeal to managers, trade unionists and administrators because there will be an emphasis upon the practical implications of research findings. But the volumes will also serve as a useful introduction to particular areas for students and teachers of management and industrial relations.

The series is jointly produced by the Cambridge University Press and the Social Science Research Council.

Other books in the series

1 *Lost managers: supervisors in industry and society* by JOHN CHILD and BRUCE PARTRIDGE
2 *Tackling discrimination in the workplace: an analysis of sex discrimination in Britain* by BRIAN CHIPLIN and PETER SLOANE
3 *Inflation accounting: an introduction to the debate* by GEOFFREY WHITTINGTON

Industrial relations and management strategy

KEITH THURLEY
Professor in Industrial Relations (with special reference to Personnel Management), London School of Economics

and

STEPHEN WOOD
Lecturer in Industrial Relations, London School of Economics

CAMBRIDGE UNIVERSITY PRESS

Cambridge
London   New York   New Rochelle
Melbourne   Sydney

Published by the Press Syndicate of the University of Cambridge
The Pitt Building, Trumpington Street, Cambridge CB2 1RP
32 East 57th Street, New York, NY 10022, USA
296 Beaconsfield Parade, Middle Park, Melbourne 3206, Australia

First published 1983

Printed in the United States of America

Library of Congress catalogue card number: 82-23464

British Library cataloguing in publication data

Industrial relations and management strategy. –
(Management and industrial relations; 4)
1. Industrial relations
2. Industrial management
I. Thurley, Keith E.   II. Wood, Stephen
III. Series
658.3'15   HG971

ISBN 0 521 25287 3 hard covers
ISBN 0 521 27277 7 paperback

VB

Contents

Contents

Acknowledgements

This book is the result of a special SSRC seminar series which culminated in a two-day conference at which the papers included in the book were originally presented. In many cases they have been substantially redrafted. As such we would like to thank the SSRC for the initiation and support of this seminar. We would particularly like to mention the help and support we received from Professor Dorothy Wedderburn in her role as both chairperson of the SSRC Management and Industrial Relations Committee and one of the editors of this series, and Gerda Loosemore Reppen, who as a representative of the SSRC attended and contributed to both the conference and the meetings prior to it. Apart from the contributors to this book, the conference was attended by several others who acted as discussants and/or session leaders. We would thus also like to thank the following for their help: Richard Brown, Professor A. Eccles, Arthur Francis, Professor L. Hunter, Ken Jones, Theo Nichols, Ed Rhodes, Professor B. C. Roberts, Stuart Timperley.

We would also like to acknowledge the contribution made to the development of the SSRC initiative by three people who were unfortunately not able to attend the conference: Professor J. B. F. Goodman, Professor H. Clegg and Professor H. A. Turner. John Goodman was the organizer of the series of seminars which preceded this special series and helped us considerably in developing our application for its continuation.

Finally we would like to thank Mrs Anne Morris and Ms Sue Allen who helped in the organization of the conference and typed much of the manuscript.

Contributors

KEITH THURLEY (Editor), *Professor of Industrial Relations, London School of Economics and Political Science*

STEPHEN WOOD (Editor), *Lecturer in Industrial Relations, London School of Economics and Political Science*

A. J. ARTHURS *Lecturer in Industrial Relations, University of Bath*

C. J. BREWSTER *Research and Development Manager, Employment Relations Ltd*

C. G. GILL *Lecturer in Management Studies, University of Cambridge*

J. G. GILLIES *Assistant Director, Industrial Relations Research Unit, St Edmund Hall, Oxford*

HOWARD GOSPEL *Lecturer in Industrial Relations, Kent University*

JOHN HENLEY *Lecturer in Business Studies, Edinburgh University*

RAY LOVERIDGE *Professor of Manpower Management, University of Aston Management Centre*

MICK MARCHINGTON *Senior Lecturer in Industrial Relations, Preston Polytechnic*

A. I. MARSH *Senior Research Fellow, Industrial Relations Research Unit, St Edmund Hall, Oxford*

JOHN PURCELL *University Lecturer in Management Studies (Industrial Relations), Oxford and Fellow of the Oxford Centre for Management Studies*

S. RICHBELL *Lecturer in Industrial Relations, Sheffield University*

PETER SEGLOW *Lecturer in Sociology, Brunel University*

viii

Contributors

TONY SHAFTO *Senior Lecturer in Economics, Lanchester Polytechnic, Coventry*

DAVID SIMPSON *Lecturer in Industrial Relations, University College, Cardiff*

ROBIN SMITH *Senior Lecturer in Industrial Relations, Durham University Business School*

A. W. J. THOMSON *Professor of Business Policy, Glasgow University*

SHAUN TYSON *Senior Lecturer in Personnel Management, Cranfield School of Management*

1

Introduction

KEITH THURLEY and STEPHEN WOOD

It has frequently been stated that the academic study of industrial relations in Great Britain has concentrated on the labour movement and therefore neglected the study of management. This assumption led to the creation of a seminar series on the role of management in industrial relations. This book is a collection of the papers presented at the final conference of the last seminar series, and an attempt to draw together the central points discussed by the participants and debate the critical issues facing future research.

The debate on management in industrial relations has moved ground over the course of preparation of the book. At the start, it was concerned with the sterility of recent discussion about managerial actions in industrial relations in the UK (Thurley, 1975; Wood, 1982). This led to a discussion of the different perspectives in industrial relations and of the different views of management itself. In organizing the seminar, we distinguished three perspectives according to their degree of concern for the concept of *strategy*. The first argued the need to relate industrial relations strategy to corporate strategy. The second treated industrial relations strategy as important but as relatively autonomous, its creation reflecting the growth of a professional, self-conscious approach to labour problems. Finally, the third stressed the informal and spontaneous nature of industrial relations (that is, the lack of strategic thinking).

Underlying the three focuses are three different organizational models. The first takes a pluralistic view, in which the political nature of organizations and the fluid nature of organizational life are stressed. This is because different interest groups are not simply competing for resources, but are also, implicitly or explicitly, trying to influence the overall direction of the organization, that is, the organizational strategy. The second takes a functional and top-down view of organizations, in which

1

both personnel and industrial relations management and corporate strategy are seen as specialist functions although the latter is ultimately the prerogative of the board. The third also takes a functional view but stresses that industrial relations is essentially about production, and that specialists in industrial relations, if they exist, are servicing and training line management. The emphasis here is on both employees and managers coping (almost on a day-to-day basis and perhaps in conflicting ways) with the uncertainties and fluctuations in both production systems, and labour and product markets.

We cannot pretend that the theoretical problems raised by these different approaches are not complex and are as yet difficult to unravel and articulate. Certainly the conventional terms in which industrial relations theorizing has been discussed (for example pluralism versus Marxism) seem inadequate for this purpose. We found that we could not even distinguish various approaches by their degree of determinism or the extent to which they depict managements as having choices. In the third group, for example, it might be argued that corporate strategy is irrelevant as the course of the organization is determined by its environment, or alternatively, that it can be taken as a 'given' for the purpose of industrial relations, which is seen as being essentially about operational management.

The study of strategy will be of little concern to those who see economic laws as sovereign, determining the course of organizational life in such a way that management has no choice, so that both its objectives and the best way of pursuing them are given; managers cannot, and hence do not, have the kind of autonomy which the term strategy conveys. The idea of strategy, however, *does* seem to imply an external force or forces which one must anticipate and try and come to terms with; strategic thinking arises from the need to cope with such pressures, not because they can be ignored. Lack of autonomy and strategic thinking are not then mutually exclusive. To argue otherwise is to make the very common mistake of associating choice with freedom, and treating its opposite as determinism.

Within the group of contributors to this book there is a discernible difference between those who argue that firms do not in reality have industrial relations strategies, those who argue that they can and should have such strategies and those who believe that, even if their managers do not recognize it, all organizations do have strategies. Both the first two views assume that there is an element of consciousness in the notion of strategy, that is, it represents a proposed and desired approach to guide future action, and as such it is the result of strategic thinking.

Those who believe that a conscious element is *not* necessary for the use of concept of strategy are in fact assuming it is necessary and valid to analyse the decisions taken by managements over time by an *ex post facto* investigation and that this will reveal a clear logic and structure to events.

The use of the term 'strategic choice' which has become common in recent organizational studies (Wood, 1980; Child, 1973a) leads to a view of strategy in which emphasis is placed on the element of choice that managements *may* have, not only in discovering and adapting the organization to suit prevalent conditions, but in shaping their organizational ends and policies. This implies that managements' objectives are not fixed but open, so that managers are not a 'neutral' group rationally deciding on organizational strategy purely in terms of given and non-competing organizational objectives. It also implies moving away from conceiving the organization in terms of given goals, with monolithic management charged with co-ordinating activity to realize them (Wood, 1979). If we accept this advance, we could go on to pose the question of the *diversity* of possible strategies for an organization at any given time. Thus the idea of corporate strategy, an overall direction in which organizations are moving as if all its members are working in the same direction, becomes problematic. It is this point which perhaps most divides industrial relations writers. There is in effect a fundamental disagreement as to *what* is contested in organizations, conventional thinking implying both a managerial consensus and a conflict between labour and management focused on rewards. Industrial relations as such is usually seen as the study of the latter conflict. In contrast, the argument for an industrial relations strategy in a firm may be based on the need to accommodate different managerial objectives and definitions of the situation, and hence to reconcile conflicting managerial behaviour, especially in multi-plant situations. Furthermore, those who stress the need to study industrial relations in the context of corporate strategy may go on to stress the potentially contested nature of all decisions pertaining to the firm or organization. Seglow's study of the BBC illustrates this very well, where the mission of the organization has been a continual source of debate and public concern.

Both the reality of, and argument for, strategy will vary depending on one's conception of strategy. If strategy is seen simply as the organization's 'natural' course of development, then the argument for strategy is essentially an intellectual one concerned with stressing the need to study it, in order to discover the 'logic' of historical development. If one stresses consciousness, then in arguing for strategy one is pleading, as the Commission on Industrial Relations (CIR) and others did, for more planning of labour relations on the part of all managers. More particularly, this argument maintains that specialists (professional industrial relations personnel) can be responsible for ensuring that such concerns are injected into top managerial decisions covering other matters of concern to the well-being of the enterprise. Some participants in the seminar group argue that there is a danger here, as Hyman's (1975) critique of conventional industrial relations makes us aware, that this amounts to a further argument for greater top-level control, regardless of which strategies are adopted. Others refuse to accept that this involves any danger, particularly since their main interest in 'management in industrial relations' lies in improving organizational performance.

It can also be argued that consideration of the choice of strategies means ultimately developing institutions for rational debate and decision within organizations and that this implies a need to represent interest groups in a particular system. Concern for a strategic approach, therefore, does *not* necessarily imply a strengthening of top management control. In taking the debate forward into the future, this is a useful starting point. The discussion of a 'strategic approach' involves a concern for organizational re-design and to a re-thinking of the authority structure and the legitimacy of management itself. There is nothing which is of higher priority on the agenda of industrial relations in the 1980s, especially as some managements seem to be taking advantage of the recession to design new ways, such as quality circles, of developing employee commitment.

As we feel the debate about management involves a reappraisal of the nature and meaning of industrial relations, we have divided the papers into two types depending on the extent to which they assume a different concept of the subject. In the first type the nature of industrial relations is largely treated as unproblematic as being concerned with trade unionism, conflict resolution and the joint-regulation of work relations. The approach of these papers reflects their authors' concern to give greater emphasis than in the past to the managerial side of industrial relations. This group of papers is contained in Part I. The second type of paper takes a different starting point and tries to explore what might loosely be termed the context of industrial relations. Here the emphasis is on the diversity of situations facing managements and hence industrial relations in different historical, national and organizational contexts. The focus is on the way in which industrial relations is both managed and conducted in different situations and this approach implicitly raises the issue of how far industrial relations can be studied as a discrete and autonomous set of activities and relationships. These papers are to be found in Part II. Finally we deal directly with the issue of the relation between industrial relations policy and corporate planning and the way in which they are linked. An expansion of the scope of industrial democracy poses the possibility of deciding business policy through joint-regulation (Wood, 1982). This suggests that the study of managerial function in industrial relations is not merely a matter of academic or theoretical debate, or simply a question in its own right, but is central to many critical policy issues.

It may be useful, finally, to note three major questions that *might* be expected to be discussed in a book on management strategy in industrial relations, but are missing here. First, there is little consideration of the relationship of labour market conditions to management strategy. Clearly the recession in European manufacturing and commercial organizations may have an effect on managerial judgements in industrial relations; indeed it is already argued in the press that workers are responding differently to the call for active militant policies by shop steward committees, because of the fear of loss of jobs. There is little hard evidence of this, however, as yet and little enough evidence of new policies by managers, assuming that workers are likely to accept managerial decisions without resistance. This is an area needing urgent research in the 1980s.

Secondly, industrial relations specialists might be correct in pointing out that there is little detailed examination by contributors of the types of criteria which management take into account in planning, say a new productivity deal or a change in the payment system. The argument on strategy has been conducted at an abstract level and is not related to specific policy issues, except as illustration of general themes. Again this is a matter for further study but our position is that such detailed research can only be conducted fruitfully where there is a proper comparative framework for ordering case study research.

The third question is the treatment of technology. This is probably not adequate for understanding the detailed logic behind managerial strategies. The potential impact of micro-processors, for example, on work shop systems of control is considerable and this raises the possibility of achieving new types of organization design, with new possibilities for more participative systems of management. Managerial strategies in industrial relations are likely to be more influenced in the future by such technical factors, and future research will have to take these into account.

These gaps in the coverage of the papers are to be expected at the present stage of the debate on managerial strategies. They point to the next stage in research when far more detailed cases will have to be investigated and the results placed in a comparative framework. In this sense, the study of managerial strategies in industrial relations has only just begun. Most of the detailed issues for discussion lie ahead. It is hoped that this book will provide a clear basis for and impetus to such discussions.

PART I

The management function in industrial relations

2
Introduction to Part I

KEITH THURLEY and STEPHEN WOOD

The increasing concern for the study of the managerial 'side' of industrial relations reflects the kinds of developments which have led industrial relations to be defined in post-war Britain as a major economic and social problem. The spread of trade unionism particularly in white-collar occupations, the growth of the shop steward movement and the strength of the shop floor, the increasing size and concentration of firms, and the associated problems of multi-unionism and multi-plant and international firms all bear witness to the complexity and changing nature of the situation. The concerns of the papers in this section are rooted in these developments, as they involve three issues:

1. managerial unionism;
2. the effect of the growing strength of the shop floor on managerial prerogatives and behaviour;
3. the extent to which managements are developing strategies and policies in industrial relations to counter this growth.

Managers and union members

The first two papers present case material concerned with what happens when managers join trade unions. Arthurs, in particular, seeks to illuminate aspects of the character of managerial unionism through a study of unions catering for managers in three nationalized industries. A number of important developments have occurred since his study but, overall, his evidence supports what others have suggested, namely, that there is no necessary reason why managerial unionism will differ substantially from other kinds of unionism, and moreover that it may be as heterogeneous as is more traditional unionism. Conflicts of loyalty which may exist for all employees are, however, likely to be greatest for managers, but Arthurs shows that any conflict between a manager's union and managerial roles is likely to be resolved in practice, principally by his attenuating his union role and through the separation of senior managers into distinct bargaining units.

Simpson focuses on editors in local journalism, and particularly on the way in which recent changes have meant that journalism has become less creative and editing has become a more managerial function. The editors, whilst members of the same union as the journalists who have become more militant, have tended to resolve conflicts of loyalty in favour of their managerial role. They may increasingly have grievances, but these, as well as their position in the task and authority system of what are becoming increasingly bureaucratic organizations, have further divided them from their subordinates. Simpson concludes that for many managers in such situations, individual rather than collective means of resolving their grievances may be preferred and be effective. Both Arthurs's and Simpson's papers serve to remind us that managements are not monolithic and cannot be assumed to have interests which are unambiguously opposed to workers' interests and necessarily congruent with those of their employers. Changes in managers' tasks may be especially important in the development of their own distinctive grievances. Unionization provides one avenue for resolving such grievances, but it is not the only approach open to them.

The erosion of managerial prerogative

The papers by Arthur Marsh and Jim Gillies, and Robin Smith and Tony Shafto are concerned with the effects of the increasing unionization and pressure from the shop floor, as well as of recent employment legislation on management. Marsh and Gillies concentrate on the reaction of line managers in three industries to the demands being made on them with respect to industrial relations. Whilst there is some evidence that there is often no great need for managers to negotiate or even communicate on a daily basis with workers' representatives, there is no great reluctance on the part of line managers to involve themselves in industrial relations matters. Just over half of the managers interviewed by Marsh and Gillies had changed their views about trade unions with the rise of local unionism, but almost an equal proportion had become more favourable towards trade unions as had become less favourable. The problem of industrial relations for these managers seemed to arise from an uncertainty about what precisely they should be doing: they were ambiguous about the extent to which they should be negotiating, consulting or simply informing workers, and felt that their firms did not communicate or develop clear guidelines on such matters.

Smith reports somewhat similar findings, focusing on how line managers see changes in their control over employee behaviour. He shows that those managers who were comparatively new to managing trade union members were more likely to see unionization as reducing managerial control than the more experienced ones, some of whom argued it might increase it. The tendency is for managers to interpret their right to manage in terms of the need to channel the emerging aspirations of unionized workforces into accepting agreed procedures and structures. The diminution of the managers' control was not resented, but the main source of concern was the feeling of uncertainty that line management had about both their organization's industrial relations objectives and their own role relative to that of the industrial relations specialists.

Shafto's paper examines in more detail the way in which shop stewards have increasingly taken on managerial functions and the part that management's policies have directly or indirectly played in this. The attempt by management to channel conflict, which Smith reports, appears from Shafto's research to have been relatively successful. Shafto argues that shop stewards have been involved in managerial decision-making, without any serious loss of managements' prerogatives or control. Trade unionists are thus seen, particularly by industrial relations managers, not as a real threat to management, since they are perceived to act, and indeed do act, in a largely co-operative fashion.

The development of managerial industrial relations policies

The three remaining papers in this section discuss the development of industrial relations policies. Purcell puts forward what might be best described as a scenario of what most company industrial relations strategies will look like in the 1980s. They will, according to Purcell, attempt to institutionalize conflict and maximize areas of common interest through encouraging, for example, union membership, participation in trade union activities and inter-union co-operation, although they will also feel obliged to try to reduce the power of strategic groups. Underlying the paper appears to be a belief that some firms have already started to develop such strategies and have certainly implemented some of the policies involved. There is much evidence, for example, that managers already recognize the value of, and indeed may actively

11

encourage, the development of closed shops. The implication is that firms will be able to reduce conflict *if* they have a coherent set of industrial relations policies and, more particularly, those of the type which Fox (1974) calls the 'sophisticated modern pattern'.

Brewster, Gill and Richbell present a paper which attempts to clarify the meaning of 'industrial relations policy' in a corporate setting. They concentrate on the difference between formal statements of policy (espoused policy) and the assumptions of actual line management behaviour (operational policy) which reflect the actual priorities governing managerial decision-making at the operational level. It is argued that managerial roles vary between those creating policy (instigation), those advising on its use (facilitation) and finally those implementing it. The implication is that management face internal conflicts over policy, its definition and the determination of priorities.

Marchington and Loveridge are concerned with the external and internal constraints on the industrial relations policies which a firm can pursue. They focus particularly on the 'participation potential' of firms and show that this is significantly affected by the product market and the type of technology. Where the market is highly unstable or the production systems are technologically complex, the organization's freedom to develop participative systems of management is considerably limited. The implication of their argument is that differences in policies do not simply reflect the preferences of senior management or are completely determined by the environment, but rather illustrate the capacity for organizational responses to environmental pressures. There is a danger then that management's perceptions are too narrow and that the full range of choices open to management are not grasped due to their 'over response' to immediate external threats.

The management function emerges from these papers as a crucial area for understanding the dynamics of change in industrial relations at the enterprise, establishment and workshop levels. It is also apparent that, unfortunately, it is extremely difficult to categorize, measure and predict the direction of change from either empirical studies of what managers do believe, or analyses of formal policies and how they develop in different organizations. In short, the theoretical frameworks available are not yet adequate for utilizing the data collected. Some of the reasons for difficulty in theorizing about the managerial influence over industrial relations issues and events will become more evident when the papers based on a broader notion of the context of industrial relations issues are considered in Part II.

3

Management and managerial unionism

A. J. ARTHURS

There has been little investigation of the unions which cater for managers or about the way in which unionized managers behave. This paper summarizes the findings of research carried out by the author into the managerial unions in the coal industry (the British Association of Colliery Management – BACM), the electricity supply industry (the Electrical Power Engineers' Association – EPEA)[1] and the steel industry (the Steel Industry Management Association – SIMA).[2]

Few unions have only managerial members and those that do have small memberships. Many are in the same unions as professional and white-collar employees and most unions where managers form a majority are in the public sector. They are often specific to one industry and differ from managerial staff associations in that they are normally more established, larger, with greater resources and many are affiliated to the TUC.

The three unions investigated in this study all operated in nationalized industries, but despite this they exhibited a striking diversity in their relationships with their employer and with other unions. This will be illustrated by considering and analysing their behaviour with respect to industrial action and the closed shop, their relationships with other unions and the TUC, and the relationship of the individual manager to his union.

Industrial conflict and the closed shop

Both the EPEA and SIMA took industrial action in the period. The explanation was to be found in both the policies of the top management of these industries and the government, and the needs of the respective leaderships of SIMA and EPEA to be seen to be involved in successful negotiations. The majority of EPEA members were in positions of authority in the industry and about a quarter were graduate engineers – not, it might be thought, a likely group to take serious industrial action for two months which they did. There are two main explanations: first, the members of the Association believed that their differentials over those they supervised and over those with much lesser qualifications than their own had been progressively eroded. An agreement which enabled them to redress – at least to some extent – the balance was frustrated more than once by government policy. Consequently the members decided that industrial action was the only way of righting the position. A second, less obvious, explanation lies in the internal politics of the Association. The almost total change in the senior lay and full-time officials of the Association in 1972 and 1973 was brought about because the old regime was seen to be ineffective. The new leadership could not afford to take the more moderate stance of its predecessors without creating intense disenchantment amongst the Association's members. Therefore, even if there were any doubts about industrial action amongst the new, more radical union leadership, they could not have afforded to indulge them. They took action which received over-whelming support, achieved nearly all their objectives and fully established the new leadership.

SIMA might be thought to be even less likely to take industrial action for it was an organization most of whose members were managers relatively new to union membership. Ostensibly the action in November 1974 resulted from a refusal by the BSC to allow national re-structuring of the salary grades in order to achieve salary awards comparable to those which had been gained by supervisory, technical and clerical staffs under local pay structuring agreements. SIMA registered a state of dispute and because, by coincidence, its Annual Delegate Conference was meeting only two weeks later, the leadership was able to debate the position with active members and gain full support for their stand. At this point the issue appears to have undergone a subtle change, for the Emergency resolution passed by the Conference concentrated on the 'uncompromising attitude of the BSC' and its 'abject refusal to negotiate with this Association in a proper and honourable manner'. Thus in the eyes of some members it had become an issue of recognition, a question of whether BSC would take SIMA seriously. Meetings of all branches were convened and overwhelming support given by nearly all of them to the stand made by the National Council, although the level of support from the branches organizing senior managers was low.

The SIMA leadership's response was determined by the problem of their credibility. The jibes about being a 'bosses' union' and not having the resources or the muscle to represent the members adequately had been thrown at SIMA by the TUC unions in the industry for some years. An opportunity arose (indeed it conceivably may have been presented) to show that SIMA was an organization that must be taken seriously. A trade union may measure its success or failure in its membership figures and the message here was quite clear: in the ten months before the industrial action the membership had risen by 816 (8 per cent), whilst in the ten months following the action membership rose by 1,615 (15 per cent).

Managers are one of the least likely groups of employees to be found in a closed shop. The individualistic ethos of most managers, even where unionized, might be expected to inhibit their acceptance of a closed shop. Yet two of the three managerial unions we are considering, whilst not accepting a full closed shop, agreed to the formation of an Agency Shop under the provisions of the Industrial Relations Act, 1971. For both unions the initial impetus for formation of the Agency Shop came from the need for protection against actual or potential poaching of its members. There is no evidence to suggest that they were motivated either by a desire to restrict the supply of labour or by a felt need to be able to better discipline members or gain greater solidarity in the event of industrial action. In neither case was the decision on an Agency Shop put to the members of the union. There is evidence from their past response to the closed shop to suggest that the membership, if fully consulted, might not have agreed.

TUC membership and relations between unions

The EPEA joined the TUC in 1942. BACM members rejected the advice of their executive on two occasions, before voting in 1976 to affiliate. SIMA would have liked to join, but had been rebuffed by the antagonism of the TUC towards its independent existence. Affiliation to the TUC was not for these three trade unions an ideological act but was based mainly upon an assessment of their organizational needs. The union leaders themselves had ideological commitments, but in order to persuade their members they had to convince them of the instrumental value of affiliation.

An issue which is relatively conflict-free, perhaps precisely because it has such a great potential for conflict, is that of the action that is to be taken by managers when another union is on strike. All three unions had a clear policy that during an official strike work normally done by a member of another union should not be carried out by managers, except when it involved the safety of the pit or stability of a plant or pit. The union's leadership view of unofficial strikes by members of other unions was seen somewhat differently and BACM had a flexible policy to accommodate the particular circumstances of a dispute and the traditions of the area in which it took place. The essence of its policy was that members should refuse to undertake work other than their normal duties unless consultation had taken place previously between Area management and BACM. Some members, especially those who were undermanagers, questioned this approach, which could in some circumstances mean managers attempting to maintain production, and they would have preferred to have the same policy for both official and unofficial strikes. Although a motion proposing this at the 1975 Annual Delegate Conference was lost by a substantial majority, this has remained an issue within BACM.

The individual member and the union

How do unionized managers handle the potential conflicts inherent in the differences of interest between employer and union and between employer and employee? How can a manager sit on both sides of the table at once? Cases of conflict between a manager's union role and his management role were studied by the author. In each case it was clear that, even where the manager was an active and committed trade unionist, he resolved any potential conflict by attenuating his union role. In many managers' jobs there arise temporary conflicts between the managerial and union roles, but a smaller number of managers face an almost continuous conflict by virtue of the nature of their work. In all three unions there was a tacit acceptance that a manager retired from active union membership when he accepted a post which involved a substantial policy-making role and/or frequent negotiations with the managerial union.

Some senior managers even resigned from the union on promotion, although they were in the minority. Many interested members felt that they could no longer play an active part in the union, but they did not keep up their membership entirely or largely out of sentiment. Although many senior managers preferred to handle their own individual grievances, some of them were prepared to ask for union advice and assistance as a last resort.

16

The separation of senior managers into separate bargaining units and separate union branches enables them to be treated differently by both management and unions. The EPEA industrial action, referred to above, deliberately excluded senior managerial staff. The SIMA action did not, but separation of senior management into separate branches allowed their reluctance to take action to be clearly registered and SIMA did not attempt to enforce any union discipline on those who did not support the action. To some extent BACM was saved from this issue because senior managers had great influence in the union and therefore there was less need to separate them into different branches or bargaining units. However, the advent of collective bargaining for nearly all NCB senior managers was accompanied by the formation of a separate bargaining unit. Therefore if BACM ever resorts to industrial action it will be easier to exclude the most senior 200 NCB employees.

Separate bargaining units and union branches give both the unions and management a framework for excluding senior managers from issues which are of fundamental interest only to the main core of the union. However, a price is paid by the union, for resentment was expressed in both the EPEA and SIMA about the reluctance of senior managers to support union action. The different attitudes of senior managers can be obscured by scattering them amongst middle management branches or forming one bargaining unit. However, this tactic can endanger union unity. The possibility arises either of senior managers' domination of the union or of their resentment at being subject to middle managers' control of the union.

Conclusion

Management policies towards managerial unions need to take into account the fact that these unions must develop mutually constructive relationships with other, very different unions, whilst not losing faith with their managerial members. Union policies towards industrial action and the closed shop may be only reluctantly accepted by managers. Senior managers have to be accommodated within the union and it is important that they neither dominate the union nor are so independent that the unity of the union is threatened. Managers face conflicts between their managerial and union loyalties which they need to handle with care and discretion, avoiding the distrust of fellow union members, whilst fulfilling their management responsibilities. The trade union organization of managers has changed substantially since this research was carried out. Increasingly, small managerial unions are merging with the white-collar sections of manual workers' unions or with larger white-collar unions. These developments raise important questions about the future of unions and managers: can a trade union cater for both managers and manual workers? Can trade unions rely on the loyalty of their managerial members? Can employers rely on the loyalty of their unionized managers? Does being a member of the same trade union as a subordinate inhibit a manager's job performance? This chapter has indicated some of the responses that have been adopted, but further workplace research is needed.

4

Managers in workers' trade unions: the case of the NUJ

DAVID SIMPSON

The increasing unionization of managers means that managers may have to be studied not only from the perspective of their representing one side in negotiations but also as employees with grievances of their own. Some of the issues to be studied may be exhibited more clearly when both managers and managed are members of the same union. This situation of managers in a trade union for 'workers' occurs in parts of the health service and local government and in certain distinctive occupations such as musicians. This paper concentrates on the editorial managers in their subordinates' trade union, the National Union of Journalists (NUJ). It is based on more extensive research (Simpson, 1981) than can be reported here. This was carried out in the editorial departments of three separate centres publishing in total one morning, three evening and twelve weekly newspapers, and in which twenty-eight managers control, organize and direct the work of about four hundred reporters, sub-editors and photographers.

Most of the editorial managers are faced with a dilemma because by virtue of mandatory chapel meetings they have to abide by the decisions of their subordinates. Furthermore they do not appear to have any single clear and unambiguous commitment either to management or journalism which can help them resolve this dilemma. Their allegiance to the profession of journalism gives them some common interests with their subordinates and the bulk of the membership of the NUJ. Professionalism, often thought antithetical to trade unionism, may indeed form a basis for strong representative bodies, as the BMA illustrates. But, as sociologists have shown, journalism is by no means a fully fledged profession.

Tunstall (1971: 69) has concluded that 'It is extremely improbable that journalism would ever acquire these professional attributes to the extent of, for instance, medicine. A more realistic objective, if the occupation wished to pursue it, would be to make journalism into a semi-profession – in the way that teaching for instance is a semi-profession', a conclusion arrived at some fifty years earlier by Carr-Saunders and Wilson (1933: 265). Thus journalism could be viewed as an occupation not having any specific code of conduct, ethical regulation or a controlling body, but nevertheless as requiring a level of vocational commitment. Indeed in the early years of the NUJ this distinction was manifest in the disagreements over its purpose, and was expressed in letters in the union journal, the *Journalist*, either proclaiming its professional base or suggesting that it be more militant in a trade union sense. This latter stance appears to be more significant in recent years if current issues of the *Journalist*, and the strikes involving the NUJ, are considered. Such a trade union position has developed in response to the commercial changes in the past two decades and it has been these that have significantly affected the role of editorial work in newspaper organizations, and the position of editorial managers within the editorial department.

The changes affecting regional newspapers have arisen because of a change in ownership (either financial or in style) and subsequently a realization by this new ownership of the changed markets within which the regional newspapers operate. The take-over of Kemsley Newspapers by Roy Thomson in 1959 heralded a new style of ownership of regional newspapers as commercial criteria became increasingly important. Thus revenue-gathering departments, advertising and circulation, assumed a greater importance relative to editorial departments than hitherto. Much of this was facilitated by the monopoly position which had existed for nearly all regional newspapers, but had never been exploited. The new breed of ownership replaced the latest and most exclusive news by a rather ordinary diet of local and institutional, but easily collected, news as there was no local competition to force newspapers to act in any other way.

The new wave of ownership placed less emphasis on editorial input for the success of the newspaper, and this not only reduced the status of the editorial department within the organization, but also required a different kind of input from them than before. As newspapers began to exploit the advertising market, newspaper size increased and thus more editorial material was required. However, as the number of journalists was not increased in the same ratio, a greater output from each journalist was required. Also as advertising input became increasingly to be planned in advance, and with given advertising/editorial ratios, the space allotted for editorial input was also known days ahead. News had then to be collected to fill a required amount of space, rather than an amount of space being made available for the news that had arisen. A pattern soon emerged of small newspaper size (because of fewer advertisements) for certain days and large size for other days, particularly towards the end of the week. All the editorial department had to do was to ensure that there was enough news collected to fill the space allotted, but this required a greater emphasis on the management of news collection and presentation than in a previous era. The luxury of sending journalists to investigate an event, often in the hope of a good story, was dispensed with in favour of the certainty of a story from an institutional source – the courts, the various council meetings and pre-arranged press conferences. All of this required organization, and more editorial managers to ensure that the right amount of news was available at specific times.

A further change occurred in the quality of editorial work required. Reporting from institutional sources is fairly routine journalism and it largely replaced the investigatory reporting which had traditionally allowed the journalist to display his or her flair and artistry. The value of local journalism was downgraded to the level of pre-programmed space filling, between the more commercially important advertising. At the same time the emphasis on the organization, direction and control of editorial work was increased, giving an impetus to the management of editorial work, an aspect previously relatively insignificant. Thus the distinction between journalistic work and its management was both sharpened and revealed.

The impact of the changes was felt by both the journalists and the editorial managers. The latter acquired greater status relative to the former whose activities they increasingly controlled; whilst the former's work was subject to managerial direction, so their working conditions (in terms of office space and equipment, and in terms of the use of cars or generous expenses to follow up on news stories) also worsened and their salaries remained relatively low. These provoked grievances which were soon communicated through chapels to the NUJ, which began, during the 1970s, to organize 'industrial conflict' to rectify such grievances.

Before focussing on editorial managers' attitudes to such grievances, one further consequence of the above changes needs to be mentioned, namely, that because of the increased concentration of the regional press, career patterns in journalism are becoming managerially orientated. The traditional training of journalists in the provinces, necessary before a move to Fleet Street, still exists, but is less important as national newspapers (and there are fewer of them) directly hire graduates. Nevertheless there is now more opportunity for advancement for those staying in regional newspapers especially where a journalist is most likely to work for one of the five major groups which control 60 per cent of evening newspaper circulation. Within these groups there are newspapers of varying size and importance, and career development by internal movement is very common, as had happened to most of the managers interviewed in this study. Further, because of the greater need for the management and organization of news collection and presentation there appears to be a proliferation of senior management posts on each newspaper. For instance, in the editorial department of the morning newspaper studied there were an editor, deputy editor, chief assistant editor, assistant editor, plus nine other managerial posts. Some of the editorial managers interviewed welcomed this development as necessary training for a move to general or commercial management within newspapers. Indeed one person interviewed had moved from deputy editor to assistant managing director, another assistant editor was being groomed for such a move, and several other editorial managers were thinking seriously about such moves. To summarize, journalism is becoming increasingly routinized, and along with this the management of editorial departments has taken on a fresh significance (Simpson, 1980a).

Editorial managers' attitudes about belonging to the NUJ were, during these interviews, especially centred on the strike action that the union was organizing. Although they sympathized with the grievances of the journalists they generally felt that striking was not the means for their solution, for after all a strike would stop the newspaper, something journalists ought not to sanction. By striking they were demonstrating that they were workers like any others, and not members of a respected occupation. Those calling for strike action were destroying the nature of journalism, and the editorial managers could not identify with such a body (the NUJ) and its actions. Initially the editorial managers searched for reasons as to why such strike action should occur (even given the grievances). One sports editor said it was graduates who had stirred up the trouble, they were all 'lefties' or 'Trots'. A deputy news editor talked of left wingers, and the chief assistant editor said, 'If they had their way they would kill the baby'. One deputy editor told of a resignation interview with one of these 'lefties', who was going to be a reporter for *Socialist Worker* and talked in terms of 'his being back with hobnail boots on'.

Such comments are, however, qualified, first by reference to what the editors thought was the changing nature of the NUJ. One editor said, 'The NUJ is a type of professional association although becoming more militant'; both the features editor and his deputy felt that the NUJ is now a trade union but has tended in the past to be more of a professional association; a news editor did however still view it as potentially a professional body. Given the relative lack of professionalism in the history of the union these comments can perhaps best be seen as reflecting a managerial perspective. For these editorial managers, whatever the grievance, the paper must come first. 'The show must go on. It is part of the mystic of journalism, the paper is a living thing', one editor remarked, when commenting on a dispute. Another, the deputy features editor, said, 'Journalism is a calling, a profession in the blood, it's there'.

Editorial managers had also found it difficult to agree with and hence operate other forms of action, such as overtime bans and work-to-rule periods. One sports editor said he had to avoid being seen when he carried on working normally and was not working to rule. 'Overtime bans', one deputy editor thought, 'would only damage the editorial material that we have and eventually further damage our status'. Thus for these editorial managers, the activities of the NUJ had made it a trade union, primarily representing the interests of their subordinates. The paradox of editorial managers in their workers' trade unions cannot be resolved for managers simply through a perception of journalism as a profession or a cherished occupation. Neither can the paradox be resolved by assuming that the NUJ represents their interests, for in the examples given of the various kinds of industrial conflict, editorial managers felt inhibited in their ability to carry out what they thought were their duties. For the majority of editorial managers the paradox could only be resolved by leaving the union, but at the time of writing (1981) this was open to great dispute, particularly within the NUJ. To be successful in a strike, any union must be able to apply some pressure on those with whom it is negotiating. At present only the editor is allowed by union rules to work during a strike and, if recent examples are used, the newspapers produced by his or her efforts are not substantially different from the normal papers and are not viewed critically by most readers or advertisers, at least in the short term. Thus from the NUJ's point of view this prolongs the strike, a position greatly exacerbated if deputy or assistant editors are also allowed to work during a journalists' strike. At one centre visited, two deputy editors had worked during a strike, but as this transgressed union rules, a call to other print trade unions for their support was immediately met by the union (SOGAT) which represented the van drivers who would not cross picket lines manned by journalists. Consequently, the newspaper on this day was printed but not published.

Yet if editorial managers did want to leave the NUJ and seek representation elsewhere there might be significant problems. Such representation might be gained by joining an existing union for managerial grades, another journalists' union or by forming a separate breakaway union. The last possibility appears to be most problematic because of difficulties of gaining negotiating and recognition rights and would be strongly resisted by the employers' association, The Newspaper Society, which has been campaigning in recent times for fewer rather than more trade unions in newspapers. There is one other body that represents journalists' interests, the Institute of Journalists (IOJ), and this appears as a possibility. The IOJ, however, is more of an association than a trade union and is more concerned with standards than with working conditions. It has less than two thousand members, admits owners as full members and, where journalists have joined, there has been resentment amongst colleagues in the NUJ and thus it has not been greatly encouraged. In these interviews the few editorial managers who mentioned existing trade unions for managerial grades as a possibility did so with little enthusiasm. Two editorial managers who specifically mentioned ASTMS had in fact been in their present position for a number of years and could only see progress, in terms of salary, through a representative body like ASTMS. In this study those with such positive opinions towards the need for representation were in a small minority. Many editorial managers felt membership of a workers' trade union to be something of an imposition, and most of them were in fact unsympathetic to the problems of the journalists. They saw the degradation of editorial work as something of an attack upon themselves.

Their solution, in effect, was to increasingly associate themselves with the general management of the newspaper centre, rather than with their journalistic subordinates. They perceived a management hierarchy as open to them. As mentioned earlier there were many promotion prospects within the editorial department, many to the commercial side, or to another newspaper within the group. Indeed the twenty-eight editorial managers interviewed had held an average of 2.46 job positions in the last five years. Such a situation was also prevalent on the commercial side with an average of 2.90 job positions (among thirty-one managers) in the previous five years. In one sense, then, the resolution of the paradox for editorial managers in a workers' trade union was to accept the position, rather than leave the union which would create great hostility, and to envisage future gains or success as achievable on an individual basis.

Managers who are members of their subordinates' trade union appear superficially in an anomalous position which can only be maintained if both have a sufficiently high level of commitment to the occupation they are engaged in and can overcome the demands and strains of a superior–subordinate relationship. In regional newspapers the commercialization process and its consequent bureaucratic effect has raised the question of whether journalism can still unite what are rapidly becoming two separate groups, the editorial managers and the journalists. Each perceives their work, and indeed the organization in which they are located, very differently. Indeed the action of the NUJ in calling for strike action has reinforced the views of editorial managers who increasingly see themselves as part of a managerial team rather than as members of the occupation of journalism.

Conclusions

The case as presented here has implications for other institutions in which managers similarly are in their subordinates' trade union. Any change in the purpose of the employing organization, commercialization in regional newspapers, cost effectiveness in the health service, for example, will highlight the employment relationship to the detriment of any unifying notion of professionalism, occupationalism or client-service. The result is the fragmentation of what was once a whole. For the journalists here this had the effect of making the NUJ more a trade union than hitherto, and for other groups elsewhere, such as in the health service, it may mean taking steps along the road towards industrial militancy. The managers, however, may respond to such changes by rejecting their representation by workers' trade unions, but not necessarily the total rejection of any form of representation. As I have shown elsewhere (Simpson, 1980b) such managers working in relatively large organizations will generally have no appropriate professional body to join, but nevertheless will seek some means to resolve their grievances.

Such means may be through individual action such as leaving the organization or merely operating at a minimal performance level. Some managers may, as suggested here, join the promotion chain on the commercial side, severing ties with journalism altogether. For others collective representation through a trade union specifically for managers, or some form of staff association, are likely possibilities. For a few of the managers under discussion here, the Institute of Journalists has provided the necessary haven although the choice will differ as between individuals, the kind of organization they work in, and the kinds of changes that may be taking place, but the end result will be the growth of a need for distinctive managerial representation.

5

The involvement of line and staff managers in industrial relations

A. I. MARSH and J. G. GILLIES

Introduction

It is generally agreed that the day-to-day conduct of industrial relations must inevitably lie with line and staff managers and subordinate supervisors. Many personnel and industrial relations specialists believe, as we confirmed in an inquiry in 1974, that such managers perform this role with no more than modest competence, a view shared, according to the findings of our 1975–6 study of such managers in the engineering, chemicals and printing and publishing industries, by many of the managers themselves. The object of this paper is to present the findings of this study concentrating especially on the issue of involvement. To what extent do line and staff managers, especially those 'middle managers' who were particularly the subject of our inquiries, become involved in handling industrial relations matters?

In all, 351 managers were personally interviewed during 1975–6, on a structured schedule of questions, and were categorized as shown in Table 5.1. The managers were taken from thirty-five companies comprising fifty-two separate establishments. Previous experience suggests that no precise statistical validity can, or ought, to be claimed from a sample of this kind. Nevertheless, the managers in our survey cover a wide cross-section of the three industries, by size of company, by product and by location.

Managers and unionization

A general view of the degree of unionization in the different departments within the three industries can be obtained from Tables 5.2a, 5.2b and 5.2c respectively. The lower level of departmental organiza-

27

Table 5.1. *Categories of managers interviewed*

Category	No. of managers
Research and development	29
Professional engineers and scientists	36
Technician managers	45
Administrative managers	47
Finance managers	36
Marketing managers	18
Sales managers	22
Production managers	83
Maintenance managers	35
Total	351

tion in chemicals is immediately apparent. At the time of the inquiry, trade unionism had penetrated more into the higher technological areas in engineering and print than it had in chemicals. Marketing and sales had little departmental union organization outside print. Among other non-manual departments, union organization was most likely in engineering and least in chemicals. In print, finance and administrative departments are less likely to be organized than most people seem to believe. Representation in the form of shop stewards or under other titles is less often to be found than union membership itself. A considerable number of those managers with departments where unionization exists may still find themselves with no direct relationship to an immediate spokesman for their staff.

The percentage of employees unionized within each category varied in the fifty-two establishments broadly in relation to departmental organization distribution. It varied, as might be anticipated, from the situation of some managers faced with no union organization to 100 per cent in the case of others, with the highest percentages (over 95 per cent) in the production and maintenance areas and the lowest in sales and marketing. As between industries the highest overall levels were in engineering and the lowest in chemicals. The bulk of managers, it turned out, tended to manage only one particular type of worker, be it manual, clerical or technical, at the same time. More than two-thirds of those in the sample were in this position. But there were some whose responsi-

Table 5.2a. Engineering industry: involvement of various categories of managers with trade unions and industrial relations (%)

| Category of manager | Department unionized | | | Manager | | | Handles individual grievances | | Negotiates with union reps |
	All groups (a)	Some groups (b)	Total (a) & (b)	With union reps	Talks day-to-day with employees about IR	Talks to union reps about IR	Without union reps	With union reps	
Research and development	33.3	44.5	77.8	44.4	55.5	44.4	55.5	44.4	0.0
Professional engineers and scientists	76.9	23.1	100.0	92.3	46.1	61.5	38.5	61.5	23.1
Technical	80.0	20.0	100.0	92.0	56.0	88.0	48.0	68.0	24.0
Administrative	65.0	30.0	95.0	70.0	60.0	35.0	40.0	35.0	20.0
Finance	57.9	26.3	84.2	78.9	73.7	52.6	52.6	31.5	10.5
Marketing	25.0	12.5	37.5	25.0	75.0	0.0	87.5	12.5	12.5
Sales	14.3	57.1	71.4	28.6	100.0	0.0	57.1	14.2	0.0
Production	96.7	3.3	100.0	100.0	46.7	96.7	23.3	60.0	46.7
Maintenance	92.3	7.7	100.0	100.0	46.1	92.3	30.8	76.9	53.8
All categories	70.2	20.8	91.0	79.9	58.3	63.9	43.1	49.3	25.7
N =	101	30	131	115	84	92	62	71	37

Table 5.2b. Chemical industry: involvement of various categories of managers with trade unions and industrial relations (%)

| | Manager | | | | | | | | |
| Category of manager | Department unionized | | | With union reps | Talks day-to-day with employees about IR | Talks to union reps about IR | Handles individual grievances | | Negotiates with union reps |
	All groups (a)	Some groups (b)	Total (a) & (b)				Without union reps	With union reps	
Research and development	15.4	30.8	46.2	30.8	92.3	15.4	92.3	7.7	0.0
Professional engineers, etc.	41.7	25.0	66.7	41.7	75.0	33.3	83.3	6.7	25.0
Technical	0.0	50.0	50.0	50.0	83.3	33.3	50.0	50.0	0.0
Administrative	30.8	38.5	69.3	46.1	84.6	38.5	92.3	7.7	0.0
Finance	16.7	33.3	50.0	33.3	83.3	33.3	66.6	33.3	0.0
Marketing	0.0	0.0	0.0	0.0	50.0	0.0	100.0	0.0	0.0
Sales	0.0	0.0	0.0	0.0	100.0	0.0	100.0	0.0	0.0
Production	80.6	6.5	87.1	77.4	64.5	77.4	41.9	58.1	25.8
Maintenance	80.0	13.3	93.3	86.7	86.7	73.3	20.0	80.0	33.3
All categories	49.0	21.0	70.0	57.0	79.0	50.0	61.0	39.0	16.0
N =	49	21	70	57	79	50	61	39	16

Table 5.2c. *Printing and publishing: involvement of various categories of managers with trade unions and industrial relations* (%)

Category of manager	Department unionized			Manager					
	All groups (a)	Some groups (b)	Total (a) & (b)	With union reps	Talks day-to-day with employees about IR	Talks to union reps about IR	Handles individual grievances		Negotiates with union reps
							Without union reps	With union reps	
Research and development	71.4	28.6	100.0	57.1	85.7	28.5	57.1	28.6	14.3
Professional engineers, etc.	83.3	8.3	91.6	72.7	72.7	54.5	54.5	63.6	18.2
Technical	78.6	0.0	78.6	50.0	64.3	42.8	50.0	50.0	28.6
Administrative	57.1	35.7	82.8	57.1	78.6	35.7	71.4	35.7	21.4
Finance	36.4	18.2	54.6	18.2	72.7	18.2	54.5	18.2	0.0
Marketing	57.1	0.0	57.1	0.0	85.7	0.0	57.1	0.0	0.0
Sales	35.7	35.7	71.4	35.7	78.6	21.4	92.9	14.3	7.1
Production	85.7	0.0	85.7	81.8	54.5	81.8	54.5	72.7	36.4
Maintenance	100.0	0.0	100.0	85.7	85.7	85.7	57.1	71.4	19.5
All categories	67.3	14.0	81.3	54.2	71.9	43.9	61.7	44.8	20.6
N =	72	15	87	58	77	47	66	48	22

bilities spanned clerical and technical staff, manual, clerical and technical staff, and in some cases staff of all kinds.

The information and skill required to manage such 'mixed' situations are presumably greater than those in which a 'unitary' representative system prevails, though it brought no special reactions from our respondents. More obvious to managers was the problem of handling areas in which employees were, either within a single department or over several departments which were managed by a single individual, members of more than one trade union (see Table 5.3). Table 5.3 does not, of course, suggest that every manager in each category is in contact with all the organizations stated, but it does underline, at least on an industry basis, the degree of multi-unionism which exists among all categories of employees.

'Talk', grievance-handling and negotiation

Problems inevitably arise over the accurate categorization of such activities as 'talking' or 'communicating' with employees, 'grievance-handling' and 'negotiation'. While an ascending degree of formality can be discerned in moving from one to the other, it is far from certain where the line should be drawn between them; some grievance-handling can, for example, cover a considerable degree of negotiation, while one type of activity does not rule out the existence of the others. Formally rather than informally defined, it seems from the three parts of Table 5.2 that relatively few middle managers think of themselves as 'negotiating'. The highest proportions doing so are to be found in production and maintenance and, in engineering and printing and publishing, especially in the more technical departments of factories. The chemical industry appears to be unusual in providing no real scope for negotiation for many of its middle managers, nor yet much grievance-handling with trade union representatives in some areas. In this industry, grievance-handling *without* trade union representatives appears to be more common than grievance-handling *with* such representatives except where production and maintenance workers are concerned. One of these approaches to grievances does not, of course, necessarily rule out the other. Given the distributions of their work forces, mixtures between organized and non-organized departments and the existence of part-organized departments, managers appear to do a good deal of both. The data generally confirm the impression that manual workers are more likely to use a single, trade union, channel for airing grievances, while

Table 5.3. *Number of trade unions represented in areas managed*

| | Industry | | | No. of unions in each category |
	Engineering	Chemical	Publishing and printing	
Research and development	6	3	7	13
Professional engineers and scientists	7	6	5	11
Technical	8	3	9	15
Administrative	7	5	8	14
Finance	7	3	4	11
Marketing	2	—	2	3
Sales	5	—	3	8
Production	14	8	10	21
Maintenance	8	10	7	13
All categories	15	12	14	22

Note: This table also contains the staff sections of some manual unions, TASS, ACTSS, MATSA, etc.

non-manual employees tend to use either channel, as it suits their purpose or inclination.

Where trade union representatives exist, engineering managers tend to talk to them outside procedure. Except where manual workers are concerned, this seems to happen less in printing and publishing and even less in chemicals. None of this, however, suggests that they do not also talk directly to their own departmental staff on a day-to-day basis, though engineering managers admit to less of this than those in the other two industries.

Nevertheless, day-to-day talking to *employees* seems to take relatively little time where most categories of manager are concerned (Table 5.4). Six out of ten managers told us that they spent less than one hour a week and almost 80 per cent less than one-half of a day. The most confirmed communicators seem to be production and maintenance managers, research and development managers and professional scientists and technicians. The chemical industry had managers who communi-

Table 5.4. *Time spent by managers talking day-to-day with employees about industrial relations, weekly* (%)

	All industries		
	Under 1 hr	1 hr to ½ a day	More than ½ a day
Research and development	53.3	26.7	20.0
Professional engineers and scientists	45.8	37.5	16.7
Technical	71.4	21.5	7.1
Administrative	62.8	34.3	2.9
Finance	70.4	25.9	3.7
Marketing	86.7	6.7	6.7
Sales	68.4	26.3	5.3
Production	43.5	39.1	17.4
Maintenance	52.0	28.0	20.0
All categories	59.4	29.5	11.1

cated the most, as well as most regularly, possibly because of lower levels of trade union organization. In the engineering industry, on the other hand, more *ad hoc* approaches were preferred.

Talking to trade union representatives also appears, overall, to take up little of middle management time (Table 5.5). One manager in every five reported doing none at all, six out of ten spent less than one hour a week, and all but 14 per cent less than half a day. Overall, less use was made of stewards in chemicals in this respect than in engineering and printing. The greatest contrasts were, however, to be found between production and maintenance managers and others. They, while still spending a modest amount of time with shop stewards, were generally far ahead of their colleagues; this was especially so in engineering. Virtually all managers reported that very little of this kind of communication resulted from initiatives from their superiors and that they themselves initiated the contact in about the same proportions as their stewards (Table 5.6).

It may be of interest that there was very little coyness among managers about their involvement with stewards, or about becoming, when necessary, involved in negotiations. Production managers were, in general, convinced that they were good at negotiating; most others tended

Table 5.5. *Time spent by managers talking to trade union representatives about industrial relations, weekly (%)*

	All industries			
	None	Under 1 hr	1 hr to ½ a day	More than ½ a day
Research and development	18.2	63.6	18.2	0
Professional engineers and scientists	32.0	40.0	28.0	0
Technical	23.5	29.4	35.3	11.8
Administrative	42.8	32.2	14.3	10.7
Finance	38.5	46.1	15.4	0
Marketing	100.0	0	0	0
Sales	57.1	42.9	0	0
Production	1.6	35.5	37.1	25.8
Maintenance	12.5	46.9	18.8	21.9
All categories	21.3	39.1	25.4	14.2

more modestly to reflect that negotiation was, after all, to be considered integral to their jobs, and that they might be expected to know the situation, and their workpeople, better than other negotiators (Table 5.7).

Managers and company practice, policies and attitudes to trade unions

Almost all the managers in the sample worked for companies with personnel or industrial relations managers. With one or two exceptions, they were aware of the existence and value of these specialists and were willing to accept their advice, though not to be made subject to their direction. In contrast to the impression which we received from the personnel directors and managers in an inquiry we conducted in 1974, these middle managers were concerned to make it clear to us that they constantly had in mind the industrial relations implications of unilateral decisions within their departments on relationships elsewhere in their concerns. Exceptions to this were to be found principally among sales managers. They were also almost universally concerned to declare their commitment to discussion of departmental matters with their employees

Table 5.6. *Who generally initiates talks between managers and trade union representatives on matters as they arise in their departments?* (%)

Industry	Managers themselves	Superior managers	Union reps
Engineering	47.3	2.0	50.7
Chemicals	45.6	2.5	51.9
Publishing and printing	47.2	4.2	48.6
All industries	46.8	2.6	50.6

and to participate in prior consultation with shop stewards. At least eight out of ten managers believed that they were currently spending about the right amount of time on the latter, though a few, some 9 per cent in printing and publishing, 12 per cent in chemicals and almost 16 per cent in engineering, thought that they ought to spend more. Most managers were equally convinced that it was essential, or often useful, to keep employees informed about company actions and policies.

There appeared to be some paradoxes in this situation. While approving consultative approaches by employees to management, and being convinced that this was the style they were personally adopting, their concept of consultation in practice appeared mainly to refer to information given by employers *after* decisions by management. And while approving the notion of wide disclosure of company policies, many of them believed that they themselves were only indifferently informed on the subject. Less than a half thought they were satisfactorily informed on industrial relations policies and many often resented the fact that senior trade unionists, and through them the members, frequently had access to information which they themselves were not given, or which became available only at a later date.

Most of them came from family backgrounds where fathers had work either of a similar or more artisan or unskilled kind than their own. Fathers falling into 'intermediate' occupations according to the Census of Population classification were in most cases also managers (in parentheses in Intermediate column of Table 5.8). About one-quarter of printing managers, rather more engineering managers, and almost one-third of chemical managers claimed that their fathers had been trade unionists

Table 5.7. *Why do you prefer to be involved in negotiating?* (%)

	Know the situation well	Know the work-people well	In touch	Good at nego-tiating	Integral with job
Engineering	68.6	54.3	51.4	20.0	71.4
Chemicals	66.7	50.0	61.1	16.7	77.8
Printing, etc.	65.0	60.0	65.0	25.0	75.0

Table 5.8. *Occupation of fathers of managers* (%)

	Professional	Intermediate	Skilled	Semi-skilled	Unskilled
Engineering	1.4	35.7 (27.8)	50.0	10.5	2.1 (27.8)
Chemicals	4.0	35.0 (30.0)	47.0	7.0	5.0 (32.0)
Printing, etc.	5.0	49.5 (50.0)	29.9	13.1	0.9 (23.4)

(in parentheses in Unskilled column of Table 5.8), and many had been trade unionists themselves (60 per cent of engineering managers, 44 per cent of chemical managers and 58 per cent of printing and publishing managers), though they rarely admitted to having held any substantial union office. Some were trade union members still, by current choice or long-standing commitment. In engineering in particular, a considerable proportion of the managers were former craftsmen.

What happens to managers' attitudes to trade unions during the course of their career is a difficult, but interesting, question to answer. We used a self-reporting approach, and the results were as shown in Table 5.9. Of the 55 per cent of the managers who reported that their views on trade unions had changed during their career rather less than a half thought that they had become more understanding or accommodating, while rather more than a half had become more apprehensive or hostile. The most apprehensive of categories of managers tended to be in technical and finance areas. At the time of the inquiry it may have been that the latter were reacting in the main to the reputation of draughtsmen in AUEW (TASS), while the latter may have been primarily concerned with what they largely saw as the advance of the unknown.

Table 5.9. *Managers whose attitudes to trade unions had substantially changed over their working lives* (%)

	More favourable to unions	Less favourable to unions
Engineering	48.8	51.2
Chemicals	41.9	58.1
Printing, etc.	46.6	53.4

Conclusion

Middle managers, while expressing interest in participation in industrial relations, and while commonly being involved to some extent with employees and their representatives in day-to-day matters of an industrial relations kind, appear to spend relatively little time in this type of activity, although wide variations exist between individuals and, in some respects, among the three industries concerned in the inquiry. It is, perhaps, the modesty of their practical involvement which makes it difficult for managers to differentiate between consultation and the giving of information and to see their role as it may be seen by others, and particularly by personnel staff. Undoubtedly, the problems arising out of company personnel policies, or sometimes out of lack of such policies, add to the managers' difficulties in appraising the situation. There is no clear indication that they have become either less favourable to trade unions or more favourable to them during a period in which trade union workshop organization has been on the increase. Managers seem, in general, willing to regard industrial relations as part of their jobs and to accept this situation with no noticeable resentment.

6
Work control and managerial prerogatives

ROBIN SMITH

The central focus in this study is the view that managers hold of their traditional 'right to manage', and how this has been affected by factors such as increasing unionization (especially among white-collar employees), changing union strategies and new employment legislation. Evidence was gathered from line and specialist managers at four large organizations: a large plant of a major multinational chemical company; a heavy engineering firm making industrial plant; an American-owned manufacturer of bus and truck components; and a regional branch of a nationalized industry in the energy field.

The managers and union control

The balance of control over job entry was seen to have changed little. During recent years all organizations had been more preoccupied with reducing labour by natural wastage and sometimes redundancy rather than in recruiting. The existence of post-entry closed shops for manual employees, clerks and technicians was almost complete in each of the four organizations, but they were not seen as constraining management's control of the recruiting process.

Control over job content, however, had increasingly become a contentious issue. Employee representatives in both blue-collar and white-collar unions had shown an increasing disinclination to accept traditional managerial authority on work allocation and task design. Paradoxically the catalyst which most frequently sparked off this resistance against authority was a management-inspired job evaluation exercise or a review of job gradings. From the line managers' point of view, no matter how objectively necessary they thought such an exercise or review was, they interpreted the subsequent events as 'misconceived

Table 6.1. *Perceptions about the impact of staff unionization on management control* (%)

	Chemical company		Bus and truck company	
	Directly involved[a]	Total[b]	Directly involved[a]	Total[b]
Management control has:				
Declined greatly	40	21.7	29	12.3
Declined slightly	57	28.3	42	36.8
Stayed the same	13	39.1	29	36.8
Increased	—	10.9	—	14.1
	N = 15	46	17	57

[a] These managers include only those who manage staff whose system of representation has changed from individual and consultative arrangements to trade union negotiation.

[b] This includes all managers in the firm who expressed an opinion on the subject of staff unionization.

interference' by specialist managers into their own – that is, the line managers' – sphere of competence on task design. They were further embittered because the specialist managers 'do not have to live closely with the consequences of their own interventions'.

It is interesting to compare a tabulation of the views of line managers new to managing white-collar trade union members with those of line managers with longer experience of dealing with manual unions on the issue of unions, and management control. Table 6.1 contains a summary of these views from two companies, one a chemical firm, the other a bus and truck component company, where the overwhelming majority of managers in staff areas saw unionization as denting managerial control. But when the views of all managers were considered, the number perceiving a drop in control fell to around 50 per cent. Some of the specialists and line managers with experience of shop floor unions argued that in the long run control need not be lost to the employer as a result of accepting unionization; indeed a minority felt it might actually increase.

Control between line and specialist managers

All four organizations had undertaken certain reforms in their procedures for regulating industrial relations. Were these reforms interpreted as affecting the balance of control between line and specialist managers?

The nationalized firm's response to union aspirations for increased job control was to take the pressure off individual managers by removing their decision-making power and centralizing it in the hands of specialists. The net effect of this is that line managers move towards a position of administration, applying solutions to industrial relations problems from guidelines laid down by specialists. Where no such instructions exist or cannot be applied the manager is asked to refer the matter to the specialist function, in order to avoid setting possibly awkward precedents. In this organization, therefore, increased union control over the job was won not so much by precedent and rule-making between the work group and local managers, but through collective bargaining between parties not directly concerned with the job itself.

In the heavy engineering firm, senior functional management expressed concern about what they regarded as the 'unwillingness' of substantial numbers of line managers to settle grievances that were considered to be within their purview. These senior executives expressed the view that it was desirable to centralize authority within their function, in a similar manner to that achieved in the nationalized firm. What stopped them was their belief that such an objective was too radical a break with the decentralized traditions of their industry, allied with the suspicion that if that objective became generally known it would 'further weaken' the morale of line managers and thus contribute to further reticence to act. Short-term costs would perhaps outweigh long-term gains. Research evidence showed that line managers were divided in their views. About 40 per cent of the sixty-five line managers primarily saw themselves as specialists in engineering, in whose working lives industrial relations intruded in an unwelcome way; whereas about a third of the group appeared to relish their involvement in industrial relations which they saw as inseparable from other management tasks.

The conflict between the line and functional managers in this firm arose because the ideology – espoused by senior executives more from tradition than conviction – to keep decision-making on industrial relations issues within line managers was seen by the latter as at variance with actual practice. The method of deciding upon and implementing new grievance-handling procedures (as distinct from the procedures themselves) was resented on two grounds: partly as an implied criticism of their hitherto informal methods of solving problems, and partly as a reaction against increasing bureaucratization of all central functions within the firm which had followed a merger five years earlier. The new procedures were pictured against a background of scepticism over other initiatives of the function, particularly systems of job evaluation, which were widely criticized. All this resulted in a wide gap in the perceptions of the two sides of managers over which side had the real influence – and the consequent failure to act of which the specialists complained.

Curiously, in the chemical firm, specialist managers complained of almost the opposite behaviour: too many grievances were settled low down in the procedure by line managers with no thought for their repercussions across other sections of the firm. It transpired that these line managers believed in a principle widely thought to constitute good industrial relations practice: that the lower the level at which a grievance was settled, the less their section would be seen as a 'problem' by higher management. This belief was given credence by the widely known existence of an elaborate programme of company succession based on comprehensive reviews of individual performance over all areas, including industrial relations. Further, they believed that training programmes contained the same rhetorical message.

But the specialist managers' perception of the situation was that their own professional skills – diagnosing industrial relations problems, negotiating with unions and preparing briefs which took an overview of company needs – were given scant chance of utilization because of overhasty settlements low down in the procedure. Secondly, they could demonstrate, by reference to those few grievances that had escaped unsettled the spheres of authority of line managers, that settlements at a high level were often no costlier in substantive terms than they would have been if settled at the point of origin. Thirdly, they recognized the importance of a full utilization of the procedure for a local union representative, who might initially suspect that the grievance of his members would not actually be resolved in their favour, but who retained membership credibility by being seen not to take the first 'no' as a final answer. Therefore, far from regarding an unsettled dispute as a black mark against the manager, they welcomed the opportunities it provided to demonstrate their skills.

The motor components firm appeared to be least troubled by questions of control between line and specialist industrial relations managers. This can be largely explained by the fact that this organization was by far the smallest of the four studied. The management group was more cohesive as a team, and felt more collective ownership over changes in the control system. Nevertheless, its members all agreed that the influence of the specialist group had extended.

Conclusions

Most line managers in the research perceived some diminution of their own authority and an increase in that of the functional specialist. But contrary to the fears of some specialists, this diminution was not in itself resented by the majority. Rather it was the marked feeling of uncertainty: uncertainty as to where the boundaries of decision-making lay, uncertainty as to the objectives of the firm in responding to a changing environment. Centralization had produced less uncertainty, but the lesson of the research appears to be that centralization is not necessarily good, but that clarity certainly is.

The managers did not believe that developments in industrial relations during the 1970s had inexorably dented management's right to manage at the work place. The common view was that the power of unions in society is too great and ought somehow to be reduced, but this was a judgment about the world of politics, rather than their own world of management. Indeed, their views on the right to manage can be characterized as essentially pluralistic. They support wider disclosure of information; there is some support for employee representation at board level (though not the kind of parity structures suggested by Bullock); and they do not see shop floor bargaining strength as inimical to their own pay aspirations. They criticize the 'conservatism' of manual workers' unions for being slow to embrace single status. Significantly, the experience of the 1970s has highlighted an awareness of their own distinctive needs as managers separate from corporate objectives. They were, however, of the opinion that in the day-to-day management of the actual process of production, overwhelmingly viewed as their special concern, they had to be vigilant in order to resist union aspirations for job control. Some saw the growth of specialists as synonymous with 'concessions' to the unions; but most recognized that challenges to traditional rights to manage were inevitable.

Thus a majority of line managers accepted that the response to these challenges lay in channelling aspirations into agreed procedures and structures. Only where the collective response was uncertain – or where it failed in its institutionalizing goal – were aspirations for greater union control seen as a real threat to their own position.

7
The growth of shop steward 'managerial functions'

TONY SHAFTO

The emerging shop steward organization

During the period 1967 to 1976 I undertook an investigation into the activities and organization of shop stewards in eleven manufacturing establishments in the West Midlands. The results of this investigation suggested that a frequently expressed view, that shop stewards were locked in continuing conflict with managers, was not realistic and that profound changes in the managerial structure of large manufacturing companies were affecting the day-to-day relationships between line managers and stewards. At the same time the functions and responsibilities of the personnel department were changing and in some cases particularly close working relationships were developing between personnel officers and senior stewards.

At a time when it was common to hear complaints from line managers that the long-term interests of the company were being subordinated to narrow and short-term financial interests represented by accountants, my study suggested that the responsibilities and influence of personnel specialists were being extended. In many cases they were becoming active participants in the decision-making processes at an increasingly higher level of management.

It is a remarkable feature that the changes in the personnel function appear to be taking place with a relatively small increase in the total number of departmental employees. But the puzzle presented by this unusual administrative feature may be solved when we note that departments appeared to be making use of a growing number of shop stewards and that the stewards seemed to form a coherent, organized structure. Evidence of close co-operation between stewards and personnel officers accumulated throughout the research. Underlying this co-operation was

45

the frequently expressed need for personnel officers to be aware of, to understand and to interpret the attitudes, aspirations, fears and problems of workers on the shop floor. The realization that such a need existed represented a significant shift in managerial thought. The use of stewards as a means of communicating the interests of the shop floor represents a particular, rather pragmatic, response to weaknesses in the existing managerial structure, especially at the lower managerial levels. It also shows a willingness to make use of and to develop an existing structure in preference to any attempt to form a new one, for example by arranging elections for separate departmental representatives to working committees. Such an attempt would, of course, have been seen by stewards as a challenge to their legitimacy as representatives, and would have been resisted by them with consequent disruption to the firm.

It could, of course, be argued that the developments observed during the research simply represented a take-over bid by management, an attempt to buy off or win over a potentially hostile force and so deprive the shop floor of its leadership in order to keep it servile to the interests of senior management. This type of take-over was indeed observed in two companies, both private, one small and one large; nevertheless, both eventually failed. One resulted in a successful challenge to and removal of a convener by a rival from the shop floor, the other led to organized and successful opposition by senior stewards to the policies and authority of a newly appointed senior executive. These attempts were very different in expressed motive, form and execution from the trends now being outlined.

These trends were greatly stimulated by incomes policies, government legislation including the 1971 Industrial Relations Act. Such developments influenced the growth of productivity bargains, which, if they are to be genuine, require considerable investigation, negotiation, and implementation. In a Black Country chemical establishment, for example, an agreement was preceded by a long investigation carried out by a committee containing shop stewards. It was recognized by the management that a far-reaching productivity agreement would affect every part of the plant. There was a concern, therefore, to ensure that every part of the plant would be represented in the negotiating procedures. At the same time protracted negotiations had to be organized. The simplest way to organize this was to make use of senior stewards as a regular communication channel who were in turn linked by a close network of shop stewards to all parts of the shop floor.

The growth of shop steward 'managerial functions'

The Industrial Relations Act of 1971 had the paradoxical effect of strengthening personnel–steward co-operation. Initially it was anxiety on the part of both stewards and management to avoid damaging and expensive public legal wrangles that brought senior stewards and personnel officers together to make sure that no recruit was hired who would be likely to object to joining a union. Subsequently the unfair dismissal provisions which have, of course, survived the Act, encouraged further co-operation, particularly over dismissals. Today the personnel department has to live with the possibility that any dismissal will lead to a costly, time-consuming and possibly public defence before a tribunal. It also has to make sure that it has the support of senior stewards and that stewards have appropriate evidence to show that they too have followed approved procedures. Tribunals have since given ample evidence of their willingness to penalize employers who have not followed approved procedures even when the *fact* of dismissal is acknowledged to be fair.

There are many other areas of co-operation. Some have been fostered by prices and incomes controls, and others by further legislation such as the Health and Safety at Work Act (1974) and the Social Security Pensions Act (1975). The purpose of this paper, however, is not so much the operational processes of change but the strategic background of management thinking and its influence on the development of the position of shop stewards.

The close co-operation developed between personnel, and some parts of line management, with stewards can be seen as part of this process of reducing uncertainty. If labour is to be recognized as a serious pressure capable of influencing the decision-making process then it is desirable to organize that force so that its reactions and movements can be predicted. With the help of, and sometimes under pressure from, the personnel office, stewards become increasingly organized, even bureaucratic in their structure within the establishment. During interviews with both senior stewards and personnel officers references were made to 'vacancies' in the agreed establishment of stewards. It was evident that senior stewards were even being reminded by personnel officers that vacancies existed and should be filled. Senior stewards gained offices which were usually manned by a rota system. Meetings of senior stewards were held preparatory to joint management–stewards meetings to discuss issues for the agenda of the joint committee. Personnel officers found that these meetings were more productive if they took the initiative in organizing them. In one establishment, even, minutes of the regular combined shop stewards meeting were taken by the personnel manager who attended the meeting.

Not surprisingly, in the light of the above, the number of shop stewards grew between 1968 and 1974. In the first period (1968–70) the average ratio of stewards to manual workers was 1:42. In the second (1972–5) the ratio was 1:35. This type of comparison is always suspect because there were few accurate records kept during the earlier period. By 1974, however, all the twelve firms visited did keep records. Nevertheless, only one establishment was able to provide accurate records to cover a ten-year period. These showed the following change:

1964   5 shop stewards for 1683 manual workers
1970 10 shop stewards for 822 manual workers
1974 17 shop stewards for 685 manual workers
1975 18 shop stewards for 800 manual workers

In 1975, however, the number of stewards permitted by agreement with the unions was twenty-seven, but senior stewards reported difficulty in filling vacancies with suitable workers.

Stewards and managerial functions

Evidence of co-operation between stewards and management is not, in itself, evidence that stewards were undertaking managerial decision processes. This involves the problem of identifying managerial functions. At first sight only senior levels are concerned with strategic decisions, that is, those concerned with the broad objectives of the firm and the main production and marketing choices made in the effort to achieve these. However, we also have to recognize that not only is there a grey area where the tactical shades into the strategic, but also many lower-level considerations set constraints to strategic policies.

We need, therefore, to consider to what extent shop stewards participated in these elements of the managerial decision-making functions, at what levels they operated, and how far their activities influenced and were influenced by the general strategy of corporate management.

If we accept the arguments of this chapter it is clear that the stewards affected the information system at the supervisory level and sometimes at the middle management level. They did so by their contacts with supervisors, their membership of joint steward–management committees and the daily interaction between senior stewards, personnel officers and departmental managers. There were also frequent formal and informal contacts between the most senior stewards or conveners and senior establishment managers. Although participation in the communication process may not be seen as being at the heart of decision-making it does seem to go further than anything envisaged in the concept of unions as representing an independent opposition to the government of management.

Whether or not stewards share or should share in the making of choices is a matter of some controversy. It is really at the heart of the notorious consultation versus negotiation controversy which Marsh (1965; 1971) has documented so faithfully. Wilfred Brown (1965: 246) went to the core of this dispute when he referred to chief executives who 'talk of joint consultation as a means of getting *advice* from employees. Most so-called joint consultative bodies are set up with ''advisory'' terms of reference. They talk about *negotiations* with unions. The fact is they are obtaining authority to make changes.' Here Brown accepts that a managerial acceptance of an obligation to meet union representatives before reaching a decision is also an acceptance that these representatives have power to influence the implementation of the decision. At the same time Brown pointed out that unions also needed to recognize 'that the negotiations with managers are, indeed, discussions about what plans management should follow, and that, . . . they are deeply involved in managerial decisions' (ibid.: 243).

Interviews with senior stewards indicated that they were fully aware of the responsibility that power would bring. One steward who defined his function as that of protecting his members, also added the rider – and insisted that this should be noted – that he also had a duty 'to keep the factory running'.

Negotiating the boundaries of constraints on management, it would appear, inevitably involves accepting some responsibility for the functions of management. Even this, however, assumes that management always initiates proposals and relegates labour representatives simply to the role of rejection, acceptance or modification. To argue that stewards are developing a more positive function we need evidence of stewards initiating proposals. In this direction, of course, the stewards can be expected to put forward proposals designed to improve the working conditions of employees. This type of evidence is not hard to find. It could be seen at the supervisory level with steward-controlled schemes to share overtime or the 'soft' jobs that enable some workers in a shop to earn more than others. At a higher level it was found for example when a convener initiated a proposal to install a new dust extractor plant involving substantial expenditure – a proposal made in spite of his members' relative apathy. Whenever any proposal involves the allocation of men or finance the steward finds himself facing the problem of choice between alternatives involving scarce resources. Dust extraction plant, for instance, has to be paid for out of profit and reduces the funds available for other purposes, including wage payments or the purchase of new production machines. An overtime sharing scheme which gives some workers a better chance of improving earnings may reduce the income of others. The steward, who at any level faces a problem requiring a choice between competing uses of scarce resources, is involved in the exercise of managerial functions.

When the steward is involved in the negotiation and implementation of major establishment changes, such as a genuine productivity agreement that includes job evaluation and re-grading, he finds himself making decisions (or recommendations likely to be acted on by formal management) that are clearly managerial in nature. A junior shop steward can support his mate's plea for re-grading because he sees the claim as an individual issue affecting one man only. The senior steward sees the claim against the background of the whole grading structure, a structure he probably helped to erect. He has to consider the implications of a decision for other shops and other workers. He may develop a wider view of this problem than even the departmental manager.

The development of fresh functions and relationships between stewards and managers seems likely to affect attitudes. At the same time the attitudes of the participants must also affect the actions they take and the relationships they develop. Observation over the period 1968–75 in establishments at different stages of development did suggest that attitudes were changing.

On the management side acceptance of something approaching a social contract was most markedly shown in the following extract from a Handbook for Works Employees issued by one of the establishments visited: 'The Works have as few rules as possible, because it is a policy to depend more on the common sense of everyone than on any rigid system. No rule is of any use unless everyone understands and approves the reason for it.'

On the steward side the movement for worker control began to exert some influence by the end of the mid-sixties and this was partly because stewards gained in self-confidence as a result of successful interaction with managers. Nevertheless, the actual number of stewards actively involved in the movement appeared to be very small. Stewards were considering, discussing and disagreeing on the issue of how far they

50

should become involved in 'management matters'. Some of the older stewards expressly denied any ambition to become any further involved in management affairs and doubted their own personal competence to proceed further. They thought, however, that others were coming along with the abilities and a wish to extend their influence into the higher levels of management strategy. By 1976 two of the companies possessed national shop steward committees seeking to negotiate directly with senior management. It is notable that the most vocal opposition to proposals for increased worker involvement in decision-making has come not from pragmatic industrial managers well aware of current shop steward power but from the financial interests and top managers of large groups whose own influence over the higher levels of corporate decision-making is the interest which is most directly threatened.

The structure of steward organization in the work place

Involvement, conscious or otherwise, in managerial functions would be expected to lead to a greater degree of formal organization of the stewards. The emergence of such a structure was clearly indicated by my own research and is supported by the work of Batstone *et al.* (1977), which was also based on West Midlands manufacturing. Power clearly lay with a relatively small group of active stewards. The degree of formality with which an élite group of senior stewards was recognized by workers and managers varied. Recognition could be linked with membership of joint negotiating or decision-making committees and expressed in written agreements, or it could simply be a part of the unwritten custom and practice of the establishment. The emergence of a dominating group of shop stewards was, however, evident in all the establishments visited.

This simplified the day-to-day work of the problem-solving and the settlement of work place disputes because it meant that personnel officers and managers knew who they could turn to for assistance in obtaining information and establishing acceptable solutions. It also provided a clear focus of power for any group of worker representatives seeking to challenge the existing structure. Such conflicts between rival groups to gain positions of influence as conveners or chairmen of steward committees were apparent in the later stages of my study. These conflicts and power struggles which included personal rivalries and animosities appeared further to indicate steward responsibility for effective decision-making.

The relationship between management and the developing structure of steward influence is far from simple. It would, however, be quite false to suppose that the day-to-day working arrangements between plant and personnel managers indicate any identity of fundamental attitudes or of any subordination of objectives on the part of either group. No manager would admit to running the plant for the benefit of the workers employed within it. Personnel, as well as line, managers were at pains to stress their obligations to make profits for shareholders and to hold their share of competitive markets.

For their part no steward could afford to be branded a 'management man'. Their often loose administration and cheerful contempt for agreed rules relating to the manning of offices and telephones probably indicated a need to remind themselves and their 'constituents' of their identity with the manual workers. The benefits they gained for the shop floor were regarded as being won at the expense of shareholders and the authority of managers who were nevertheless expected to continue 'to manage'. Industrial relations appeared still to be regarded as a zero sum game with only very limited opportunities for mutual benefit. The more political of the stewards saw themselves as being the defenders of socialist principles against the capitalist instincts, not only of manager and shareholder, but also of the shop floor worker. The committed Marxists saw no paradox in working with management at the micro-level of work place negotiation, whilst seeking to change the existing financial and managerial power structure at the macro-level. It was the younger stewards, closer to the younger managers in background, education, training and skill, who were most clearly separated from management in attitude and in their desire for change in the pattern of ownership and control of the industrial system.

In spite of practical co-operation between management and an organized steward structure and the involvement of the steward in effective managerial decision-making, the stewards still remained essentially the representatives of the shop floor, attempting to maintain constraints on the managerial use of labour as a factor of production.

8

Management control through collective bargaining: a future strategy*

JOHN PURCELL

The purpose of this paper is to suggest how in practice large corporation management in the late twentieth century will attempt to maximize the achievement of their general business objectives not through opposition to unions but by collaboration. Eight core elements in such an industrial relations strategy can be identified. These are:

1. the encouragement of union membership and support for the closed shop where appropriate;
2. the encouragement of membership participation in trade unions;
3. the encouragement of inter-union co-operation and the development of joint shop steward committees;
4. the institutionalization of irreducible conflict;
5. the minimization of areas of avoidable conflict;
6. the maximization of areas of common interest;
7. the reduction of the power of strategic groups;
8. the development of effective control systems.

1. Encourage union membership and support the closed shop where appropriate

The objective of the corporation in dealing with trade unions is twofold: to ensure that the union leaders with whom it negotiates represent and reflect the view of all employees covered in negotiations; and that in discussions covering or affecting a number of groups of employees, all groups have a collective voice. Thus, in the corporation where the bulk of employees are already unionized, groups of workers who do not have

*This is a revised and considerably shortened version of a paper originally published in *The Control of Work*, edited by John Purcell and Robin Smith (Macmillan, 1979).

a collective voice by virtue of not being union members become a source of difficulty. They are essentially disenfranchised. It costs the corporation little to encourage union membership among all groups of employees and the concession of a closed shop does little to increase union power but much to improve order and stability in union organization.

Encouragement of union membership, prompt union recognition, concession of the closed shop where unions want it, and deduction of union dues from source give the corporation a degree of stability which may otherwise be lacking. Assisting in the achievement of trade union principles can be seen as a useful basis for building co-operative relationships with trade union officers, official and lay.

The corporation's management (hereafter the corporation) recognizes that stability in industrial relations is achieved through the development of good working relations between negotiators from the beginning. The intention is to create a set of relationships supported by appropriate procedures for the settlement of disputes so that a strike comes to be regarded as a sign of failure *by both sides* when it is used.

2. Encourage membership participation in trade unions

The corporation accepts that industrial relations is conducted between its representatives and those of the union. This indirect participation through collective bargaining and consultation implies emphasis on a relationship between professionals on both sides. Perhaps inevitably, and certainly by management design, good personal relationships will usually be achieved between the negotiators. Where stewards are not co-operative, management will endeavour to ensure that they achieve little. The co-operative or 'reasonable' shop steward will be rewarded with some success in negotiation. Tangible progress in negotiation confirms the steward's effectiveness in the eyes of the constituents. Management hopes that the unco-operative steward will be unable to satisfy the members' needs and will lose office or resign in frustration (cf. Beynon, 1973: 158, 214). But can the strong leader be really controlled?

It is here that the strength of the apathetic majority is brought in to play. The corporation assumes that unions wish to be democratic and that authority rests with the members. The corporation therefore will set out to encourage accountability to the members by offering extensive facilities for union meetings and communications.[1] By helping the unions to be truly democratic – that is, they follow the wishes of the largely conservative bulk of the membership – the corporation expects that union leaders will find that some of their more ambitious or radical policies do not have the support of the membership while management's 'reasonable' offer is accepted.

This strengthening of union communication channels does not mean, however, that the corporation will rely exclusively on the union to inform employees of management proposals and plans. In some circumstances management will engage in a propaganda campaign to persuade employees of the benefits of an offer or the inevitability of a management decision, involving for example redundancy. This could be taken a stage further in exceptional circumstances where management feel that the bulk of members would accept the offer but their negotiators are showing little sign, on grounds of principle, of wanting to reach an agreement. As a last resort management can announce that as from a certain date anyone reporting for work would be deemed to have accepted their final offer. In this case management appeals directly to the workforce ignoring the union officers, as they have done recently at British Leyland.

3. Encourage inter-union co-operation and the development of joint shop steward committees

In large establishments multi-unionism is the norm (CIR, 1974: Tables 16 and 30). Given this, one clear objective of the corporation is to ensure that the unions work together and that no single union is able to pursue its own claims without the approval of the others, and in effect engender a feeling of company unionism.

The corporation will try to achieve this in a number of ways. Perhaps most importantly it will realize that the degree of control it exercises over itself, in the sense of ensuring that effective power resides at the level of senior management at establishment level, will be a major influence on the structure and functioning of the shop steward organization. Thus first, the corporation will develop strong personnel departments with executive authority although the myth of local departmental management responsibility will be perpetuated. In effect, once approval of the board has been reached, the personnel department at senior levels will formulate policy, negotiate acceptance and monitor progress on implementation. Shop stewards will quickly recognize that power resides among senior management and will feel the need to develop appropriate central control in their own organization.

Secondly, the need to avoid sectional bargaining will be recognized. This means among other things careful choice of payment systems. The ideal payment system is one in which all movements in pay are centrally determined, flat rate or simple measured day rate schemes for example. However, in some circumstances incentives may be needed. Following the principle of central control, the first choice might be a factory-wide scheme along the lines of added value systems. Even if an individual piecework incentive scheme is operated, this will be based on annual negotiations establishing the base rate and the rate at which job time is converted into money values (the conversion rate). In this way, provided management maintain control of the system, relatively little negotiation takes place at the shop floor and wage drift is likely to be more limited than in traditional piecework.

Management will recognize that they cannot draw up the shop steward committee rules themselves, but will use their influence to suggest basic principles, such as that all claims must be ratified by the shop stewards' committee, that majority decisions are binding, and the convener should lead all negotiations above section level. Instructions will be issued to managers not to negotiate sectional claims unless they have been authorized by the stewards' committee. In the event of such an unauthorized claim being pursued the corporation will wish to develop concerted action with the shop stewards' committee to oppose it.[2]

4. Institutionalize irreducible conflict

Senior managers will recognize that their objectives are usually in fundamental conflict with most trade union objectives, the securing of employment and the pursuit of higher incomes. The corporation approaches this problem from two angles.

First, it emphasizes the need for co-operation and partnership. That is to say it develops a façade which denies, or at least portrays as irrational, this basic conflict of interests. The intention is to foster a belief in the minds of its employees that industrial action which damages the company will be equally damaging to them in reducing job prospects and causing insecurity of employment. It plays on the essential contradiction in union objectives of maximizing both employment and income.

Secondly, and more importantly, management policy aims to create a set of institutions and procedures through which conflict can be expressed and resolved, at least on a temporary basis, without recourse to overt industrial action. Conflict is institutionalized by creating both

56

the avenues in which legitimate claims and grievances can be raised and the machinery in which negotiations can be conducted, such as joint negotiating committees. The intention is to develop a set of beliefs among union leaders that their claims can best be resolved by utilizing conflict resolution mechanisms which *they* have created with management: in short to develop a feeling that using the procedures and abiding by the agreements is the action of responsible trade unions and recognized and rewarded as such by society. At the same time the corporation will recognize that in the last resort industrial relations is about the power of competing interest groups. And, although institutionalization is concerned with creating peaceful channels through which that power can be used, sometimes power has to be expressed forcibly to show it still exists. Some strikes may be useful in the pursuit of good industrial relations as defined by the company.

5. Minimize areas of avoidable conflict

The role of top management is to integrate the wide variety of interest and pressure groups in the company into the most effective combination possible. This frequently means that to maximize the whole, each sub-system is sub-optimized. Production managers, for example, may not be allowed to operate at the most efficient level since they must meet the requirements of sales or personnel. Faced with these constraints it should not be surprising to find that sometimes they undermine these long-term goals in order to maximize output, for example by allowing or sanctioning excessive overtime. The resultant conflict in industrial relations, with other workers wishing for similar benefits, will be defined by corporate management as avoidable and thus requiring the development of appropriate policies.

First, the corporation will look to its control system to give them early warning of such difficulties. Secondly, it will limit the discretion that line managers have to take decisions on a unilateral basis. Thirdly, where flexibility is required, top management will endeavour to limit this within certain bounds and ensure that action is taken in conjunction with local shop stewards.

Finally, the corporation will pay particular attention to procedures for grievance and discipline. The adoption of a *status quo* clause, for example, is seen as beneficial in that it allows disputed moves by management to be examined and negotiated. But management will clearly recognize that it always has the right to implement the desired changes when the procedure is exhausted, if no agreement is reached.

6. Maximize areas of common interest

One major element of the industrial relations policy is to utilize and reinforce an acceptance of a common interest between workers and management through policies which create an impression of participation and partnership whilst maintaining management's right of last say.[3] The intention is to foster a bargaining relationship with the trade unions which integrates the two sides and depolarizes the situation. This implies that the company will engage in behaviour which legitimizes the role of the unions, develops trust between the parties and encourages friendliness between the negotiators. To achieve this it is necessary to broaden the base of negotiations and consultation from terms and conditions of employment (where some conflict is irreducible) to other questions, traditionally considered part of the management prerogative, where common interests can be exploited. Joint working parties of managers and stewards discussing such subjects as job evaluation, quality or new technology, provide an appropriate opportunity for this to occur.[4]

In effect, through the joint working parties, employees and their unions take an increasing responsibility for the policy or plan of action which the working party agrees. The experience of working closely in collaboration with management helps break down the traditional antipathy between management and labour and allows trust between the two sides to develop. At the same time by exposing trade union leaders to the competitive position of the company, external conflict with other firms is emphasized with the effect that internal conflicts tend to be minimized (Coser, 1956: 87–95). The joint working party is also a forum where union representatives can learn about the nature of business and the role of management. In this way the role of management as agents of capital is minimized while management's function of co-ordination and control in the pursuit of efficiency and growth is highlighted. In effect, in a subtle way, managerial power based on property ownership and employee subservience becomes replaced by, or is believed to be replaced by, managerial authority based on technical expertise.

The development of industrial democracy involving more extensive consultations, and in some cases worker directors, is a logical progression in the means of achieving and maintaining control. The corporation's approach to industrial democracy will be based on the belief that 'the problems of change can be reduced by greater employee involvement in the making and implementation of decisions which lead to such a change' (CBI, 1976: 63). This involves the development of activities and structures to emphasize a common interest in overall organizational objectives.

7. Reduce the power of strategic groups

The six earlier policies are concerned with the creation of a system of industrial relations which is to the maximum benefit of the corporation. Senior managers recognize, however, that these policies do not guarantee success. Corporate personnel departments will increasingly try to identify areas and groups of employees whose position in the organization gives them the potential to disrupt the business with serious consequences. The intention will be to devise ways in which either the power potential of such strategic groups is reduced or the likelihood of the power being used to coerce the company minimized. This will involve first, the reduction in the dependency of the organization on a particular group; secondly, inhibiting the development of solidarity and beliefs in the legitimacy of industrial action; and thirdly, ensuring that if power is tested the outcome will weaken rather than affirm the group's perception of its power. The corporation will have to make a basic choice of whether to break up a strategically powerful group or, if that is not possible, of either isolating it geographically and organizationally from other sections (Purcell *et al.*, 1978) or trying to subsume it into a wider unit so that the group has no exclusive bargaining rights.[5]

The corporation will also examine the possibility of reducing its dependency on particular groups, for example by standardizing production in a number of plants, or by increasing stock levels so that it can continue to supply in the event of a dispute, especially if stocks are held on separate sites. In the same vein the ability to keep production going from buffer stocks has the benefit of limiting the impact of a sectional strike. Realization of this may weaken work group solidarity and belief in the ability to succeed in a strike.

8. Develop effective control systems

Finally the problems to be considered are those involved in management's application of their industrial relations policies. Two types of difficulty may be expected. First, there may be a failure to apply agreements or decisions, and secondly, there is the difficulty of detecting informal practices and customs before serious damage has occurred leading to claims for comparable benefits. The corporation will look to its formal information and control systems as a means of inhibiting the development of informal adaptions and to give managers information on the extent to which these deviations are occurring so that appropriate action can be taken to ensure that future decisions are based on an accurate picture of industrial relations.

Management will be concerned to give line management information of how well they are managing their sections in terms of measurable data such as earnings, productivity, breakdowns and recorded grievances in order to inhibit behaviour which deviates from established rules or norms. Secondly, these controls may then be used to provide information on the adequacy of the target or rule itself. Thirdly, control systems to assist strategic planning and policy formulation will be the particular concern of corporate management themselves, so that the company is never forced to react to circumstances without careful consideration and much forethought.

Conclusion

Fox (1974: 302) has termed the type of industrial relations policy described in this chapter as the 'sophisticated modern pattern'. Here 'management legitimises the union role in certain areas of joint decision-making because it sees this role as conducive to its own interests as measured by stability, promotion of consent, bureaucratic regulation, effective communication or the handling of change . . . it recognises that its discretion is being limited in certain areas of decision-making, but it legitimises these limitations and therefore does not counter with low-trust behaviours and attitudes' (ibid.). Fox's justification for this seeming paradox is based on the view that 'the satisfaction of these marginal aspirations strengthens the legitimacy of the system in the eyes of those subordinated to it, thereby enhancing rather than weakening managerial effectiveness' (ibid.). The corporation's ability and willingness to deal with the sort of issues which trade unions raise in negotiation ensure that in the eyes of employees it is a 'reasonable' employer which makes it unnecessary, as far as they are concerned, to ask more fundamental questions. Conflicts are defused before class consciousness and solidarity have time to develop and general class issues arise.

Fox has predicted that this 'sophisticated modern pattern' will tend to be highly unstable as 'it represents an equilibrium situation, and in a constantly changing world any equilibrium is uncertain and precarious' (1974: 307). Corporate management is unlikely to take this argument too much to heart. Rather, they will note the remarkable tranquillity of many major companies which have sought to develop modern sophisticated policies in industrial relations in the last fifty years, despite the quite extensive social, political and economic changes which have occurred. Corporate management will, of course, recognize that problems and failures are bound to occur and that few, if any, actions in industrial relations are taken without risk. In terms of priority they will lay particular stress on policies to institutionalize conflict and maximize areas of common interest once the relationship with the trade unions and supporting union organization in the company has been established. They will realize that the achievement of these two objectives is crucial to maintain that relationship *and to control*. They will note that while it may be tempting in times of economic recession to return to the blunt instruments of enhanced managerial power, this will be likely to be at the cost of long-term stability, order and predictability which are the central aims of the corporation's industrial relations policy. It is simply foolish to alienate trade unions when they are weak and at a time when they are more than usually predisposed to co-operate with management strategies.

9

Industrial relations policy: a framework for analysis

C. J. BREWSTER, C. G. GILL and
S. RICHBELL

Definition

Since the publication of the Donovan Report (1968) much emphasis has been placed on the importance of formulating and implementing company-wide industrial relations policy. Such a policy has been seen as a means of assisting management to establish and maintain a coherent and consistent framework for the conduct of industrial relations.

However, despite the importance attached to the notion of a company industrial relations policy, the subject has received little attention in industrial relations literature, and when it is discussed the concept of an 'industrial relations policy' is rarely defined. In our analysis an industrial relations policy is seen as a set of proposals and actions which establishes the organization's approach to its employees and acts as a reference point for management. These proposals and actions are selected, either consciously or unconsciously, by those with formal authority in the organization.

Taking its constituent parts helps to clarify some issues. It consists of a *set* of factors; emphasizing that no single management statement or action can be evaluated totally in isolation. The definition includes *proposals and actions*. Even where an organization does not have a written industrial relations policy, there will nevertheless exist a series of shared expectations among the management about industrial relations. A policy must be *selected from possible alternatives*. Implicit here is a recognition that the operation of an industrial relations policy takes place within a set of contextual factors which limit managerial discretion. However, this must be qualified by acknowledging that it may be possible for the contextual factors to be altered.

Our definition also indicates that a policy must be established *by those with formal authority in the organization.* The idea of responsibility resting at the top level has become conventional wisdom in official government publications and was highlighted by the CIR (1973: 9) who stated that the board and top level managers have final responsibility for industrial relations policy. The definition states that the policy *acts as a reference point for management.* As Hawkins (1971: 204) observed:

> An assumption which underlines the concept of a policy in industrial relations as much as marketing, production or finance – is that the realisation of a company's objectives is heavily dependent on a consistent approach. Without a set of guidelines, consistency in day to day management can be very difficult to achieve unless there is tight central control of decision making.

The overriding objective in formalizing an industrial relations policy is to assist management to establish an ordered and consistent framework for the conduct of industrial relations. This means a formulation of principles or settled rules of action to which operating management is subject.

Finally, in our definition, policy *establishes the organization's approach to its employees.* We do not imply that this is necessarily done either deliberately or knowingly, or that the selection from possible alternatives is a necessarily or totally rational process uninfluenced by habit or custom.

Espoused policy and operational policy

As a first stage in conceptual development we propose distinguishing between espoused and operational policy. The *espoused policy* is a summation of the proposals, objectives and standards that top level management hold, and/or state they hold, for establishing the organization's approach to its employees. When policies are formalized, it is the espoused policy which management commits to paper. It is this form of policy with which discussions of industrial relations policy are generally concerned. We need not assume that these objectives and standards are ever considered as a whole, or that they exclude mutually exclusive aims or, finally, that they have been consistently and rigorously examined.

The organization will hold espoused policies in other areas of business such as marketing and finance, but in larger organizations it is usual for these to be integrated into some form of corporate plan

(McCarthy and Ellis, 1973: 103). There is a tendency for what we have termed the espoused industrial relations policy not to be integrated into such a plan, and so no formal allowance is made for the inevitable interaction of the industrial relations policy with other policies within the many constraints acting on the organization.

The *operational industrial relations policy,* in contrast to the espoused policy, is the way senior management are seen to order industrial relations priorities *vis-à-vis* those of other policies through the mechanisms of restrictions, control and direction that they impose on line management. This ordering of priorities, which reflects senior management's value system, is often done unconsciously. The operational policy is influenced by both its espoused counterpart and custom and practice, but it also reflects more than either of these. It is transmitted to line management by means of directives, or through the monitoring processes involved in customer service, marketing and budgetary and profit control. The operational policy is the way that senior management control the organization and, crucially, through the control, reward and punishment of line management. It is largely through the reward/ punishment system that line management assesses the internal value system of the organization. By this means the operational policy affects the way line management acts in an immediate and direct way which the espoused policy does not.

The espoused and operational industrial relations policies inevitably will differ. By their nature, policies cannot cover every eventuality. Espoused policies will be narrower: either specific to particular circumstances, or general statements of intent, to be interpreted or ignored by line management in accordance with the less clear but more dynamic operational policy. Nor is it possible in the creation of such policy to determine exactly the way it will be implemented and the effects it will have. Even where a conscious attempt is made to bring espoused and operational policies into line, it is unlikely that those responsible for them would be able in practice to assess their effects so minutely that there would be no disparity between them. A crucial element in our distinction is that in the very common situation where espoused policy and operational policy are different, line management will in effect follow the operational policy. The significance of this is that it is the operational policy which is experienced by the workforce, and it is that and their response to it that determines industrial relations, not the espoused policy.

Espoused and operational policy – some examples

The distinction between espoused and operational policies, and its importance, can be illustrated from our research. One example concerns line management operating on the ramp in an airline. Some of the airline's espoused policies are formalized in the 'operations manual' to which every manager is supposed to conform. These include for example the need to abide by Civil Aviation Authority (CAA) and British Airports Authority (BAA) procedures, the allocation of work within shifts and agreements reached with the unions. Other espoused policies are unwritten; for example, the managers in the ramp area are aware that they are supposed to keep within certain overtime limits, that they are expected to talk frequently to the shop stewards, that they are to avoid industrial action, and even that they are to prevent loaders not actually engaged in loading being seen 'hanging around' by the public.

But the managers are also aware of other pressures upon them. In particular, the enormous costs of hardware, the restriction of competition between airlines on the same route to 'service' (prices being controlled by cartel) and the pressure on such facilities as aircraft stands and baggage handling equipment are well known to all airline managers. These mean that aircraft 'turnround times' must be kept to a minimum. The managers are aware, too, of policies outside the formal industrial relations area (for example, 90 per cent of all flights will have passengers' baggage in the terminal within thirty minutes of touchdown).

The espoused policies are themselves inconsistent; it may not be possible to obey all the CAA and BAA regulations, allocate the work as laid down, talk to the shop stewards, restrict overtime and meet the thirty-minute performance standard. Furthermore, the espoused policy may not be operative; it may be no more than pious aims or statements, breached with impunity and unrewarded when followed. In this situation, line management has to select between conflicting directives or, in an area in which there are no directives, to take a unilateral decision. This selection is made on the basis of the manager's assessment of the priorities within the organizational value system. This will be done by reference to the whole organization – is the company's espoused industrial relations policy more important than its espoused policies on customer service or marketing? And in a more restricted sense – which industrial relations directives (espoused policy) have priority over which

Table 9.1. *Extent of managerial information on industrial relations policy*

Degree of information	No. of managers	% of managers
Well informed	31	12
Adequately informed	97	37.6
Poorly informed	120	46.5
Missing cases	10	3.9

others? And, ultimately, in an action sense – which of the things I can do will be acceptable to senior management and which will not? Choices are made in accordance with the manager's understanding of the on-going operational policy.

In our example, the ramp management are aware of and may support the company's espoused policy of restricting overtime. Yet the operational policy is that a fully manned shift to ensure a rapid turnround is more important and, if this can only be covered by offering additional overtime, then it will be done. The ramp management are also aware of, for example, and support the new agreement with the union that all loaders must wear safety shoes. But the operational policy is that a higher priority is given to ensuring that no work stoppages occur, and so management tolerates loaders who arrive for work in plimsolls.

These are examples of cases in which the espoused industrial relations policy is either published or widely known. There are many areas in which the espoused policy is less clear. A recent survey in the air transport industry questioned 258 managers about their knowledge and understanding of the espoused industrial relations policy (Brewster and Connock, 1978). The results are given in Table 9.1. The managers were also asked how well informed they would like to be, and their responses are presented in Table 9.2. These tables show that many managers are unclear about the policies that their airlines are asking them, formally, to pursue. Nonetheless, despite their lack of knowledge of the companies' espoused policies, the managers were getting on with their jobs, were dealing with staff and, in so far as no action had been taken against them, apparently doing so at a level of performance that was at least tolerable to their superiors. They were working to the operational policy.

Further evidence of differences between espoused policy and opera-

Table 9.2. *Managers' desired level of information on industrial relations policy*

Level of information	No. of managers	% of managers
Present level satisfactory	72	27.91
Like to be a little better informed	63	24.42
Like to be a good deal better informed	115	44.57
Missing cases	8	3.10

tional policy is found in the case study of a petrochemicals plant (Richbell, 1979). One dimension of the change to participation which was consciously built into the espoused policy was that there should be a greater flow of information via face-to-face interaction between management and workers. One method of furthering this aim was to incorporate the use of section meetings into the formal model of communications. However, investigation revealed that the incidence of section meetings was not as high as the formal model implied. Indeed Table 9.3 shows that only 35 per cent of the total workforce sample received information in this way, and in some subgroups the percentage was as low as 17. These results, indicating that many line managers held few or none of these meetings, show a discrepancy between the new espoused policy of holding section meetings and what actually happened. The fact that the incidence of section meetings was not monitored and that managers were not reprimanded for not holding such meetings would seem to imply that the change in espoused policy was not accompanied by a corresponding change in the plant's internal value system.

This failure to effect a change in face-to-face interaction is further illustrated if we examine the percentage of the workforce who received information from first line management (supervisors) on developments in the implementation of the participative agreement. Table 9.3 shows that the range was between 43 per cent and 10 per cent. Overall, only 29 per cent of the workforce received such information.

There had been in fact no organized attempt to explain the philosophy of participation to supervisors or to discuss how this approach would affect their work. No special communications were set up to ensure that the supervisors had the necessary information to further face-to-face

Table 9.3. *Extent of managerial interaction with the workforce*

| Source of information | % of sample receiving information | | | | | | |
| | Craft workers | | Process workers by department | | | | Total workforce |
	EEPTU	AUEW	A	B	C	D	
Section meeting	50	37	17	17	53	43	35
Information from supervisor	30	30	43	33	10	27	29

interaction. The lack of such facilities probably led to an interpretation that, within the organization's value system, these aspects of espoused policy were not given high priority by the instigators of the policy.

Such failures to bring operational policy in line with changes in espoused policy may, in part, be attributable to the more general problem that instigators tend to assume a united management team which is ready to support whatever policy they introduce. Frequently line managers are not consulted until after a decision to effect changes in industrial relations policy has been taken. Successful implementation, particularly where the change is fundamental, requires the line managers to be convinced of the need for change. The CIR (1973: 10) emphasized that 'industrial relations policies can hardly be expected to succeed without the agreement and acceptance of those who implement them'. This is particularly so where the espoused industrial relations policy requires line management to take a more active industrial relations decision-making role.

One aspect of the Co-operative Wholesale Society (CWS) study (Gill, 1974) was the provision for a greater degree of decentralization in the industrial relations decision-making role. This was considered essential in a diverse multi-plant organization embracing many industries and product groups. The CWS policy also provided for the development of a much stronger personnel function within the groups themselves with the establishment of joint negotiating committees at unit level chaired by the senior line manager at the unit concerned. The Industrial Relations Department greatly underestimated the training programme that was required in such a large and complex organization, and the implementation time scale was considerably extended. Despite the heavy involvement of the industrial relations specialists in the implementation process, line managers still preferred to refer industrial relations matters to the specialists and were reluctant to assume the responsibility themselves. The CWS policy has since been revised to assume a less rigid and more flexible stance. This was largely because line management still preferred to do things 'in their own way': thus indicating a preference for the long established operational policy rather than the new espoused policy imposed on them.

Managerial roles and policy

The CWS example underlines an important aspect of the distinction between espoused and operational policy, namely, the roles performed by different groups within the managerial hierarchy. Using a similar approach to Hunt (1975), we identify three major categories of management involved in industrial relations policy: *the instigators, implementers and facilitators*. The *instigators* determine industrial relations policy. They are usually a small group of senior personnel. In some organizations they may be the board of directors or senior members of the head office of a multi-plant company or, in other cases, the decision may stem from one or two senior individuals within a company. The personnel department may or may not be involved in this level of the decision-making process. Illustrations of this are drawn from our case studies.

In the petrochemicals plant discussed earlier, for example, instigators of the participation scheme were a group of senior managers comprising the works general manager, his deputy, the heads of production, engineering, and the personnel department. Although this was a multi-plant company, the decision to adopt a participative approach to the formulation of a productivity agreement had been made by these instigators at the plant level.

In the CWS study, the new espoused policy was instigated by the Industrial Relations Department in conjunction with an outside consultant, and was then agreed by the chief executive officer and the senior management. This draft policy was then submitted to all group general managers and group personnel officers for their comments prior to final ratification.

In the airlines, it is possible that the instigators may not even be resident in the country of implementation. For, although the policy of most airlines is to provide pay and conditions broadly comparable to the 'national carrier' in each country in which they operate, most major policy decisions are made at headquarters. In the foreign airlines studied, all the changes to espoused policy were either initiated or at least approved by overseas headquarters. In one British airline new policies initiated by a newly appointed personnel manager were agreed and promulgated by a small team consisting of the personnel manager himself, the managing director, the operations manager and the general manager (technical).

It is important to note that the role of the instigators is not restricted to the espoused policy. They also determine the operational policy, although they are rarely aware of this. Their values, the organization's value system, are indicated to those further down the managerial hierarchy by the control systems, the areas which are monitored and the kinds of performance that are rewarded or punished. In practice the lower managers adapt their behaviour to conform with their perception of this operational policy, rather than the espoused policies.

The second category, the *implementers*, comprises the main body of the managerial hierarchy (excluding the instigators) and it is their actions, or lack of action, which reflect the operational policy. The line manager (or his equivalent in occupations where this term is not used) assesses the various demands upon him and acts in accordance with both his own abilities and limitations and his understanding of what senior executives require of him, or what we have called the organization's internal value system. Support for the espoused policy among the implementers is variable and this is understandable when changes in industrial relations policy, particularly those involving a conscious attempt to alter operational policy, may be threatening and produce feelings of insecurity among them. Operational policy develops in response to a set of pressures (including espoused policies) but, in hierarchical organizations its implementation will depend largely on managers' assessments of their superiors' wishes. Over time the line manager obtains a very detailed understanding of operational policy as he is rewarded, punished, well thought of, or reprimanded. A change to the policy means that his previous understanding is no longer valid. He has to begin the process of testing, guessing, and trial and error again in order to identify the new operational policy.

In addition to these two main groups, it is possible to identify a further sub-group – the *facilitators*. These are the experts or specialists in industrial relations who are involved in advising and assisting in the implementation of industrial relations policy. The facilitators are likely to also hold membership of one or other of the two main groups. Where the instigators are involved in decisions to implement major change in industrial relations policy, the facilitators may become more visible and active as a small group and the difference between their function and that of the implementers, in relation to policy, may become more visible and obvious. This was so in our petrochemicals example with its move from distributive to integrative bargaining (to use the terms of Walton and McKersie, 1965). Here, the personnel specialists found that their contact with the employee representatives increased significantly and led to a separation from, and in some cases to conflict with, the line managers. Furthermore, the role of the facilitator may also become more important in such situations. In this example involving changes in managerial style, the personnel department was very active in its development. The facilitators become particularly important where the change involves specialist techniques and knowledge and has no precedent. Applying the concepts of Lawrence and Lorsch (1967), it would appear in this case that participation became a major vehicle for facilitating the integration of the various differentiated functions and departments of the organization, and that the personnel department, as the experts cast in a supporting role, became a vital element in the successful functioning of this method of integration.

Conclusions

The main focus of this paper has been to establish two sets of concepts which extend the analysis of industrial relations policy. These concepts are the espoused/operational policy and the managerial role distinctions of instigators/implementers/facilitators. Our case study examples indicate that the operational policy both in terms of its features and content has the greater long-term effect on the quality of industrial relations, while the espoused policy tends to have less direct effect. The latter's main impact is governed by the extent to which the espoused policy is integrated into the operational level.

The context within which the industrial relations policy operates will also have major effects on the quality of industrial relations. The influence of the context is often felt more at the operational level as various contextual constraints and pressures acting on the policy may encourage a more adaptable and expedient approach. For example, a change in the organization's financial position or marketing strategy will often have a direct effect on operational policy. It is perhaps in the content of the espoused industrial relations policy that the influence of the contextual factors is least, and where there is the most scope for initiating new policies without reference to environmental constraints. One exception to this tendency is government legislation where changes often have a rapid impact on the espoused policy, particularly the content, but filter through to the operational policy more slowly.

The existence of divergence between espoused and operational policy has been indicated. Instigators are more likely to achieve their aims if they are aware of this divergence and of their responsibility for its existence. For the degree of divergence depends on the extent to which changes in espoused policy are accompanied by complementary changes in the organization's value system. Changing the latter requires instigators to restructure the order of priorities within the organization and overtly to adapt the reward system to emphasize the new structure.

10
Management decision-making and shop floor participation

MICK MARCHINGTON and RAY
LOVERIDGE

Introduction

Classical organization theory involved a search for generally applicable principles and techniques in order to develop efficient and effective decision-making structures. The anticipation was of one 'ideal' management system (Lupton, 1971: 18–19). Nowadays, however, the emphasis is on the particularistic or contingency perspective. This regards the design of an effective organization as necessarily having to be adapted to cope with the contingencies which derive from the circumstances of the environment. But nevertheless this is clearly still related to a logic of efficiency. Not surprisingly trade union demands for employee participation are viewed in the same light, and a characteristic of most management submissions to the Committee of Inquiry on Industrial Democracy (Bullock, 1977) was the potential effects on efficiency – primarily problems – related to any extension in involvement.

For participation to be acceptable to management, it would have to lead to increased efficiency and not its converse as some management bodies fear.[1] If organizations have developed structures which are responsive to the exigencies of the external environment, then participation represents a problem since it brings to bear a different rationale and the possibility of multiple perspectives on any given problem presented by the environment. Consequently, managements are likely to resist this intrusion unless it is shown to be capable of enhancing effectiveness. Certainly, it is management who introduce the majority of schemes, so analysis of their current systems of decision-making is of crucial importance to any discussion of shop floor participation. This has, of course, been noted by Walker (275: 446–51), in his attempt to isolate a number of determinants of participation; he introduced the term

73

participation potential which consists of the structural and situational factors confronting the enterprise. His other determinants – managements' acceptance of workers' participation and the propensity to participate – have been adequately dealt with elsewhere.[2] For the purposes of this paper, we will concentrate on an examination of participation potential and the way in which the environment may serve to constrain the opportunities for the shop floor to become involved in decision-making. Although the analysis will be based upon the structural factors, this is not meant to imply that these alone determine the possibility for participation. The exact interplay of structural elements constraining participation and management's attitudes, perceptions and ideology is always a difficult problem to disentangle and we will regularly refer to management perceptions of the environment. Indeed, as Child (1973a: 247) notes in his critique of contingency theory, it is inadequate 'to conclude that environmental circumstances determine intraorganisational features in any direct relationship since important elements of choice are found to empirically intervene'. We feel, however, from our observations, that environmental influences have a significant impact on management decision-making, and it is for this reason that we are assessing these influences in greater depth. We will use data from two companies under investigation – each one from a different industry, and displaying very different characteristics in terms of participation potential – and we shall particularly focus,[3] as others have, on the product market and technological constraints (Hebden and Shaw, 1977; Guest and Fatchett, 1974; Terry, 1977).

The nature of the product market

A number of recent studies of workplace industrial relations have identified the significance of the product market, particularly for situations of indeterminacy. A passage from the investigation of the footwear industry by Goodman *et al.* (1977: 23) illustrates this admirably:

> The major features of the product market are the relatively slow growth in total demand, the intensity of competition, the recent dramatic increase in import penetration of the home market, the enhanced importance of fashion, and marked seasonality in the nature and level of demand. All these factors have important implications for industrial relations, perhaps most notably in the frequent changes in both volume and type

of production . . . Most firms 'make to order' and consequently flexibility and speed of response are at a premium,
particularly in the fashion sectors.

The effect of the market on decision-making is demonstrably apparent;
conceptually it can be analysed in terms of three related but distinct
factors. First, we need to assess the *degree of competitiveness* of the
market; to what extent the firm is dependent upon general movements
in the market rather than able to dictate terms. Secondly, we need to
examine the rate of change or *stability* of the market; whether it is characterized by seasonal trends, contracting or expanding, and the degree
to which these trends are predictable. Finally, we can look at the *orientation* of the market; whether a company is geared to industrial buyers
or consumers, to what extent the product is fashion-orientated or subject
to repeat orders. Clearly the product which is a component for another
industry – in which capital investment is high – provides a more deter-
minate environment in the short term.

Each of these factors can vary along a continuum, one end of which
is characterized by relative stability and certainty, the other by indeterminacy. A furniture firm, which we studied, is very much towards the
latter, and in many ways similar to the footwear situation outlined above.
The firm competes in the luxury kitchen and bedroom markets. It has a
workforce of approximately seven hundred, of which five hundred are
on the shop floor. On site, there are two manual unions: FTAT (Furniture, Timber and Allied Trades Union), which organizes the vast majority of the workforce including maintenance fitters, electricians and
internal transport as well as the more usual woodworking trades, and
TGWU, which has unionized the lorry drivers. All the shop floor are
unionized as, indeed, are all the staff up to the level of superintendent.
For the trade, working conditions are generally pleasant, especially the
assembly and packing areas which are well-lit and quiet.

The market is predominantly fashion-oriented, with designs being
continually updated and modified in order to stimulate customer demand.
When a product has been marketed for a number of years, it is removed
from the range or given a complete overhaul. Fairly minute changes in
product design frequently take place; for example, on ranges introduced
over a two-year period modifications were soon made to a number of
the parts. Moreover, changes to metric measurements have doubled the
number of available products. Although the basic design of units within
any one range is similar, each unit has a number of alternative colours,

and these too are constantly changing. Consequently, the amount of individual types of unit available at any one time is in excess of several hundred, and these are continually altering in size, shape and colour.

This kind of environment tends to result in energies being primarily directed towards it. Flexibility is at a premium and regular top-level management meetings are held in order to balance activities and develop new products for the market. Survival depends very much on responding quickly and competitively to changing customer tastes. As Burns and Stalker (1961: 671) note, many of the skills in the electronics industry were contributed 'to the focal task of determining sales policy and . . . deciding on the outward appearance, performance standards and price of sets'. On occasion, this resulted in the development of products which, although commercially marketable and recognized as a valuable addition to the field, were not technically possible. One such instance demonstrated the way in which the technical programme was not developed until several years after the 'product' had been launched (ibid.: 72). Below, we will present a similar example for the furniture firm. It is apparent that, occasionally, important strategic decisions are made without reference to specialist technical management, let alone shop floor representation.

Furthermore, as one might expect, in addition to its fashion orientation, the market is fiercely competitive. No one firm holds more than about 15 per cent of the market, and the influence of the leader at any one point in time rapidly diminishes as new firms enter the industry. The firm under review is one of the leaders, but its share is considerably less than 10 per cent. Even though the size of the market expanded considerably over the last five years, no one company has been able to increase its share to any great degree, partly because of the regular increase in new manufacturers. Recently, however, overall production of kitchen units has been declining and all the competitors have been adversely affected to some degree.

Beynon (1973: 155–8) observed similar characteristics in the car industry. The market sets very definite limits on the extent to which security or prior consultation can be guaranteed. He describes a situation in which men were laid off with only a few hours' advance warning. Similarly, Stewart (1970: 173) offers a piece of advice for managers when she states that 'the would-be manager who wants an uneventful life . . . would be wise to go into a monopoly, preferably with a product with a stable market'. Once again, in order to remain competitive, emphasis has to be placed on flexibility and adaptability;

requirements which run contrary to the principles of involvement and discussion prior to decision-making.

At the furniture firm, demand varies over very short cycles; orders from week to week can vary by as much as 200 to 300 per cent, and therefore forward planning is extremely imprecise. Forecasts are often proved wrong and companies are reticent about manufacturing for stock since the product mix may change drastically at short notice. Companies work to six- and eight-week delivery periods and production programmes are computed accordingly, although constant readjustments are made to these on a daily, and even hourly, basis. Management systems are geared very much to incoming order statistics, almost to the extent that morale varies directly with the number of orders. Although shop stewards have access to order statistics on a weekly basis, the variations are so large that little constructive discussion can take place; rather, meetings are often characterized by discussion praising or criticizing sales staff, instead of assessing either the causes or consequences of these figures.

We can see, therefore, at the furniture company, a very unpredictable and indeterminate product market, one subject to continual change and increasing competition. In order to take advantage of changes in the situation, rapid readjustments have to be made and quick decisions have to be taken. The market context militates against stability and certainty. Managers feel they have to react quickly in order to take advantage of a market situation or to ensure that production is not halted. They feel that there is no time for discussion prior to action and that the speed required for decision-taking does not allow them time to ensure commitment or encourage alternative ideas from shop floor representatives.

Two examples serve to demonstrate this point. First, at a time when the market was depressed and the company was attempting to cut costs, management devised a plan for reducing the stock of raw materials to an absolute minimum. This meant, in effect, that chipboard would only be bought in the day before it was required; since this was delivered by other firms, problems arose and shortages occurred on several occasions. However, the policy was not formally altered. Late one afternoon, a load of chipboard arrived several days earlier than required and management decided that, rather than run the risk of further shortages, they would unload and store the material. The stewards were in a meeting at the time and, on discovering the apparent change in policy, demanded a statement from management as to why they had not been informed of the new situation. Management justified their decision in terms of previous shortages and present availability; the stewards understood the viewpoint but felt they could not condone management's precipitate action. Although the issue went no further, this demonstrates the way in which the timing of decisions is so crucial to shop floor participation. External factors, that is, a delivery in this case, had led to the need for a quick decision without regard for the need for involvement.

The second example concerns a major change in policy and illustrates the manner in which external exigencies lead to non-participation, not only of the shop floor, but also of members of management. The prime opportunity to test customer opinion is at the National Exhibition held each year. In this case, the firm produced a new design and, in the light of tightening markets, decided to exhibit the model primarily on the basis of its external appearance without sufficient evaluation of its engineering or production features. Little or no discussion took place with the production management prior to the launch. The response was enthusiastic and orders were taken since this was seen as an important way in which to 'corner' the market. Production management (and stewards) were resentful of the non-involvement, even more so when a number of the parts were found to be unobtainable or impractical. Delivery dates were exceeded, production targets were never reached and substantial re-design took place. Clearly, what had happened was that top management became so concerned with the problems of the market that they had failed to consider technical or interpersonal implications. Decisions had been made by a small management team operating in an entrepreneurial manner – a system of decision-making largely incongruent with the more stable and long-term nature of participative techniques. This, in effect, not only demonstrates the indeterminacy of the external environment but also the way in which management systems *may* develop in response to this.

The technological environment and production system

The major consequence of unstable, competitive and fashion-oriented markets lies in the potential impossibility for prior involvement of the shop floor if quick decisions are to be made. As we noted at the outset, some of this non-involvement is certainly due to management themselves; to some extent, management *legitimates* non-involvement by reference to the external environment. But, as we have seen, the market sets limits on the opportunities for participation; to an extent, the same is true of the technological system at the kitchen firm. However, as we will see by comparison with our second company – a metal-working organization employing approximately 2,500 people of whom 1,500 work on the shop floor and are organized (to about 85 per cent coverage) by GMWU, AUEW, EETPU – 'scientific expertise' can also play a part in legitimizing non-involvement by management.

Within the technological environment, we can also identify three potential sources which influence decision-making. First, there is the *stability* of the technical market; the regularity with which new machinery is introduced and the amount of forward planning that can go into its choice. Secondly, there is the *degree of interdependence* within the production system; the degree to which one operation is dependent upon others, the speed with which problems in one section can affect or be transferred to others. Finally, there is the degree of *scientific complexity* of the process; the need for scientifically qualified management and research support staff. This may result in non-involvement due to 'lack of expertise' rather than 'lack of time', as in the cases discussed so far.

At the furniture firm, the technical operation is basically simple – chipboard is cut to size, drilled, machined, partially assembled and finally packed. The rapid growth in the market has led to constant changes in machinery available for the job. Some machinery – especially for the cutting and drilling operations – is virtually obsolete in a few years since new machines will have been produced which can do functions in a fraction of the time. Indeed, one drilling machine was replaced after only three years by a newer version capable of performing a greater number of operations in a substantially shorter period, and requiring little or no time for setting up for variations in ranges. Since, also, some machines are central to the whole flow of operations through the rest of the factory, the effect of reductions in time spent on certain activities is soon multiplied throughout the whole process. Therefore, in order to keep up with competitors, machinery is regularly changed.

Although the overall process is not complex, each unit is composed of a large number of separate parts, requiring precise integration at the appropriate part in the production flow. Each unit comprises, in addition to each operation, hinges, screws, supports, plinths, extrusions, instructions and packaging materials. Clearly, unavailability of any one of these parts leads to production stoppages; since a unit can be manufactured in a few hours once it has been cut to size, effects of shortages are soon experienced elsewhere in the operation. A large number of these parts are bought elsewhere and problems in other firms soon transferred to the furniture manufacturer. In other words, management systems are, once again, fairly dependent upon the external environment, whether it be in terms of the speed of technological change or production dependence on other operations.

In our observations of production managers, particular issues continually re-emerged during the course of any one day, and each decision taken quickly leads to another set of implications to be dealt with.[4] One manager spent most of his day attempting to ensure that parts were in the correct place when required, that deliveries would be on time, and that the production plan had not been revised at short notice. Clearly, in such an indeterminate environment, decisions do tend to be made on the spur of the moment and managers do appear to spend most of their time moving from one crisis to another. Not surprisingly, the shop floor become exasperated by continual changes being made without their knowledge or their involvement, and a substantial part of meetings was devoted to complaints about such issues. Junior management often had to defend their actions without themselves having been informed of the reasons for changes. If lower levels of management are not aware of changes or the reasons for them, there is little potential for participation by their subordinates or by the stewards with whom they come into contact, unless stewards go to higher management. Even with a well developed formal structure for employee involvement – as in the case of this plant – participation may be constrained by virtue of other factors, notably the external environment, or management's perception of it.

For the purpose of contrast, we can briefly describe these two factors at the metal firm. The technology is more stable than in the kitchen industry; furnaces which are used for melting down nickel have not changed a great deal in design over the last twenty years, and many new items of machinery are not that different from those which they replace. In most instances, changes in machinery can be planned for over a number of years and, as in the forgings industry, machinery becomes obsolescent mainly through old age rather than because of new inventions. The new techniques which are introduced – such as powder atomization – can be planned and introduced over a lengthy time period. The method of production is of a large batch nature and production programmes can be planned accordingly. Although there is generally a specific flow of work through the factory, operations take longer than, and timing is not so critical as, in the furniture factory. Very few of the products require packaging, except in boxes, and no printed leaflets or instructions are required for insertion. Overall, the product at the end of the operation is essentially melted, treated and manufactured raw materials (nickel and other metals).

Although timing is not a crucial factor as in assembly operations, the shop floor is regularly excluded from decision-making since management feel they are not suitably qualified. Since the process involves chemicals and metals, many procedures are well known in advance; for example, metals have to be treated to a specific temperature in order to melt. Managers possess qualifications in this field – many with degrees – and resent the intrusion of 'non-qualified' personnel. Many had worked in research laboratories earlier in their careers, spending several years experimenting with new ideas. They had developed a technical and scientific knowledge which the shop floor did not possess. Indeed, by virtue of their qualifications, they felt they had earned the right to be managers; quite clearly, participation in their decision-making activities tended to be viewed with some suspicion.

Conclusions

From this examination of participation potential, we can see the way in which this may vary between organizations dependent upon their market situation and technological environment. This is most noticeable in relation to the time factor. Basically, if firms have to respond quickly to changes, employee participation – which most students admit does take longer than authoritarian management – is difficult to put into practice. In contrast, firms operating in more stable environments may be able to devise systems to guarantee a fuller exposure of impending problems. However, if these firms make scientifically complex products, this may also limit the potential for involvement. In other words, the external environment may exert quite an influence on decision-making structures.

Once again though, the problem arises as to what extent decision-making is influenced by structure rather than management ideology or style. It would appear that management's *perception* of the environment is probably the most critical variable. In our case studies, management attempted to legitimate its use of authority through superior knowledge of the environment. In the case of the furniture manufacturer, the style and beliefs of the managing director affected the ideology of the company as a whole. Since he perceived the product market as such an uncertain factor, he felt that only an aggressive entrepreneurial and highly personalized style of decision-making would be effective. In the metal firm, scientifically trained managers tended to dominate due to the greater stability of the product market. Centralized control structures were such as to leave them freedom for decision-making in the technical and task-related areas, those in which they gained both job satisfaction and legitimation as managers.

In both cases, the grounds for establishing legitimacy tended to preclude joint regulation within those areas perceived as crucial to the future well-being of the firm, that is, production control and new products in the furniture firm, and product design and engineering in the metal firm. Employee involvement was accepted by management in those areas which were of lesser importance to them, ones in which decision-making was not seen to be a priority for them. In other words, joint decision-making was confined to the relatively 'safe' aspects of the business whilst unilateral decision-making continued in those areas felt to be crucial to the future well-being of the firm.

In conclusion, therefore, we can see the importance of examining both management ideology and the external environment in order to gauge management's perception of the prevailing uncertainty. In both firms, we have noted that non-participation may be attributed to management style as well as influenced by the indeterminacy of the external environment. Clearly both factors are crucial in determining the potential for shop floor participation in management decision-making.

PART II

The context of management strategies in industrial relations

11
Introduction to Part II

KEITH THURLEY and STEPHEN WOOD

In Part I, the contributors were mainly trying to pioneer empirical research on management policy in industrial relations. In discussing these cases, it was recognized that decisions on industrial relations policies reflected a range of managerial objectives in the production, marketing and financial fields. For management, industrial relations can hardly be treated as a discrete set of issues, even though managerial specialists in industrial relations have often to concentrate on the detailed merits and limitations of procedures and systems. It is one thing, however, to start from the industrial relations activities and policies of managers and to admit following this that many additional factors have to be taken into account. It is another thing to recognize that the *context* of management strategy is the crucial determining influence on decisions in industrial relations. The detailed discussion of alternative policies in collective bargaining, for example, may then not be a matter of whether managements are influenced by Clegg or Donovan, or any industrial theory, but rather the need to develop consistent policies, following, for example, the logic of launching a new product or of opening up a new market.

This second approach is followed by contributors to Part II. They focus on the *context* of the decisions, but emphasize different aspects of that context. Some authors assume a direct link between formal corporate strategy and industrial relations policies; others see this relation as more complex, as it depends on internal organizational relations within the firm. From different vantage points and with different focuses, collectively, they extend the debate beyond the question of defining industrial relations policies and strategies *per se*.

There are, in general terms, *three* approaches to studying context:

(a) *'Macro' explanations of managerial roles and actions*

It is possible to try to explain managerial actions by the general role of managers in society and the beliefs that go with it. A class theory or an élite theory of management would fall into this category. Such theories require an explanation in historical terms of the origin of the structures of which management is judged to form a part. A typical explanation starts with the form of economic development and traces the implications of this for political control and managerial authority.

In Gospel's account of the development of employee/employer systems and structures in Great Britain (from the eighteenth century to the mid-twentieth), he is very conscious of the possibilities of utilizing managerial theories of the firm or neo-Marxist analysis to provide a general explanation. He reviews a set of employer policies from the 'putting out' system to the creation of centralized labour departments in large conglomerates, laying emphasis on the advantages to the employer of utilizing particular systems and structures in certain situations. There could certainly be said to be a long-term trend towards greater bureaucratization. However, Gospel is also well aware that it is easy to exaggerate such a trend and he is particularly concerned with the fact that older employee systems and structures survive alongside the new. Subcontracting, for example, survives and flourishes in certain industries; federal decentralized firms, where local market strategies can be pursued and local payment systems utilized, exist together with the large-scale professionalized and centralized personnel and industrial relations departments of other multi-plant firms. Strategy and structure, the twin concepts of Chandler (1962; 1977), are inter-dependent across the various aspects of managerial decision-making. This implies that the variation in employer policies and strategies noted are likely to persist. In this way Gospel questions the validity of any simplified macro-level causal explanation of managerial strategies. He is rightly content at this stage to set down the broad evolution of different employee systems and structures, to point to some of the plausible reasons behind the development of particular systems and to raise the problem of the *lack* of change in so many industries and firms.

John Henley tackles the same issues by making a comparison of employer policies and industrial relations in two rapidly industrializing Third World countries, Kenya and Malaysia. Both have a common heritage of British colonial rule and both have many British-owned firms and have been influenced by British ideas on personnel management, labour relations and trade unionism. But Henley also points to the way that the pressures of 'macro' level economic, political and social objectives involved in the rapid development of newly independent nations place considerable constraints on employer policies. In particular, and in contrast with Great Britain (in the countries he discusses), there are much closer and more direct relationships between company policies and the State. Trade union behaviour is strictly limited in scope and controlled by direct legislation and managerial prerogatives are clearer and also protected by the State. He argues that the industrial relations and personnel policies of firms are directly linked to the need espoused by governments to encourage multi-national enterprises to invest in the countries concerned and to develop high productivity in export-oriented industries. Typically this can be done by paying relatively high wages and through the provision of job security and a protected status for permanent employees in such industries. The implication is that newly industrializing countries are driven towards a 'dual structure' in the economy and that there is a direct political objective in the encouragement by the State of 'modern' employer/employee relationships in the expanding modern industrial and commercial sector of the economy.

Having made this case on 'macro' grounds, Henley then shows that there are significant differences between Kenya and Malaysia in the types of policies typically followed by employers in the 'modern' sectors. The Malaysian companies, compared with Kenya, follow policies which place much greater emphasis on psychological 'rewards' to employees; they attempt to stimulate loyalty and identity with the company and try to offer long-term employment in return for commitment, similar in this respect to the Japanese model. An easy and superficial explanation of this is found in the cultural heritage of South-East Asia, compared with Africa. But can 'culture', on its own, explain a certain set of decisions by managers? Clearly, it can be accepted that a particular society may encourage its managers to place a high priority on certain criteria in business decisions. Those decisions will also, however, be directly influenced by the particular constraints of the situation in which they are made. There is therefore a rationality to such decisions, although it is bounded by cultural factors and the institutions and practices accepted as legitimate in that society. This implies that there is no real possibility of *directly* predicting trends in employer behaviour or trade union response from a *general* macro-level theory of development.

(b) *Economic rationality and managerial actions*

The developments of the neo-classical theory of the firm by Simon (1957), Marris (1964) and others sought to retain the concept of economic rationality but to extend this to judgements about employment contracts in local labour markets, decisions on the political and legal constraints of investments and choices of managerial priorities. The concept of market rationality was thus enlarged to deal with optimizing between or within a range of objectives, social, political and economic. In this way, it becomes possible to compare the types of strategic choice open to managers in organizations with different types and mixes of objectives. Thomson adopts this approach to compare industrial relations strategies in the private, the public non-market and market sectors. He is able to set up a broad classification showing the differences between the factors affecting decision-making in the three sectors. The focus of his argument is on the different objectives of management (profit, growth in market share, public service), the tendencies to centralization in the public sector and the way in which lower managerial actions are constrained in these different sectors. This enables him to argue that a close relationship exists between the economic and administrative contexts of organizations and the type of industrial relations structures and procedures found in those organizations.

The chapter written by Tyson questions, or at least qualifies, this argument. For him, it is less possible to accept a causal relationship between the environmental situation of an organization and the development of industrial relations and personnel policies without explaining *why* the specialists in industrial relations and personnel management (and, by implication, line management) respond in the way that they do. He tries to demonstrate that a close examination of the actual constructs used by such specialists in their thinking about role relationships and personnel problems tends to reflect organizational cultures rather than a clear set of occupational norms and beliefs. His evidence is certainly not conclusive, but it does point to the similarities in values between personnel and industrial relations staff in each organization. He also shows that there are considerable differences between personnel specialists employed in different types of organizational environment. Tyson suggests that the very role of the personnel specialist leads to an accommodation between organizational and personal values – partly because it is essentially a 'process' role in which adjustments and modifications in the views of actors and interest groups are constantly being negotiated, and partly because personnel specialists are frequently asked to represent the organization and define its particular identity and character.

The Tyson argument qualifies but is not essentially opposed to that of Thomson. Both are concerned with the rationality assumed and used by actors in different contexts. Thomson develops the contrast between the goals and constraints in different sectors of the economy, whereas Tyson is more concerned with the criteria actually used in managerial decision-making company by company. It is important to note that Tyson appears to doubt that personnel specialists will be able to develop strategic changes in policies and approaches, given the accommodation process built into their roles.

(c) *The organizational context of managerial decisions*

We turn lastly to a specifically organizational approach to the analysis of managerial actions. This third approach lays emphasis on differences between organizations in terms of goals, structure, functions and behaviour patterns. The argument is that managerial roles are essentially organizational roles concerned with decision-making, control and the implementation of decisions in specific situations. Managers are likely to come up with different industrial relations strategies, according to the organizational context of decision-making.

The first case analysed by Seglow deals with a public sector corporation, the BBC. In his analysis he follows along similar lines to Thomson. He demonstrates that the goals of the organization were altered fundamentally by competition from commercial television. This competition took the BBC out of the non-market public sector into the public market sector. The pressures this generated had a strong impact on managerial policies and provided both new constraints on and new stimuli for taking industrial relations decisions. At the same time, the new organizational situation altered the power position of the unions and indeed of individual members of the BBC who could go and work for ITV if they were dissatisfied. Conflict became more overt and the numbers and seriousness of disputes escalated.

The case shows two important aspects of the change process by which industrial relations were transformed. First, the 'organizational culture', so important in Tyson's argument, itself changed under extreme pressure to raise performance. Secondly, industrial relations strategy – if it is developed – is the response to a particular set of organizational problems. It does not emerge on its own.

The Loveridge chapter develops these points using data from the engineering industry in the West Midlands (the source of much previous argument about the nature of industrial relations in the UK, especially that of the Donovan Commission). The first thrust of Loveridge's thesis is that there is no necessary long-term trend of bureaucratization, based on concentration of capital, leading to a strong functional development of personnel management. In spite of growth in the size of enterprises, the size of plants is not necessarily affected nor the extent of diversity in the way those plants are run. This is not just a lag or delay in developing tighter, more standardized procedures and policies. Companies strive to keep a more decentralized system, particularly in industrial relations, as they have to contend with constant shifts in the product and local labour market situations and with conflicts between the policies and objectives which are relevant to these situations. Industrial relations strategy is therefore not simply an extension of corporate strategy. On the contrary, it is best understood in terms of inter-dependence between a whole set of corporate and establishment policies and strategies. As Loveridge concludes, 'strategy in the external environment impacts upon strategy in the internal concerns of the enterprise and so shapes and constrains managerial action in both areas'.

The organizational context of industrial relations strategies is therefore *not* simply a question of the shifting goals of the organization or of the 'culture' of the organization. It means understanding the conflicts between alternative goals and policies followed by and argued between different groups and sections *within* the organization. The emphasis by organizations on 'fragmented systems' of control is best understood as a deliberate response by management to conflicting pressures from different functions and sections. Loveridge makes a general interpretation of British managerial policy and extends his argument far beyond interpreting particular cases. He sees organizational constraints as the probable cause of the lack of radical change in industrial relations strategies and policies.

To consider the context of managerial strategies in industrial relations leads to a consideration of the different conceptions of strategy according to the theoretical framework used. It also raises the question of why a 'strategic' approach does not seem to be adopted by so many enterprises in the United Kingdom. A full discussion of these issues is therefore attempted in Part III, in the concluding section of the book.

12

The development of management organization in industrial relations: a historical perspective

HOWARD GOSPEL

Until recently there has been only limited scholarly work in Britain placing the development of employers' labour policies in historical perspective. For the most part business historians have concentrated on the organizational, financial, and commercial aspects of the business enterprise and have tended to neglect the labour and industrial relations side of business growth and developments. Even the best company histories, such as those of Unilever, Courtaulds, ICI, and Pilkingtons, focus on the more formal and evident aspects of labour relations. Labour historians, for their part, have traditionally concentrated on the organization and activities of trade unions, the notable exceptions being Hobsbawm (1964) and Pollard (1968). In the contemporary industrial relations literature there are few studies which focus on the employer–manager side of the industrial relations systems, though in the past ten years there has been a recognition that management should be one of the topics high on the research agenda (Bain and Clegg, 1974; Wood, 1982).

Other academic disciplines and approaches do, however, offer some potentially useful perspectives for historical analysis. In economics it is not so much the neo-classical theory of the rational profit-maximizing entrepreneur, but more recent managerial theories of the firm which are relevant. There is, for example, Williamson's transaction cost theory of organizational form and hierarchies: this interestingly compares closely with Chandler's quite independent historical study of company structure and strategy (Williamson, 1975; Chandler, 1977). Sociologists for a long time have been interested in organizations, their environments, and control systems. Woodward (1970), for example, identified three basic types of managerial control – 'personal' control through direct supervi-

91

sion and the development of managerial hierarchies, 'administrative' control based on more impersonal rules specifying required behaviour, and 'mechanical' control embedded in machinery and production processes. From a different perspective, neo-Marxist writers have viewed the development of the firm and managerial structures as social control devices and means of extracting surplus value (Marglin, 1974). Drawing in part on the work of Braverman (1974) on the labour process, others have recently developed typologies of employer strategies. In the British context, Friedman (1977) has talked about the strategies of 'direct' control by close supervision and coercive restraints, and 'responsible autonomy' where some control is delegated to workers and they are treated in a more cooptive manner by employers. In the USA, Edwards (1979) has identified a gradual development of employer strategies from 'simple' control by foremen and relatively unsophisticated piecework systems, through 'technical' control via machines and methods of work organization, to a 'bureaucratic' stage where employers seek to develop elaborate systems of internal hierarchies, rules and procedures to control workers. Drawing on some of these concepts and frameworks, there is considerable scope for a historical analysis of the growth of managerial structures and strategies in the employment field.

The aim of this chapter is to identify some of the institutional arrangements and structures of control which firms have used for the management of labour. It deals with the organizational means and personnel through which firms recruited their workforce, organized the work process, disciplined and rewarded workers, and dealt with trade unions. The emphasis is on the diversity of structures, why they came into existence, and how they changed over time. It is hoped that this examination of structure will be a useful starting point for understanding employer strategies. The chapter focuses primarily on the late nineteenth and twentieth centuries, but in order to place later systems in context it begins by considering some earlier methods of labour management.

The putting-out system and the rise of the factory

Under the early putting-out system the merchant–manufacturer or master–artisan supplied raw materials and sometimes simple tools and machinery to a dispersed labour force who worked in their own homes. For a certain quantity of physical output they were paid a price stipulated in advance. The putter-out or his agent would then collect the output and arrange its sale. From his point of view the system had several advantages: it required minimal capital investment; if offered flexibility in the face of changes in product demand; risks were spread over a number of discrete operating units; and from the point of view of labour management, there were savings in the cost and trouble of recruiting, supervising, and maintaining a workforce.

The system which developed early in textiles spread in the eighteenth century to other industries such as footwear and metal working. It never, however, developed in mining, iron smelting, or glass, chemical, and paper manufacture, industries where capital costs were higher and where production was not as easily divisible into separate processes.

Marglin (1974) has contested the traditional explanations of the demise of the putting-out system. He has argued that it was superseded not for any technical or efficiency reasons (the latter being defined as greater output, without a corresponding increase in inputs), but because factories offered capitalists a permanent position in the production process and a better means of discipline and control over workers. More recently Williamson (1980) has retorted with an assertion of the efficiency and transaction cost advantages of later capitalist forms of organization over the putting-out system.

A number of points need to be made here. It is too simplistic to dichotomize efficiency and control in seeking to explain the development of organizational forms. The two must be seen as interrelated. Though Marglin directs our attention to control, he does in fact see this as an intermediate goal, with the ultimate objective being the extraction of surplus value and capital accumulation. He admits that factory organization may also increase efficiency over time. However, Marglin plays down some possible immediate efficiency advantages: reduced transportation expenses, lower buffer stocks, reduced wastage of materials and possible benefits of assigning workers to jobs on the basis of their comparative advantage. Williamson, on the other hand, accepts that there might be labour control advantages in moving from putting-out to factory organization, but the ultimate factor determining organizational forms is seen by him as relative efficiency and transaction costs. Thus, though in both frameworks labour control might be seen as an intermediate goal, the two arguments are nonetheless incompatible; unfortunately, they are also untestable.

A more fruitful approach is to examine the historical record for any actual problems and opportunities which have confronted capitalists, focusing on the structures and strategies with which they have experimented. Such an approach will enable the development of factory organization to be seen at least in part as an initial response to problems of labour control. In turn, the development of new organizational forms can then be seen as facilitating the use of new strategies and techniques, such as different forms of motive power and new systems of work organization. However, these techniques might increase efficiency, quite independently of their effects on labour control. Marglin is, then, correct to stress that the development of factory organization was not just determined by technology or efficiency, but was socially determined; however, he fails to add that new structures permit new strategies while also generating new problems.

This leads on to a further point. The putting-out system was only slowly superseded by factory production. It continued to exist side by side with factory organization and even expanded in scale in the late eighteenth and early nineteenth centuries. It was a convenient way, during periods of high demand, to expand production. It continued to exist in handloom weaving into the early nineteenth century, into the mid-nineteenth century in footwear, framework knitting, and some of the metal working trades; and it has survived to the present day as outworking on the fringes of the clothing industry. Moreover, the factory system which superseded it was very often one based not on direct but on other delegated structures of control.

Inside contracting

It is sometimes assumed that with the development of the factory system, the owner came to employ and control his workers directly. This was often not so, for the owner, in many industries, relied for labour management on a system of internal subcontracting. Because this was an important, but often overlooked, form of labour management, this section examines it in some detail.

Under the system of 'internal contracting', the owner of the factory or mine or site provided the physical environment. Like the putter-out, he supplied raw materials, usually he provided the machinery, and he arranged for the sale of the product. But though the workers were gathered together on his premises, they were not his direct employees; rather they were under the control of one or more subcontractors who hired the labour force, supervised the work process, and received a rate from the entrepreneur for the finished goods. The income of the subcontractor consisted of the difference, on the one hand, between the wages he paid his employees plus the cost of any working capital he might provide and, on the other hand, the price of his sales to the entrepreneur. For the owner, the advantages of subcontracting were that many of the risks of operating could be shared with others, who might also provide small amounts of capital. The system offered some cost predictability, and, from the technical point of view, problems of production could be transferred to those who might be more skilled in the trade. From the point of view of labour management, further advantages of the system lay in the saving in cost and trouble of recruiting, monitoring, and disciplining a workforce: labour administration could be delegated to others. For the subcontractor himself, the system allowed a man, usually a skilled craftsman or experienced worker, to retain a high degree of independence in the production process and to make a profit, whilst avoiding the problems of procuring large-scale capital and raw materials and of selling the finished product. If the subcontractor's own income was squeezed by the owner reducing the contract price, he in turn could cut his own employees' wages and thus hope to retain his profit margin.

This system was widespread in nineteenth-century Britain. It was prevalent in the building and civil engineering industries; the canals, railways, and large factories and buildings of the nineteenth century were all built under the subcontract system (Coleman, 1965). It was widespread in coalmining, where the mine owner usually sank the pit and installed the machinery, but where a subcontractor or 'butty', as he was often called, would recruit the miners, provide the working capital, and deliver the coal to the proprietor at a certain rate per ton. It was extensively used in the iron and steel trades (Allen, 1929; Carr and Taplin, 1962); it was an important form of industrial organization in engineering (Roll, 1930; Schloss, 1892); and it was common on a smaller scale in the metal workshops of the West Midlands (Fox, 1955).

A system which bore many similarities to subcontracting was the 'helper system', which was also common in nineteenth-century industries such as textiles and iron working. Under this system, the skilled craftsman hired his assistants or helpers and paid their wages from his own earnings. These semi- or unskilled assistants performed the routine tasks such as feeding machines, removing or finishing the end product, or simply just assisting the skilled principal. The latter, however, had more restricted managerial functions than the subcontractor, usually worked under a company foreman of some kind, and seldom had more than half a dozen helpers, often sons or daughters or young apprentices. Unlike the subcontractors, these master craftsmen were more likely to see themselves as workers rather than managers and were among the earliest to organize in unions (Clegg, Fox and Thompson, 1964). Of course, from the entrepreneur's point of view, one of the main similarities between the subcontract and helper systems was that they relieved him of much labour management, including the recruitment, supervision, discipline and payment of workers.

The subcontract and related helper systems were, I have suggested, forms of labour administration in the nineteenth century. As one late-nineteenth-century observer wrote, 'Subcontract, in fact, is practically ubiquitous' (Schloss, 1892: 120). Nevertheless, the system did come under pressure in a number of industries in the late nineteenth century. For example, in various coalfields, though subcontracting was already on the decline earlier in the century, the final quarter of the nineteenth century saw the final decline of the traditional entrepreneurial form of subcontracting. The reasons for this were mainly economic and technological. The exhaustion of the more accessible coal seams meant deeper, more highly capitalized, and more heavily manned collieries. Under these circumstances, the owners saw the need for more direct control and more systematic exploitation of their pits. An associated development was the growth of trained professional colliery managers in the late nineteenth century. The opposition of the mining unions to subcontracting, though it played some part, seems to have been less important than the technological and economic factors influencing management (Taylor, 1960).

In the metal and engineering trades of Birmingham and the Black Country, under the economic pressures of the late 1870s and 1880s, the subcontract system began to give way to new methods of production and labour management. This change occurred first in the manufacture of guns and small arms. Falling prices and foreign competition forced the bigger firms to seek cost reductions by substituting machinery for manual skill, and this in turn gave them a greater incentive to employ directly their own semi-skilled labour. Later, in the late 1880s and 1890s, increasing demand in certain trades, especially those connected with the newer sections of the engineering industry, led to further capital investment, an increase in the size of the typical unit, and the introduction of new systems of planning and more capital-intensive production processes. The entrepreneur, in order to control and take advantage of these systems, was forced to become more directly involved in labour management (Fox, 1955).

Subcontracting was thus an important stage in the development of labour management in British industry. It would be wrong, however, to see it as a totally distinct stage which was finally superseded by the end of the nineteenth century. Even in its heyday it did not exist in all industries. It did not exist on the railways and was not introduced in some of the newer continuous process industries, such as large-scale food processing or chemicals. Furthermore, even in subcontract situations the system often existed alongside more direct methods of management; for example, in engineering, though component manufacture and certain operations might be controlled by inside subcontractors, final assembly would very often be completed by non-contract employees under the supervision of company foremen. It should also be remembered that subcontracting continued in various forms well into the twentieth century, though it took on more of the characteristics of 'team work' and helper systems. In coalmining, for example, the so-called 'little butty' system, a form of collective piecework under a butty, existed in certain coalfields well into the interwar years (Goffee, 1977). It existed in the motor car industry in the 1920s, where, in some firms, gangs of workers worked to an output contract, under which they were collectively responsible for the organization of their work (Friedman, 1977). And it continues to operate today in construction, an industry still characterized by small firms, unpredictability, and relatively simple technology.

The foreman and more direct systems of control

The wage-earning foreman, employed directly by the company as part of a hierarchy, did not take over from the subcontractor in any very definite way. As has already been suggested, subcontractors and company foremen could exist side by side in the same plant or on the same site, and company foremen would themselves have acted as small-scale subcontractors. Some of the earlier foremen, deputies, gangers and taskmasters were themselves former subcontractors (Schloss, 1892: 102, 116, 139). This is not surprising, given the fact that most of them had usually risen from similar origins and they achieved their position largely because of their knowledge of the trade.

In many respects the traditional nineteenth-century foreman performed the same functions as the subcontractor. He controlled the production functions of planning, the allocation and speed of work, and working methods; he also controlled the personnel functions of hiring, firing, promotion and demotion, as well as discipline, payment, and the handling of grievances. The crucial differences between the foreman and subcontractor were that the former did not employ his own labour; the wage or salary he received as a company employee was his main source of income, and he did not have the same entrepreneurial interest in costs and profits.

In terms of status, the bowler-hatted foreman stood above the over-seer and working chargehand and usually way above the ordinary work-man. He was relatively well paid as compared with manual workers and office staff (Pollard, 1968: 163–85; Williams, 1915: 283, 309). Above the foreman might be a few officials such as plant engineers and accountants, and above them would be the works manager, often a member of the owning family. Outside the workplace the foreman was a man of prestige and influence, and, generally, to be promoted to fore-man was a significant step upwards. The foreman was thus seen as part of management by both the owner and the workers. However, his status varied, from industry to industry and no doubt from firm to firm; in general terms, it is probably true to say that in small firms his standing was nearer to that of the owner than in larger firms; on the other hand, in some firms in craft industries, the prestige and authority of the highly skilled craftsman were not much lower than those of the foreman.

The foreman of the late nineteenth and early twentieth centuries was very much the master in the workplace and was the key figure in labour management (Melling, 1980). One engineering employer described the foreman this way:

> 'In most works the whole industrial life of a workman is in the hands of his foreman. The foreman chooses him from among the applicants at the works gate; often he settles what wages he shall get; no advance of wage or promotion is possi-ble except on his initiative; he often sets the piece-price and has power to cut it when he wishes; and, lastly, he almost always has unrestricted power of discharge. These great pow-ers are exercised by men chosen generally for their energy and driving power.' (Quoted in Webb, 1917)

A key expression here is 'driving power', for this was the basis of nine-teenth-century foremanship, a method of getting production out by means of direct and coercive control, particularly where semi- and unskilled workers were concerned. The foreman was in practice the source of many of the works rules, and it was his duty to apply those drawn up by others. There was no court of appeal against his ruling: as the same engineering employer reported, 'it is almost impossible for the workman to get past the foreman to see the manager or a director, and even if he should succeed, the management has practically no choice but to back up its agent'. However, despite this authoritarian and often capricious behaviour there is evidence that strong personal loyalties could grow up, and in some circumstances the workman would follow the foreman from job to job, and even company to company, in a way reminiscent of the subcontractor (Bendix, 1956: 55–6).

The considerable power of the foreman was to continue largely unchanged up to the First World War and even beyond. But even in the pre-war years there were signs of a gradual diminution in his power and authority. Where trade unions were strong, union rules or collective agreements placed restrictions on the foreman's right to hire, to allocate work, and to fix rates. A more important reason for erosion of the foreman's power and discretion was the pressure on management organization. There were a number of influences on the firm: greater competition, problems of increasing size, technological change, as well as new management ideas deriving from accountants and engineers. Under these influences, even before the First World War some firms were attempting to rationalize and systematize their production and employment systems.

Management began to recognize the need to monitor and discipline their foremen so that they could in turn more closely control those whom they supervised. Consequently, there was more interference from the central office and monitoring of the foreman's performance. In this way senior management sought to control this traditional and often idiosyncratic group. In the larger firms there was also a gradual trend to shift various functions which had traditionally been the foreman's to centralized staff departments; selection and dismissal, production planning, payment, quality control started to be parcelled out to specialist departments. In the case of one engineering works, for example, where labour had traditionally been taken on in an informal *ad hoc* manner by the foreman, a more elaborate system of examination and selection via a central office was introduced:

> Different methods are now employed in engaging new hands.
> They are now seldom taken up from the entrances by the
> foreman, but must apply at the works' Inquiry Office and
> begin to pass through the official formula in that way, or the

> foreman is supplied with names . . . This is another indica-
> tion of the times, a further development of system at the
> works. (Williams, 1915: 276)

Thus by 1917, Sidney Webb could write that appointments and dismissals were, following American practice, increasingly being made by
special employment departments or by relatively senior managers with
special responsibilities for labour (Webb, 1917: 21–3). In the area of
wage administration, firms were experimenting with new techniques
which tended to reduce supervisory functions. Above all, the extensions
of piecework and the development of more sophisticated premium bonus
systems reduced the foreman's ability to regulate wage rates. Incentive
schemes were a way of stimulating the pace of production, while cir-
cumventing the foreman's traditional 'driving' method of exacting greater
effort.

Paradoxically, these changes were accompanied by an increase in the
number of foremen. At the same engineering works cited above, for
example, supervisory staff more than doubled between 1900 and 1915.
The newer foremen tended to be better educated, being 'reckoned good
at arithmetic or able to scratch out a rough drawing' (Williams, 1915:
75, 304). However, they were less powerful than the older type, more
dependent on top management for their positions, and more heavily
committed to enforce company rules. Their greater dependence did not
mean a closer relationship with top management; quite the contrary, for
the rise in the number of foremen, the increasing size of the companies
and plants, and the growing differentiation in the management hierarchy
brought about a reduction in the personal contact between foremen and
top management.

By the First World War, this process of rationalizing lower management organization and integrating the foreman more closely into new
management systems was still in its infancy. Even if they wanted to,
top management could not have moved quickly to reorganize supervisory structures because there often did not exist any effective alternatives for enforcing work discipline. Thus the traditional pivotal role of
the foreman in workplace labour management remained.

Employers' organizations and delegated multi-employer control

British employers in the late nineteenth and early twentieth centuries
frequently relied on employers' organizations as a means of labour con-

trol. Employers' associations were in fact their main defence against emergent trade unionism in the workplace and became an increasingly important source of formal rules governing employment relations. Such organizations had a long history, for as Adam Smith pointed out, 'Masters are always and everywhere in a sort of tacit but constant and uniform combination not to raise the wages of labour above their actual rate . . . Masters too sometimes enter into particular combinations to sink the wages of labour even below this rate' (Smith, 1776: 81–2). In the final quarter of the nineteenth century there was, however, an increase in the numbers of employers' organizations and in their stability, and national federations were established in some of the main British industries, including cotton, shipbuilding, shipping, footwear, and engineering. In part, these organizations were a response to the rise in trade union membership and to the 'new unionism' of the late 1880s. But they were also a reaction to the economic pressures of the time: for as markets expanded and competition intensified employers sought either to reduce the competition on wages between themselves, where this was feasible, or to reduce production costs by keeping a closer control over all aspects of wage costs and by eliminating the practices of the craft unions.

The employers' organizations performed three main functions. First, though in some industries such as shipping and railways they were initially openly anti-union, in others they operated more to defend broadly defined managerial prerogatives and to curtail trade union activity at the workplace. This became increasingly the pattern from the early twentieth century onwards. Secondly, employers' organizations often took the initiative in establishing relations with the trade unions' district and then later national disputes machinery. These were used by the employers to bring some stability to industrial relations in their industries, and to defend managerial rights through collective action. Thirdly, employers' organizations gradually developed substantive agreements on wages and conditions. Before the First World War these were mainly district level agreements, but during the war and in the immediate post-war years the consolidation of national associations allowed them to be extended to national level. As suggested above, this could be a way of taking wages out of competition and in some industries was used to support collusive product market arrangements. The reliance by companies on these organizations meant that issues such as the handling of relations with unions, certain aspects of wage fixing, the regulation of other employment conditions, and disputes handling were outside the firms' sphere, and thus the rule-making activity of entrepreneurs, their managers and foremen was limited. In a sense employers were delegating labour management to external organizations. Top management came to rely on their associations, just as they relied on foremen, as a way of avoiding direct handling of labour matters, which further slowed down the development of internal management structures and enterprise-based industrial relations strategies.

The extension of internal hierarchies

The emphasis so far has been on the importance of delegated structures of control. However, this is not to deny that plant managers concerned with production played a large part in labour management. By the early twentieth century these general production managers and the foremen under them were important figures in labour control on the shop floor. Increasingly they were assisted by plant engineers and accountants in the middle ranks of a developing managerial hierarchy. Unfortunately we know little about the recruitment, numbers, and activities of these managers, and further research into this is still necessary. Nearer the point of production, since the late nineteenth century, there had been an increase in the number of 'speed and feed' men, rate fixers, and progress chasers. These were involved with the introduction and administration of new incentive payment systems, such as premium bonus schemes, which spread through British industry from the late nineteenth century onwards. Later, during the inter-war years, as Littler (1981a) has shown, formal scientific management, primarily in the form of time study and often connected with Bedaux schemes, brought the introduction of work study managers and a further elaboration of internal hierarchy.

Other managerial groupings started to crystallize in the late nineteenth and early twentieth centuries. Paternalism and welfare activities had a long history in British industry. However, towards the end of the nineteenth century welfare work began to be relocated from the community into the workplace. For the first time specialist staff were appointed to administer company welfare programmes. Early pioneers of welfare work were firms such as Rowntree which appointed its first full-time welfare officer in 1891. They were firms often with Nonconformist and Quaker backgrounds in industries such as food processing and consumer goods which employed large numbers of female workers. Often the welfare officers were women and spent much of their time on health and working conditions, recreational matters, and education. They did not have a role in the central policy making of the enterprise. Most of them would only occasionally be consulted on wage determination, broader questions of factory discipline, and union matters. However, some of them did slowly and indirectly become involved in such matters: they became involved through their work in recruitment and training; they might also be consulted on dismissals; some of them serviced works councils and consultative bodies; others monitored piecework systems and the level of performance; and most of them were involved in keeping records on lateness and absenteeism. However, up to the First World War, there were probably fewer than one hundred such welfare officers in British industry (Niven, 1967: 21–44).

During the war there was a considerable extension and elaboration of welfare work, largely with encouragement from governments, and increasingly with respect to male workers. This extension of welfare work did not take place without opposition. In the first place many workers resented welfarism and unions were suspicious of the motives behind it. A common view was that 'most welfare workers discourage organisation and only try to increase output' (Webb, 1917: 143). Many workers felt that it was 'a dodge to get more out of them, and there is no doubt that welfare pays . . . In America it is part of scientific management, where the essence of scientific management is centralisation of authority and the subordination of the workers, and the employers take the view that when the workers become independent the welfare supervisor gives them back their authority' (quoted in Webb, 1917: 143–4). Foremen were also suspicious, not surprisingly since an increase in the duties of welfare workers tended to be at their expense.

Furthermore, some employers and managers were suspicious, seeing welfarism as unnecessarily indulgent. It was viewed by many as a costly policy that might work in prosperous firms such as Rowntrees or Lever Brothers where trade unions were weak, but which could not work in more unionized and conflictual situations. There is no evidence that employers' organizations encouraged welfare workers, and many of those firms which had them imposed on them during the war saw it as an interference with managerial prerogatives and dismissed their welfare officers immediately wartime regulations lapsed (Niven, 1967: 46–53). Yet, on the other hand, some firms introduced welfare programmes after the war. By the mid-1920s there were around one thousand firms with welfare managers, and among them were an increasing number of men, reflecting the enhanced status of the function in the management hierarchy and its increased orientation towards male workers (ibid.: 56–7, 76).

During the inter-war years welfare slowly developed by way of what was first called 'employment management' into 'personnel management'. So-called employment departments had existed for some time in a few firms; for example, the large engineering company of Renolds Chains had established one in 1906 and the chemical firm, Brunner Mond, had such a department from 1916 onwards (Renold, 1950: 14; Reader, 1975: 6). What had previously been welfare departments in firms increasingly had their name changed to employment or personnel departments. Many of the functions carried out by these personnel managers remained the same as those performed by the former welfare officers. For example, recruitment was important, though increasingly more emphasis was placed on interviewing, testing, and systematic selection. As one personnel manager wrote, in reference to the traditional *ad hoc* system, 'the engagement of labour is a highly specialized function and not incidental to supervision' (Niven, 1967: 77–8). Also wage and salary administration became more technical, along with new forms of incentive systems and the beginnings of job grading. In addition, personnel managers increasingly came to deal with trade unions and to be involved in collective bargaining and the administration of agreements. Where personnel managers did not develop out of welfare, they came from a number of other backgrounds: some were clerks, employed to maintain wage and employment records, who were gradually upgraded because of their knowledge of procedures, agreements, and pay systems; others moved from the 'harder' end of labour management, namely, production and work study; and a few came direct from large government bureaucracies. By the beginning of the Second World War there were, however, still only 1,800 personnel specialists with jobs and qualifications which made them eligible to join their professional organization, the Institute of Personnel Management. It was the circumstances of wartime production which gave a further stimulus to personnel management, and by 1945 the number had grown to five thousand (Crichton, 1968).

Federal structures

So far this paper has dealt with the firm as though it was a single unit enterprise. It is now necessary to go beyond this to examine management structures. By 1919 at least a quarter of the two hundred largest manufacturing firms in the UK were multi-unit enterprises; by 1930 this had risen to two-thirds, and by 1948 to over three-quarters (Hannah, 1980: 54). The mergers and acquisitions of the 1920s were the major source of this growth. These enterprises were usually organized as holding companies, that is, federal organizations of constituent firms loosely controlled by a parent company. Control by the holding company was often restricted to legal and financial ties, and decisions about buying, production, and marketing were largely taken autonomously by the operating subsidiaries, which in many instances continued to trade under their original names. During the period under consideration, proprietorial and family influence and traditions remained strong throughout such holding companies and their subsidiaries. Even where a family no longer controlled a majority of the shares, they often retained board positions and played a large and major part in day-to-day managerial decisions. Such patterns of ownership and organization were common in iron and steel, engineering, shipbuilding, textiles, and the food and drink industries.

These firms may have remained as loose federal structures partly because of tradition and a lack of innovative imagination. Such structures, however, offered certain advantages. For the senior managers it was a way of spreading risks across a variety of separate operating units. Autonomy in buying, production, and selling enabled them to respond flexibly to changes in product demand. It also, of course, saved on the costs of developing a central managerial hierarchy and standardized systems of control. Though the initial impetus for federal structures came from such financial, marketing, and administrative considerations, labour factors may have reinforced the value of these structures. For senior managers in the parent companies, especially where they might have come from finance capital backgrounds, it was easier to delegate local labour responsibilities to former owners and their local managers. It was a way of building on the already existing social foundations. Membership of employers' organizations and multi-employer systems of control also encouraged federal fragmentation: for the unit of membership of most employers' organizations was generally the individual plant, and holding companies could not join directly. This, and especially the procedural systems operated in industries such as engineering, reinforced local autonomy in labour matters.

At plant level, in an industry like engineering, this form of management was an extension of earlier systems of delegated control, as outlined above. Production managers, often ex-craft apprentices, though also coming from work study backgrounds, played a large part in labour management. Personnel departments were rudimentary, and personnel officers were very much responsible to local line managers. The foreman also played an important role in production and, depending on the state of trade, this was often shared with shop stewards. In practice this meant industrial relations rested on shared understandings and joint decision-making through 'mutuality'. Though the 1898 and 1922 settlements, forced on the engineering unions by the Engineering Employers' Federation, had formally asserted managerial prerogatives, they had also recognized collective bargaining and 'mutuality'. Where market and technological factors were favourable, joint control over the work process was important.

This federal approach, articulating with earlier delegated structures, continued to be an important structural form into the post-Second World War period. Indeed Loveridge in Chapter 17 describes how such systems of labour management exist today in companies such as GKN, Tube Investment, and Delta Metals. Despite the increased size of these firms, the employment of more professional management, and sometimes pressure from trade unions for more centralized systems, they still retain federal structures and pursue what he calls 'local labour market' strategies based on 'uncertainty transference', fragmentation of the labour force, extensive use of incentive systems, and local custom and practice. Risks are shifted to workers so that they bear the costs of a downturn in product demand. Shop stewards are involved in the operation of delegated control structures, performing the classic role of 'badly paid personnel managers'.

Centralized structures

Some multi-plant firms, whether growing through internal expansion or by merger, developed more centralized structures. In the inter-war years firms such as ICI, Unilever, Pilkingtons and Dunlop developed centralized structures, partially functional, partially multi-divisional, based on the development of extended managerial hierarchies and centrally administered departments. The individual plants and subsidiaries of such firms enjoyed much less autonomy in financial, production, and marketing matters than did the subsidiaries of federally structured firms. The degree of centralization varied, however, and depended on the homogeneity of the company's products and on the preferences of the senior executives. As they developed in the 1930s and 1940s these firms, though they still had members of the original families on their boards, came increasingly to be run at all levels by professional managers. However, they were still a small minority among the largest enterprises before the Second World War; Hannah, for example, estimates that there were probably only a dozen firms organized on distinctly multi-divisional lines by 1948 (Hannah, 1980: 53). They were to remain a minority well into the post-war period.

In terms of labour management these firms had a choice: they could decide either formally to decentralize, or they could centralize and internalize their control structure. This decision would depend on a number of factors, including the product range and the degree of autonomy in other areas of management. A firm such as Unilever, with a diversified product range, chose to decentralize, although the small head office department pursued more coordination in some divisions than in others. On the other hand, ICI at a very early stage decided to centralize its labour management function. It provides an appropriate example of a particular type of structure. The company established its Central Labour Office in 1927. This was based at headquarters, was accorded high status within the company, and from the beginning reported directly to a senior board member. General labour policy emanated from the department and little independence was allowed to local factory managers. From the beginning the larger factories had their own labour departments, but their role was to administer the system established by head office staff. Local management had control over engagement and dismissal, recreational activities, the running of works councils, and purely local administrative matters. The main features of policy, changes in wages and working conditions, and negotiations with trade unions were tightly controlled by the Central Office.

The policy developed and administered by the Central Office contained some interesting and relatively novel elements. There was a works council system offering a form of representation and participation via a consultative framework of committees which bypassed the unions. However, from its creation, ICI did recognize trade unions and tried to institutionalize relations with them. As Henry Mond said, 'The trade unions are extremely useful to us in bringing to our notice matters that we should not otherwise be aware of, and at the same time they are not in a sufficiently powerful position to make themselves aggressive or difficult to deal with. It seems to me clear that our main line of policy should be firm but friendly' (quoted in Reader, 1975: 66). The unions were dealt with centrally through an industrial relations council in which directors, backed up by personnel management staff, met with union full-time officers. ICI also developed profit sharing and staff status schemes. The latter, established in 1928, was the most interesting. Under the scheme, manual workers with more than five years' employment were eligible for staff status. The main benefits of this were a weekly wage, with elaborate arrangements for extra time at above normal hourly rates; the right to a month's notice; payment for bank holidays; and payment of sick pay up to six months in any year. Promotion to this grade was entirely at the discretion of management, and was used to promote loyalty to the firm and to tie workers to their jobs. Finally, throughout the 1930s, ICI worked towards a uniform centrally administered wage structure, at first based on work-studied incentive schemes, but by the late 1930s it was considering company-wide job evaluation. On the details of the wage structure the Central Labour Office worked with a large and powerful central work study department. It was only the war which slowed down the introduction of a company-wide wage structure. It is significant that ICI, having developed its own internal personnel function and its own centralized labour policies, left its employers' organization in the mid-1930s.

Even by the 1960s this centralized structure of labour management had been adopted by only a few companies – at least for their manual workers. It was, however, more widely used for managerial, technical, and white-collar staff. In part this may have been because the latter types of workers were more homogeneous. But also senior managers may have felt the need to control more directly these members of staff and to tie them to the firm. Referring to the idea of an internal labour market, the Commission on Industrial Relations (CIR) in its study of multi-plant companies pointed out, 'there can be a need to move such staff from one plant or division to another' (CIR, 1974: 39). But this centralized approach clearly offered wider advantages and facilitated certain strategies: it encouraged long-run planning of labour policy; it facilitated a planned and coordinated wage structure; it permitted firms to develop internal labour market policies; and it could be used to bureaucratize relations with unions. For some of these reasons it was encouraged by the Donovan Commission, by the CIR and by other government-sponsored bodies. However, this is not to deny that there were some disadvantages in highly centralized and internalized structures. In the 1960s there was some movement towards decentralized systems, as the CIR put it, to 'improve individual plant productivity and eliminate inefficient practices' at plant level. These moves, it added significantly, were 'not in response to trade union or work group pressure but as a result of a determination by management to improve productivity' (ibid.: 36). However, such decentralization was usually centrally coordinated, and on the whole has probably been offset over the last two decades by a movement towards more centralized or at least divisionalized structures. As the same official report stated, 'A number of companies are moving towards the common treatment of all their employees' (ibid.: 15).

Conclusion

General management strategy is more the concern of other chapters in this book. However, strategy and structure cannot be separated; the relationship between the two is highly interdependent. It is hoped that this chapter has shown how structure both follows and embodies strategy and in turn can either constrain or facilitate further strategic choices. Thus the development of an internal hierarchy of foremen, work study engineers, and personnel managers was a response to the development of direct control strategies, and in turn such hierarchies facilitated the development of more bureaucratic forms of labour administration within the firm.

The changes in the development of management structure described above embody both the pattern of historical evolution and the diversity of contemporary arrangements. In the first place, each form of organization corresponds roughly to a stage in the development of some of the main British industries and firms. In the second place, though, the speed and totality of change should not be exaggerated. The timing of change has been different between and within industries and the various forms have often existed side by side. Thus, at the present time, the putting-out system still exists, especially as homework in wages council-type industries, where processes are easily subdivided and where demand is variable. Internal contracting as a form of team work under a gang leader survived until recently in mining and on the docks, and still remains in building. External subcontracting, though not considered in this paper because of the way it merges with ordinary commercial dealings between firms, performs some of the same functions as these other structures in that it enables firms to maintain an internal labour force while laying off risks to others. It is an often neglected aspect of management organization (Friedman, 1977: 120–9; Littler, 1981a). For their part, employers' organizations had begun to decline in importance during the inter-war years, and this continued at an even faster rate after the war. However, where they have maintained a labour control and a market function, they still remain important in certain industries, for example in building, printing, paper, clothing, textiles, and footwear. At the level of the firm there has been no simple or widespread conversion to the centralized integrated model; federal structures remain important in many companies. Nevertheless, though this diversity exists, the long-term trend is probably towards internal centralized structures, with delegation or divisionalization increasingly coordinated by senior managers.

Why this diversity? It is difficult to explain by relying on either theories of increasing employer control or by the drive for greater efficiency. Both have an influence on managerial strategy and structure. For employers, although control over the labour force is an important intermediate goal, certain structures may suit different environments more than others and in the longer term prove more efficient. Such structures are clearly more likely to be adopted and to survive. Yet organizational structures reflect choice by management, behind which lie arguments of individual managers and sections on the need to adopt a certain approach to marketing products, competing with other firms and developing new products. Strategies and structures are thus interdependent and together constrain individual management actions.

13

Corporate strategy and employment relations in multinational corporations: some evidence from Kenya and Malaysia

JOHN HENLEY

Introduction

The industrial relations policies pursued in the less developed countries (LDCs) are of interest to observers from industrialized economies for a number of reasons. First, since much of the industrial development is carried out by multinational corporations (MNCs) deploying technology previously unknown to the host economy on 'green field' sites, there is an opportunity to examine the application of strategic planning techniques to the structuring of a modern labour force *de novo* with few overlays of custom and practice. While such economies may provide analogues of the past industrial history of metropolitan economies, subject to the 'late development effect' (Dore, 1973), there is also the possibility that they represent scenarios of the future for global industrial relations, should unemployment rates rise in the industrialized world to levels comparable to those generally prevailing in the Third World.

Related to the first theme is another source of interest: the role of the state in industrial relations. The state in industrialized economies has increasingly abandoned its 'nightwatchman' role for a more interventionist one and there of course has been much debate in the west about the relative autonomy of the state. Newly independent, ex-colonial states provide some interesting paradoxes for theories of the state for, at independence, political power did not by and large devolve on the property owners but on a social stratum of 'property hunters'. As Njonjo (1971) observes with respect to Kenya: 'The politically dominant middle class employs the state machinery to create wealth with which to under-write

111

its power . . . It is in reality a poor class: its wealth in land, cars, real estate etc., is mortgaged and dependent on the good will of the state.' According to this view, in the absence of an independent middle class, the state primarily serves to protect the interests of foreign capital in the regulation of industrial relations. Moreover, since most industrialization is dependent on protectionist incentives that are financed by taxation of exportable agricultural products and mineral export, all local employees of MNCs are beneficiaries. Hence the notion of a 'labour aristocracy' to explain both the local labour movement's lack of concern for the impoverished rural population and its tendency towards economism rather than radicalism (Arrighi, 1970; Arrighi and Saul, 1969).

A third issue, which sets aside the finer nuances of investment motivation, is implied in the concept of strategic planning through 'management by structured foresight' (Steiner and Miner, 1977), that is, the extension and expansion of the world economic system with bureaucracy as the dominant form of its social organization. In so far as the management of the labour process in LDCs corresponds to the 'rule of the rules' it is consistent with the inevitability of the bureaucratization of the world (Kerr *et al.*, 1973). Bureaucratization of relationships avoids the problems of face-to-face dependence relationships yet protects the rationality of collective action. However, efficiency always remains problematic and a function of motivation to work. A social issue here is therefore the extent to which international personnel policies in MNCs are deliberately tailored to harness local or national cultural values in order to motivate the workforce.

This paper discusses labour relations in Kenya and West Malaysia, both of which are, broadly speaking, capitalist economies deriving many of their institutions from the period when they were part of the British Empire.

Context: the development of industrial relations institutions

Both Malaysia and Kenya experienced insurgency prior to independence and although the labour movement of each adopted a similar oppositional stance in the struggle for independence, the outcome was very different. In Malaysia the initial post-war attempts at trade unionism, under a predominantly communist and Chinese leadership, were partially successful in redressing the regressive incomes policy of the reconstruction period but resulted, in 1948, in armed revolutionary conflict with the colonial administration struggling hard to re-establish British rule after the Japanese occupation. By contrast, in Kenya the labour movement remained the only legitimate national African organization during the State of Emergency, 1952–60.

The communist hold over the Malayan labour movement was broken primarily by legislative and judicial restrictions and ultimately by force following the declaration of a State of Emergency in June 1948 (Stenson, 1970; Morgan, 1977).

The colonial government then proceeded to reconstruct a more compliant trade union movement which, according to Rudner (1973), by the time self-government was attained in 1955, had acquired a new self-confidence in spite of its previous failures and employer hostility. Yet it still encountered a government deeply suspicious of communist infiltration and willing to deploy at least as many legislative obstacles against the development of a strong national trade union movement as the previous colonial administration. The Trade Union Ordinance of 1959, like its colonial predecessor, was intended to be a 'realistic measure to bar subversion and ensure industrial peace'.[1] Under its provisions trade unions are restricted to organizing 'similar' occupations or trades, with the effect that omnibus federations remain banned. The case against the Ordinance is still maintained by the Malayan Trades Union Congress (MTUC) which, of course, is barred from legal protection as a trade union since it covers unions from various trades, occupations and industries. A serious consequence of the Ordinance has been the restriction of the size of trade unions and the development of a multiplicity of 'peanut unions'.

Other important restrictions on trade union organization include prohibition of individual unions from subscribing to federations or using their funds for political purposes. The rule that trade union officers are required to have at least three years' experience has been used to restrict attempts to organize workers in 'Pioneer Industries'.[2] Perhaps most crucial, the Registrar has the absolute right to interpret the application of the rules defining 'similar occupations or trades'.

The other key legal instrument for regulating trade unions is the Industrial Relations Act, 1967. This Act provided a system of arbitration for all sectors of the economy.

Following the third State of Emergency, which was declared after the inter-communal riots of May 1969, the Industrial Relations Act was further extended to curb the right to strike and to define a wide range of managerial prerogatives that were not negotiable. As the law now stands it is illegal to go on strike in Malaysia over managerial decisions relating to promotion, transfer of labour, the right to fill a vacancy, to dismiss or to reinstate a worker (Danaraj, 1976). It is also illegal for the unorganized to go on strike, though the individual has the right to take his grievance to the Director General of Industrial Relations, for conciliation or arbitration by the Industrial Court.

Summarizing the development of industrial relations in Malaysia, two strands stand out with consequences for the growth of the institutional framework. The first has been the continuing threat to political stability from communist insurgency dating back to the Japanese occupation and the struggle for control of Malaysia immediately after the war. At least in the minds of the present-day rulers of Malaysia, the labour movement has not yet been purged of its association with the Chinese community's involvement in the Malayan Communist Party (MCP). This has resulted in the under-representation of Chinese workers in trade unionism and the dominance of Indians, who have only weak political links with the government through the minority Malaysian Indian Congress faction in the Alliance government.

Secondly, the government's continuing policy has been to subordinate labour to broader considerations of national economic development on the grounds that the ruling Malay faction's survival depends on restructuring the Malaysian economy so that, above all, Malay participation in all levels of the economy is increased. The pressure on the government to regulate the labour movement seems to have remained consistently high, in spite of a high economic growth rate and an expansion of enumerated wage employment. This growth of the economy stands in contrast to the comparatively stunted growth of the trade union movement. Strike activity has tended to be cyclical, dampened by increasing restrictions as activity accelerates (see Table 13.1).

In Kenya, in contrast to Malaysia, the labour movement was remodelled towards industrial unionism before it could become radicalized. Moreover, it was much smaller and less experienced than the pre-independence Malayan movement, reflecting the lower level of industrialization of Kenya. Indeed, the Labour Department of the colonial administration was able to pursue successfully a policy of collaboration with the nascent labour movement. Though unable to forestall nationalism, the Department was able to channel their specific demands along economistic lines. Thus it was instrumental in persuading Kenyan employers to raise wages in exchange for industrial unionism to forestall the growth of any politicized general unions (Clayton and Savage, 1974). An agreement was signed between the Federation of Kenya Employers and

Table 13.1. Number of strikes, workmen involved and mandays lost, 1958–75

Year	Malaysia			Kenya		
	No. of strikes	No. of workmen involved	No. of mandays lost	No. of strikes	No. of workmen involved	No. of mandays lost
1958	69	9,467	59,211			
1959	39	6,949	38,523			
1960	37	4,596	41,947			
1961	58	9,045	59,730			
1962	95	232,912	449,856			
1963	72	217,232	305,168	282	54,881	191,023
1964	85	226,427	518,439	231	67,038	158,060
1965	46	14,684	152,666	186	82,250	286,071
1966	60	16,673	109,915	130	42,554	130,574
1967	45	9,452	157,980	129	30,160	110,903
1968	103	31,062	280,417	93	20,428	50,003
1969	49	8,750	76,779	110	33,718	109,092
1970	17	1,216	1,867	79	18,739	58,720
1971	45	5,311	20,265	69	13,553	32,778
1972	66	9,701	23,455	94	27,510	42,006
1973	66	14,003	40,866	84	14,475	42,267
1974	85	21,830	103,884	71	22,144	92,421
1975	64	12,124	45,749	26	4,148	8,754

Note: Figures for Kenya are not available before 1963.
Source: Ministry of Labour records.

the Kenya Federation of Labour in 1958, establishing trade union jurisdiction on industrial lines which has ever since continued to form the basis of trade union development (Amsden, 1971).

Two years after independence, in 1965, the government passed the Trades Disputes Act which in effect consolidated the restrictive legal framework of the colonial period.[3] Strike activity became in practice illegal and disputes were made subject to compulsory arbitration in the Industrial Court established by the Act. There is, as in Malaysia, an intermediate process of conciliation but, in cases reaching deadlock, the Minister of Labour has always exercised his right to refer them to the Court. Trade union acceptance was bought by offering union officials a means for achieving a degree of personal security through the introduction of a 'check-off' system whereby all employers with more than four union members were required to remit members' dues to trade union headquarters. While strike activity declined sharply after the 1965 Act, membership continued to rise to over 40 per cent of the total paid workforce by 1972.[4]

The government has considerable influence over the unions' parent body, the Central Organization of Trade Unions (COTU), since the President of Kenya appoints its high-ranking officials, after the officials of individual constituent unions have elected them. He has not been bound by their choice in the past. The Minister of Labour also has a representative on the major policy-making bodies of COTU. To gain legal protection, unions must be registered with the Registrar of Trade Unions and submit to scrutiny of their internal management, particularly with regard to elections, finance and changes in their constitutions. The political control afforded the government by legislation affecting the conduct of industrial relations, naturally, hinges on the willingness of the authorities to enforce codes of practice. As Sandbrook (1975: 26) notes:

> Both stringent legislation restricting the possibility of internal union opposition and state supervision of the internal processes of unions may be used to enhance the personal security of incumbent officials. If this strategy of isolating union leaders from the rank-and-file pressures succeeds, it transforms leaders responsive to their members' aspirations into *de facto* public servants responsive to the 'public interest' as defined by the political authorities.

The most recent restriction on the activities of trade unions in Kenya has been the introduction of an incomes policy. Wage guidelines were issued to the Judge of the Industrial Court by the Minister of Finance in 1973. These were to be followed when determining wage awards and other terms and conditions of employment or when the Court accepted voluntarily negotiated collective agreements for registration. Amendments have been made periodically to the guidelines each year since then.

Contrasting the development of trade unions in Kenya and Malaysia (see Table 13.2), one aspect stands out – the close link between the Kenyan labour movement and a faction of the political leadership immediately after independence which fostered a government policy of incorporation of labour leaders in a web of state patronage. This link has never developed to the same extent in Malaysia because of the labour movement's early association with the MCP. Three parallel trends, however, can also be discovered: first, a basic continuity in labour policies from the end of the colonial period through to the present day, with a key role assigned to the registrar of trade unions and an industrial court; secondly, the willingness of the government of each country to subordinate the interest of labour to national economic priorities as defined by the ruling élite; and, finally, communalism[5] has tended to weaken both labour movements, in that trade unions have provided a rallying point for disaffected interests from the communities who have felt relatively poorly treated in the distribution of power. In Kenya, the labour movement is one of the few institutions in which non-Kikuyu have remained preeminent. In Malaysia, the Chinese expelled during the Emergency have not been able to regain their former position for fear of being labelled as insurgents. The field has thus been left open to Indians, and to an increasing extent Malays. The former are relatively well organized in plantation agriculture; the latter dominate the public sector.

Having briefly outlined the development of labour relations in the two countries, it is now necessary to consider the manner in which relations of production are managed at the level of the enterprise.

Managerial strategies of human resource utilization in LDCs

Low wages relative to those prevailing in industrialized economies are a universal feature of developing countries and any direct foreign

Table 13.2. *Industrial relations systems in Malaysia and Kenya*

	Malaysia	Kenya
1. Key industrial relations legislation	Trade Union Ordinance (1959) Industrial Relations Act (1967)	Trades Disputes Act (1965) Trades Disputes (Amendment) Act (1971)
2. Legal basis of trade union organization	No federations Similar occupations or trades Officers must have 3+ years' experience	Only guideline constitution Industrial unions encouraged Tight regulation of internal government
3. Trade union organization	'Peanut unions' 251 unions 425,000 members (less than 10% of labour force unionized) No 'check-off'	30 unions 300,000 members (40% + of labour force unionized) 'Check-off'
4. Central organization	MTUC only allowed as friendly society No direct government regulation	Central organization (COTU) tightly controlled by government President approves officers after election by constituent trades unions
5. Right to strike	Restricted to narrowly defined wage issues	Illegal since August 1979
6. Status of trades union leaders	Excluded from direct political involvement	A few leaders are MPs Route into national politics

investment automatically benefits from low-cost labour. However, the prime motivation for investment is rarely the availability of cheap labour. The major objective for investment in LDCs at first is usually the extraction of minerals or production of agricultural commodities as raw materials for the manufacturing industries of the industrialized economies.

A second stage of direct foreign investment occurs when underdeveloped countries start to pursue an import-substituting type of industrialization. Profits are ensured by tariff barriers and other trading privileges such as tax holidays, cost-plus pricing and favourable arrangements for transferring profits to the parent company are frequently offered to multinational companies. By contrast with extractive industries trading on world commodity markets, wage costs might relatively easily be passed on to local consumers, particularly since such costs may often represent less than 10 per cent of gross output, so small is the locally produced value-added and so high the imported cost of plant, components and materials. In short, the profit yield from 'transfer pricing' arrangements is likely to be more lucrative than any marginal increment to be gained from paying low wages and offering poor conditions of employment.

Marxists will often argue that a third stage of direct foreign investment is that primarily motivated by the availability of abundant supplies of cheap and versatile labour in developing countries to replace higher costs in advanced economies. Plants are established to form a stage in a vertically integrated production process that is internationally controlled. The actual manufacturing process located in the LDC typically involves intensive use of unskilled and semi-skilled labour and only limited investment in fixed assets. Production consists of the assembly of parts imported from plants in other countries under the parent company's control, and the end product is exported to yet other plants owned by the firm. Malaysia has several examples of this type of industrialization, concentrated exclusively in the electronics industry.

Each type of investment motivation provides its own distinctive constraints on the strategies available for structuring and developing the labour force. In the case of primary extractive industries, the parent company has little in the way of production expertise or patents rights with which to defend control of local operating companies. Its major power lies in its influence in and control over commodity markets and to a lesser extent its access to new production technology through its global operations. The threat of nationalization of assets remains a real possibility. With wage costs frequently representing over a quarter of gross output in such industries, there is little scope for buying off wage labour. Instead personnel policies are directed towards co-opting local management into the world of expatriate privilege. This is not a new policy since the traditions of expatriate tea and rubber planters merely have to be transferred to the new generation of local managers. The vast houses, retinues of servants, subsidized education schemes, private clubs and so on are already established. One Kenyan tea company even continues to send its senior African managers on 'home leave' to Britain.

Labour productivity is controlled through detailed production statistics from each estate and attendant processing factory. The labour force is unskilled apart from a small corps of skilled maintenance workers, and is housed in company-owned compounds where the population is predominantly male. Estate managers adjust the labour force to seasonal variations in the demand for labour by developing a group of high productivity workers who are assigned somewhat better and less crowded housing and other small privileges, while the rest of the workers are hired or fired according to the demands of production. Trade unions are weak and under-resourced, reflecting the low wage levels of members.

Manufacturing industries have a greater range of personnel management strategies available to them. The complexity of the subsidiaries' management and operational systems is greater than in an extractive industry, where there are relatively few imported inputs into production and no marketing function is necessary. Technological dependence on the parent company and its extensive control over the supply of production inputs, and the secondment of expatriates to managerial and technical positions all contribute to emphasizing the importance of the foreign link and reinforcing the bargaining power of the subsidiary in its relations with the host country. From bargaining power flows the potential for generating higher levels of profits. Power, of course, can be exercised in a number of ways, depending on the priorities of the power holder. Exponents of the 'good corporate citizen' model of industrial relations can argue that in import-substituting industries, where international quality standards prevail, the production conditions necessarily compare with those in developed countries, but that such conditions are not created in competitive sectors of the economy. Workers in such industries receive higher than average wages and superior fringe benefits such as the provision of medical services, transport to work, and canteens. Since workers are engaged in the processing of valuable intermediates on expensive imported machinery, employers need to build up a stable and disciplined labour force through specialized in-company training. By virtue of their special skills and disciplined behaviour these workers are insulated from the pressures of the high level of unemployment found in the economy as a whole. They can even enhance their privileges by exercising their labour market position to persuade employers to pay them more. The presence of economistic industry-based trade unions in these foreign-owned subsidiaries might be interpreted as evidence of the monopoly power of employers and the segmentation of labour markets.

An alternative characterization of company industrial relations policy emphasizes the importance of 'labour control'. It is argued that the development of a company-oriented labour force is more a myth than a reality, since assembly line technology does not require a skilled labour force and there is no need for employers to encourage workforce commitment. Fear of unemployment is quite sufficient to do that. Factory workers need no special skills to assemble products from fully knocked down kits or sets of imported components, as long as they are willing to accept the physical stress and discipline of routine assembly work. Managements who pay relatively high wages using assembly line production techniques, it is argued, are no more benevolent than Henry Ford when he introduced the 'five dollar day', because workers would not accept the discipline of the assembly line without compensation for the increased intensity of work. If the work is not specialized in its skill requirements, then there can be only very limited reasons why workers cannot be recruited from anywhere. Of course, the presence of a strong trade union capable of resisting an employer who wishes to fire mutinous or unproductive workers would provide an important incentive for moderating a 'labour control' approach to labour relations. However, as we have observed above, both the governments of Kenya and Malaysia have sought to contain the formation of powerful trade unions.

The adoption of a variant of the 'good corporate citizen' approach or a 'labour control' approach to the utilization of human resources will be reflected in actual employer strategies for hiring and retaining labour, maintaining high productivity, developing the labour force through training and containing trade unionism. In the next section typical employer strategies used in Kenya and Malaysia are compared and contrasted. They are chosen selectively to illustrate the variety of strategies found in practice.

Company policies in Malaysia and Kenya compared

'Credentialism' or the 'diploma disease' (Dore, 1975) in hiring policies is widespread in Kenya, coupled with strict adherence to the 'rate for the job' maintained through job structures, compartmentalized into as many as five status levels, with entry ports being restricted according to education. Training policies display a similar rigidity, with a strong emphasis on certification of each stage or unit completed. Ironically the explosive growth of the educational system and the supply of secondary school leavers into the labour market has meant that many of the better-paying firms attract candidates willing to offer themselves for the lowest-skilled jobs, although formally qualified for jobs at least two entry ports higher. At the same time, evidence from the administration of government trade tests suggests that formal schooling is a very poor predictor of test performance (Godfrey, 1977).

Clearly, credentialism in hiring policies cannot adequately be explained simply by reference to employers' ability to select potentially high productivity candidates. It would seem to be more of a defensive response to the enormous pressure from job seekers which also serves to increase the unequal advantage of those from more developed areas with access to better formal education. It also has historical roots in the differentiation of skill by race during the colonial period and continues to form the basis of legitimation of managerial cadres and protects the existence of substantial numbers of expatriates in senior technical and financial roles. By tending to devalue experience, it also undermines the basis of job control of Indian craftsmen and of the 'mistri' system of informal skill transfer (King, 1977). Since trade union organization is industry-based, there is no incentive to resist management's policies of differentiating the workforce according to job-related criteria, provided the application of job evaluation and promotion procedures are consistent and 'fair'. In Malaysia, employers seem far less concerned with formal qualifications. Partly, the explanation appears to be connected with the association of formal training courses with efforts to increase participation rates of Malays in an industrial system in which both informal and company-managed schemes of skill transmission are well established. By contrast with Kenya, there is a highly developed tradition of Chinese industrial craftsmanship stretching back to the origins of the tin mining industry in the nineteenth century. A survey by the Ministry of Labour and Manpower in 1975 of holders of certificates issued by the National Industrial Training and Trade Certification Board does not suggest any great success for its scheme of accreditation. No less than 48 per cent were unemployed and only 37.7 per cent were in relevant occupations, yet, according to the National Manpower Report (1978), demand for skilled workers is supposed to be so buoyant that it is predicted to outstrip available supplies by two-thirds by 1990.

Despite growing governmental pressure, the thrust of employment policies in Malaysian companies seems internally oriented, that is, towards creating an organic enclave in which the employer seeks to promote the welfare of his employees in return for commitment to the organization. For example, collective agreements specify incremental age-related wage scales for all workers, with as many as seventeen steps for skilled workers and a minimum of five steps for unskilled labour. Moreover, companies pay an end-of-the-year bonus of up to two and a half months' wages, again specified in the collective agreement. Malaysian employees of multinational companies are also subject to substantial managerial efforts to create a 'family bond' through lavishly financed company-wide 'events' and house journals that urge workers to greater dedication and vigilance in promoting high quality output. The two most popular events are mass 'walks' in which all employees, including senior executives, compete for special prizes, and company-financed functions, invariably laid on for the complete workforce.

While remaining sceptical of external training, Malaysian employers stress the importance of selecting trainees for skilled jobs from the existing labour force once workers have established their dependability. To this end many firms review the performance of the complete labour force at least annually. Moreover, collective agreements allow employers to keep workers on probation for as long as six months and the maintenance of a casual wing of up to 20 per cent of temporary workers is widespread even by wage leaders. Some employers use sub-contractors to man the manufacturing process, but this is more general for ancillary services such as factory cleaning, grounds maintenance and catering services.

The casual wing of the labour force of multinational companies in Kenya would appear to be growing, although it is less extensive than in Malaysia; but sub-contracting is very rare, being restricted to security services and a limited amount of outworking in garment manufacture. Even in plantation agriculture it is not as extensive as in Malaysia. The explanation of this difference between the two countries would seem to lie in the relative newness of the majority of Kenyan industry, the experience of labour shortages in the 1950s, the lack of linkages between many 'import-assembly' firms and the local economy (Kaplinsky, 1978), and managerial preferences for retaining direct control of production processes in situations where prices are determined by bargaining between the company and the government.

Productivity in Kenyan industry is primarily maintained through the supervisory cadre who are exposed to considerable training effort. In Malaysia, 'supervision' is referred to as a problem, as a result both of the increasing sophistication of imported production technology and the inability of older supervisors to cope with the parallel rise in the educational level of new entrants to the workforce. The strategy of seeking commitment from the labour force places much greater responsibility on the actions of supervisors than under a 'labour control' strategy. Machine-based production systems also make the use of target incentives unnecessary.[6]

The enormous inequality existing between the various grades of managers and the manual workforce in terms of such things as income, opportunities for job mobility and the general quality of life cannot but attract the interest of the able and ambitious worker towards promotion; thus it is difficult for unions in both Kenya and Malaysia to recruit and retain effective shopfloor representatives. In both countries differentials between managers and unskilled workers rise to twentyfold and labour turnover is under 5 per cent in wage-leading firms with virtually no voluntary resignations. However, generally speaking, managerial policy is directed towards incorporating the trade union as a 'loyal opposition' as an aid to bridging the legitimacy gap between the shopfloor and management. In any case, with a highly organized and professional employers' organization to defend company interests in the Industrial Court, the direct cost of discharging workers is rarely severe in either Kenya or Malaysia. Concern for maintaining a good corporate image is a greater moderating influence on arbitrary management behaviour.

The process of institutionalizing labour relations in the specific form of company unions or branches based on individual organizations is rather more explicit in Malaysia as a result of the government's policy of restricting the growth of general or occupational unions. However, patronage of trade union officials by companies is commonplace in both countries. Relatively few Malaysian unions have any fulltime officials, while Kenyan unions normally have at least one paid official. Even so, they are poorly paid by the union since the income from members is small. With respect to Kenya, Muir and Brown (1974) estimated trade union average current expenditure in 1972 to be only equivalent to US $4 per member per year, with assets of US $3 per member. Malaysian unions are not better financed considering the higher income levels prevailing, with average expenditures of US $9.2 per member per year and assets of US $6.3 per member in 1974. With minimal resources to draw on it is hardly surprising that those likely to be willing to offer themselves for election to union office are those employed by companies willing to give extensive time off with pay for trade union business and these tend to be employees of subsidiaries of multinational companies.

This policy of fostering trade unionism may seem to contradict the tenets of strategic management, since the primary consideration should be to preserve freedom of action. However, in import-substituting enclaves, managerial priorities depart radically from those relevant for the management of core production units located in industrialized economies and subject to competitive pressures. By encouraging the development of well organized but disciplined company trade unionism, management creates a constituency which can be used as a basis for defending protective trading agreements threatened by governments or, more probably, by indigenous entrepreneurs. A 'high wages' policy, of course, also raises the entry costs for competitors. Legal restrictions in both Kenya and Malaysia prevent trade unions organizing the unemployed, casual workers or sub-contractors so that there is also no organizational incentive for trade unions to concern themselves with other than company-specific issues. In addition, highly differential wage structures inside firms tend to undermine occupational or craft-based interest groups, as does the prospect of promotion generated by rapidly expanding manufacturing output which in both countries has been sustained at over 10 per cent for several years.

An indicator of the importance assigned by management to 'good', that is harmonious and above all calculable, labour relations is the central position held by the employers' associations in both Kenya and Malaysia. With open unemployment rates of 15–20 per cent, the wage structure and system of labour relations needs careful management to avoid political repercussions in the form of government directives to take on extra workers who then become underemployed. Thus the management of MNCs are supportive both of the employers' associations' campaigns to encourage members to stand firm against worker 'indiscipline' and of governments' policies to restrict trade unions since both activities enhance the attractiveness of employment in the relative tranquillity of such factories, at little cost. The fiercely competitive and unregulated conditions prevailing outside the import-substitution enclave, of course, also help to reduce the cost of living of their workers in so far as they consume the products of the competitive sector (Jeffries, 1978; Peace, 1979).

To summarize, in both Malaysia and Kenya the management of MNC subsidiaries manufacturing import-substitutes seem willing to encourage the institutionalization of company-based trade unionism as a 'loyal opposition'. However, there are significant variations in the philosophy of management they seek to impose on the workforce. In Kenya it is more directly instrumental in the sense that the emphasis is on the rate for the job and direct controls to ensure that workers appear regularly to perform their allotted tasks and do not malinger or steal company property. There is little attempt made to win over the workers' commitment to the organization. For example, in a high-wage brewery, the bottling hall was monitored by closed-circuit television and, at regular intervals, by security guards to make sure that workers were not tempted to drink any of the beer.

In Malaysia, the managerial philosophy is more permissive. Though there are complaints about absenteeism and stealing, little direct action is taken. By contrast with the weak emphasis on direct control over individual workers, many companies are active in monitoring and developing the skill level of all their workers and promoting identification with the firm through widespread adoption of age-related incremental wage scales and welfare policies with a familial emphasis. Malaysian employment policies would seem to represent an amalgam of Western institutional forms and Chinese cultural values and practices. For example, one British-owned company adopted a 'house' system, obviously modelled on the English public school, for organizing social and sports programmes, yet the purpose was to encourage a 'family bond' with the firm.[7] By contrast with Kenya, firms had Chinese and to a lesser extent Indian managers well entrenched in the highest financial and technical positions. The situation is changing to some extent since the advent of the New Economic Policy and the requirement to recruit more Malays into the managerial cadre, but it remains to be seen whether this will result in a shift towards instrumental individualism.

In Kenya the managerial cadre at all levels is generally of more recent vintage than in Malaysia (Greaves, 1978). As many senior posts are still held by expatriates employed on two- to four-year work permits and the small number of local senior executives tend to have close links with the political élite, corporate strategy tends to be dominated by short-term considerations of profitability and debt repayment. While manufacturing output has risen dramatically, this has largely been through better plant utilization and the establishment of new factories rather than through expansion of employment in existing plants. Dependence on expatriate technological expertise, in particular, reduces the real power of managers to little more than acting as supervisors of the foreign-designed managerial control systems that go with imported technology. Above all, managers are easily replaceable in small standardized production facilities either locally or, in emergency, with expatriates flown in from the international management pool of the parent company.

The development of employer strategies over time

The process of establishing manufacturing subsidiaries of multinational corporations in developing countries is invariably dominated by expatriate managers. Moreover, 'turn-key' project teams usually consist of engineers whose orientation is to engineer-out all possible problems from the production system, in particular the need for skilled workers and human intervention in the production process. Accompanying the introduction of a new factory are standardized managerial control procedures and programmes for operator training which tend to divorce the expatriate management team from its local counterparts; expatriates design and introduce procedures, while local management supervise their execution. At the outset, then, it is to be expected that the emphasis is on operational and technical issues. Once the plant is running as a viable production system and the expatriate presence has been reduced, there is some scope for moving away from an externally imposed management system.

Both the Kenyan and the Malaysian governments' policies in the industrial relations field have been designed to provide the minimum of restrictions on employers' freedom of action. In Malaysia the government's 'pioneer industries' policy provides explicit limitations on trade union rights to organize in infant industries, while both countries encourage company unionism and economism and prohibit political activity by trade unions. Except in export-oriented manufacturing and plantation industries, managements favour a high wages policy but the managerial philosophy on which it is based seems to vary between the two countries with more emphasis on human resource development in Malaysia and more emphasis on labour control in Kenya.

If the structure of high wages and superior fringe benefits is not to collapse, then the firm, in the long run, must be able to reap the benefits of increased productivity. Given limitations on the size of production units for small developing countries, this implies greater capacity utilization and, therefore, an expanding export market. In the short run, governments may subsidize import-substitution industries through taxation of the agricultural or mineral exporting base or by increasing indebtedness. In the long run, expansion of production is a priority both for management and governments in order to enhance the rate of profit and maintain the capacity to purchase the quiescence of the labour force. With significant oil and mineral reserves, Malaysia is in a more fortunate position than Kenya where the foreign exchange constraint is now providing a brake on further investment in import-substituting industry (Development Plan, 1974–83). In Kenya, in spite of a high wages policy, there have also been falling real wages as the worsening balance of payments situation has led to shortages of imported inputs and reduced demand for manufactured goods. Trade unions have been powerless to challenge company policies of tightening discipline because workers have been unwilling to risk their relatively advantageous position in a generally declining labour market.

In Kenya the closer integration of the political with the managerial élite, the greater power of the expatriate faction in a less industrialized and poorer economy and the absence of an indigenous industrial tradition have all meant that it has been relatively easy for employers to rely on the instrumental motivation of the labour force. It is, however, difficult to disentangle cause and effect. Perhaps it would be more accurate to explain the greater emphasis on bureaucratic and authoritarian labour relations in Kenya as the outcome of a process of mutual reinforcement: that is, the application of the instrumental logic of corporate strategy to a labour force with a predisposition towards accepting a calculative work ethic results in an emphasis on rate-for-the-job principles of remuneration and a managerial style that assumes that low levels of commitment to work prevail.

While political influence in the industrial sphere is increasing in importance in Malaysia, there remains a very significant part of the market economy that is relatively insulated from state intervention. In Kenya, the state's potential for intervening either for or against labour or capital is much greater because of the relative ease of access of members of the state executive to major companies and because of the leverage afforded by state patronage of the trade union leadership through protective legislation. The absence of either a strong and independent managerial class or labour movement means there is little resistance to encroachment by the state into industrial relations matters.[8]

In Malaysia the national interest, or at least that of the ruling Malay faction, is not nearly so close to that of private industry as it is in Kenya. While the Malaysian government is very concerned to prevent the integration of any broadly based working-class movement, it is willing to encourage the pursuit of individual grievances against employers through an active labour inspectorate and industrial court system. In MNCs the specific institutional and administrative frameworks provided by the different parent companies are modified over time to support a unitary managerial ideology that stresses a manager's responsibility for looking after his employees as part of his general duty to society.

Conclusions

This chapter compares labour policies pursued in the manufacturing subsidiaries of multinational corporations located in Kenya and Malaysia. It has been suggested that while both countries have rather similar government policies relating to industrial relations, company practices vary significantly. In seeking to explain divergences a number of different factors were discussed. First, the age of a factory is likely to have a general influence on policies. During the initial start-up period the influence of the expatriate 'turn key' team of production engineers will tend to permeate labour policies with a strong emphasis on control of the production process and mechanistic personnel procedures to enforce discipline. While relatively good working conditions are offered to the workforce they are the *quid pro quo* for accepting company discipline as absolute.

Secondly, the persistence of a significant expatriate management group tends to be associated with authoritarianism in labour policies. This tendency is well documented with respect to European managers working in the USA and American managers working overseas (Zeira *et al.*, 1975; Alpander, 1973). In many ways this is merely a perpetuation of the 'turn key syndrome', that is, expatriates on short-term contracts with a task and production orientation which is inconsiderate of and detached from local sensitivities. With expatriate–local communication primarily about programmed production decisions there is little scope for bridging the understanding gap created by differences in cultural background. In Malaysia, where the expatriate influence is much weaker than in Kenya, there is much greater emphasis placed on training and developing the workforce and even a limited amount of participation in welfare programmes.

Thirdly, the general level of economic activity exercises a pervasive influence on managerial priorities. With no growth and a government less willing to tolerate monopoly profits, Kenyan managers have few incentives to adopt a long-term approach to the development of the workforce. With rising domestic demand and a strong balance of payments situation in Malaysia it is easier for managers to take a longer-run view of labour productivity.

Fourthly, the specific social structure and political system of any country may itself contribute to or inhibit any move towards authoritarianism in labour policies. In Malaysia the situation of the Chinese community imposes certain limitations on the exercise of power in spite of its superior position in the economic system. The constituency of the predominantly Malay workforce matters to the senior Chinese executive. By contrast, in Kenya there are fewer possibilities of countervailing political power from the shopfloor because of the closer alignment of political and economic power.

In summary, it is possible to discern both a trend towards tight labour control and towards longer-term labour force development in the subsidiaries of multinational corporations operating in Kenya and Malaysia. In the absence of any resistance from either the managerial cadre or the shopfloor, labour policy is likely to be reduced to an appendage of scientific management and computerized budgetary control. However, as branch plants mature and the local employees begin to learn the rules of the game a more flexible approach with some adaptation to local conditions may emerge. Even so, the possibility remains that labour relations will become more authoritarian should the political, social and economic conditions prevailing in a particular country result in the destruction of what little bargaining power ordinary workers possess.

14

The contexts of management behaviour in industrial relations in the public and private sectors

A. W. J. THOMSON

Although there has recently been a good deal of interest in the differences between the public and private sectors, there has been little systematic examination of such differences, whether of management behaviour or of the contexts which might be held to produce such behaviour. This chapter is therefore an attempt, largely on *a priori* grounds, to examine three different contexts within which public and private sector managers operate in the industrial relations field, and to offer some observations on the possible effect of these differences on behaviour. It is of course the case that the public sector itself is far from homogeneous, and generalizations about it must inevitably be limited in their applicability; in particular there is a distinction to be made between the market and non-market parts of the public sector, and in the tables which form the basis of the commentary this division is used to create three, rather than two, sectors in the economy.

Differences in economic structure

Table 14.1 tabulates the major distinctions of economic structure and for reasons of space only a short commentary is possible. The most clear-cut distinctions are between the private sector and the non-market public sector, since while market forces and the price mechanism are all-important to the former as a system for the distribution of resources, they are replaced by a budgetary mechanism in the latter. In the private sector the market operates through consumer demand for products or services, which dictates the nature and extent of output, the amount of investment, and, in conjunction with cost factors, the price at which the

Table 14.1. *The private, public non-market and public market sectors: selected dimensions of economic structure*

Dimension	Private sector	Public non-market sector	Public market sector
1. Competition	Competitive, usually international	Monopolistic, sheltered from competition	Monopolistic for own products but substitution by other products creates competition
2. Determination of types of goods or services produced	Consumer demand. Diversification with changes in demand	Indirect demand through political process	Consumer demand but little scope for product differentiation
3. Determination of quantity of output	Consumer demand for goods and services. Cutbacks or expansion relatively rapid	No direct measure of output. Measured by amounts of inputs, especially money and staff	Consumer demand, but time lags in reaction to demand, creating shortages or over-capacity
4. Pricing of goods and services	Market pressures, although price leadership frequent	No price mechanism (indirectly inferred through voting process)	Cost based but with some governmental manipulation for social purposes and some exploitation of monopoly position, e.g. cross-subsidization
5. Performance criteria	Profit and growth in market share	Public service	Economic viability mixed with public service
6. Investment decisions	Market opportunities, dependent on private reserves and the capital market	Non-economic decision based on estimates of public need and public capital availability	Governmental decision ostensibly based on test rate of discount but also on employment and public capital availability considerations

	Solely from market	From taxation. No direct connection with services provided	From market, but subsidies as fallback in case of financial losses
7. Source of revenues			
8. Volatility of product demand	Considerable short-run volatility in many cases	Not easily measurable due to lack of price mechanism. Rather supply manipulated according to political and macroeconomic considerations	Mainly secular changes in demand, although predictable volatility according to seasonal, diurnal and trade cycle factors
9. Homogeneity and rate of change of technology	Heterogeneous technology. Often rapid rates of change but some areas of slow change	Homogeneous technology for given services. Generally slow rates of change	Homogeneous technology but frequently rapid rates of change
10. Capital–labour ratio	Variable from highly capital intensive to labour intensive	Highly labour intensive	Variable from highly capital intensive to labour intensive
11. Size of administrative unit of organization	Variable but small on average	Large	Large
12. Nature of labour force	Predominantly blue-collar in manufacturing, more white-collar in services	Predominantly white-collar	Predominantly blue-collar
13. Labour demand	Function of factor mix and product demand	No ready means of deciding establishment; partly created by self-determined professional standards	Relatively rapid in most cases
14. Wage elasticity of demand for labour	Relatively high	Low	Relatively low
15. Rate of productivity change	Relatively rapid	Not measurable, but slow. Tied to quality rather than quantity	Relatively rapid in most cases

output is sold. Companies are competitive, although some more so than others, and organizational objectives are geared to profit and growth. In the non-market public sector the lack of a price mechanism as a means of determining output and raising revenue puts the onus for decision-making into the political sphere, where the relationship between the provision of services and the means of paying for them is inevitably remote, denying any direct role for consumer demand in revealing preferences. To be sure, economic theories of democracy such as those of Downs (1957) have been devised to deal with this problem, but they can only establish broad principles. Likewise economic criteria such as cost-benefit analysis can be utilized, but only for alternatives within categories, not easily between them. Even the determination of output is difficult in the non-market public sector: either the cost of the inputs must be used, or crude qualitative measures such as teacher–pupil ratios. It follows that the measurement of productivity is often almost impossible.

The public market sector, consisting mainly of the nationalized industries, is more complex; it is ostensibly similar to the private sector in that its industries operate according to the price mechanism and are expected to achieve economic self-sufficiency. However, the main differences between the two are more practical than theoretical. A National Economic Development Office (NEDO) report (1976) noted that 'a good deal of confusion has arisen from drawing on private sector analogies' and pointed to various features which distinguished nationalized industries from private sector enterprises, including the strategic positions which they occupy in the economy, the political and social pressures to which they are subject and their freedom from the ultimate financial discipline of bankruptcy. Overall, therefore, while there certainly are market constraints on the nationalized industries, their operation in practice has moved them a long way from the context of the private sector.

A further factor is the monopoly which the public sector has of its products, although there are some, such as health and education, where elements of private enterprise do exist, even if they are not practical short-term substitutes except for a very few consumers. Governmental services and at least some of the public corporations are also very labour-intensive, with few opportunities for the substitution of capital; they also tend to have a high white-collar component. The size of administrative unit is also generally larger than in the private sector, partly, but not only, because services are standardized across the country insofar as possible. Standardization of services has also tended to mean standardization of technology, and at least in the non-market part of the public sector a slow rate of technical change. Consequent upon the above factors, the public sector is generally more bureaucratic in its modes of operation, more similar in the tasks performed by various groups of workers and thus in the industrial relations field more likely to be organized in a centralized structure. In fact the only link which the non-market sector has with the private sector is the need to draw labour from the same pool and thus to compete in terms of wages and conditions of employment.

Differences in industrial relations structure

Table 14.2 indicates the several distinctions between the industrial relations structures of the private and public sectors, of which only a few require comment. First, the private sector as a whole is less highly unionized than the public sector. Although of course many private companies are completely unionized at the blue-collar level, this is not true of many others, and even in large companies few if any have the high degree of organization found in the public sector amongst white-collar and managerial groups. Secondly, public sector collective bargaining remains highly centralized at a time when bargaining in the private sector has become increasingly decentralized, although retaining certain aspects of an industry-wide structure. This change has come about over the last two decades, and is primarily due to the different economic and administrative contexts in which the two sectors operate. In the private sector, large numbers of separate employers with different economic situations have resulted in diverging industrial relations conditions within industries; in the public sector there is only a single employer in most instances, and where there are many, as in local government, the standardizing influence of central government on local unit decision-making has made local authorities act in concert *vis-à-vis* their employees. The result has been that no significant degree of informal organization for bargaining purposes has emerged in the public sector, with a few exceptions. Thirdly, largely as a result of changes in bargaining structure, the traditional industry-wide dispute procedures in the private sector have frequently fallen into disrepute. In the public sector, which has in any case made greater use of consultation and third-party decision-making, procedural mechanisms have been more persistent, although some of them have also been challenged or changed in the last few years.

Table 14.2. *The private, public non-market and public market sectors: selected dimensions of industrial relations*

Dimension	Private sector	Public non-market sector	Public market sector
1. Extent of unionization			
a. Manual	Variable but high in manufacturing and large companies, low in services and small companies	Very high	Very high
b. White-collar	Low	High	High
2. Union structure	Highly complex in some cases with competitive unions	Relatively clear occupational jurisdictions, although some competition in health and education	Generally clear jurisdictions, although some demarcation problems and some competition by small unions
3. Extent of informal organization	Frequent many diverse occupational groups from powerful informal organizations	Little informal organization	Limited informal organization
4. Bargaining structure	Decentralized bargaining within industry-wide structure	Highly centralized bargaining	Centralized bargaining, except in steel
5. Codification of collective agreements	Low, although rising	Highly codified	Highly codified
6. Scope of bargaining	Narrow at industry level but wider in decentralized bargaining	Wide	Wide

7. Nature of bargaining relationship	Adversary	Traditionally cooperative through Whitley system, but trend to adversary	Adversary
8. Extent of consultation	Limited; not very effective in most cases	Central to industrial relations system	High, but questions as to value
9. Nature of conflict resolution procedures	Traditional industry-wide procedures giving way to plant procedures, but still essentially informal settlement at plant level	Formalized, centralized procedures. Some trend towards decentralization	Formalized, centralized procedures
10. Use of third parties in conflict resolution	Low, although rising	Traditionally high but declining	Relatively high
11. Nature of wage system			
a. Manual	Generally tied to performance, directly or indirectly, although diminishing use of PBR systems	Traditionally time rates, but performance increasing	Performance related systems increasing
b. White-collar	Generally merit. Few identified scales at higher levels	Published incremental scales at all levels	Job evaluation. Incremental scales at most levels up to top management
12. Relation of wages to local labour markets	Responsive but still diverse patterns	Generally not responsive	Not responsive, although some grade creep
13. Ultimate wage criteria	Labour market and what employer can afford to pay primary determinants. Some comparability	Primarily comparability. Ultimate wage determination by Treasury, not separate agencies	Product market and comparability, concern with position in wage hierarchy

Table 14.2 (*cont.*)

Dimension	Private sector	Public non-market sector	Public market sector
14. Extent of differentials	Market determined	Low. Wage and salary structures egalitarian and compressed	Low. Wage and salary structures egalitarian and compressed
15. Job security	Relatively low	High. Traditionally important in job attractiveness	Generally high. Attention paid to relocation and redundancy benefits where jobs lost
16. Patterns of industrial conflict	Few large official strikes. Many unofficial plant or work-group strikes	Relatively few strikes. Non-cooperation and demonstrations as means of industrial action	Occasional large strikes. Some unofficial strikes
17. Impact of industrial action	Low on public at large but frequently high in relation to production, both direct and indirect	Relatively low, although high visibility	Very high on both public at large and related production

Fourthly, again largely for structural reasons, patterns of industrial conflict have tended to differ in the two sectors, with a high proportion of unofficial strikes in the private sector but relatively few in the public sector. On the other hand, large and long-lasting strikes have mainly taken place in the public sector in recent years. Fifthly, wage systems in the private sector also reflect a lesser degree of centralization, being differentiated according to employer, while in the public sector wage systems are more standard, normally with published incremental scales for white-collar employees, although there has been some extension of performance-related systems amongst blue-collar groups. Sixthly, job security has generally been greater in the public sector, even allowing for diminishing total employment in many of the nationalized industries.

Although these differences mainly reflect underlying economic and political factors, the distinctions took some time to emerge. By the early 1920s what has come to be called the 'traditional' structure of collective bargaining had largely been created, with industry-wide bargaining covering public and private sectors alike. Although collective bargaining was thus adopted as the major means of determining wages and conditions, there was no public policy to institutionalize union membership as such, except in the public sector, where governmental policy encouraged union membership at all levels. In the private sector unionization was a function of the power of the unions and their attractiveness to employees, and the result was blue-collar unionization in large companies in manufacturing and relatively little organization in small companies and service industries. Patterns have changed towards increasing white-collar and service industry unionization in the post-World War II period, but the public sector remains much more heavily unionized.

Thus the structure of collective bargaining in the whole economy was highly centralized in the interwar period, with a very low discrepancy between industry-wide rates and actual earnings. This was also a period, however, of very heavy unemployment, which reduced the possibility of wage drift and supplementary bargaining. In the postwar period full employment radically changed the situation in the private sector, and the lack of plant-level institutions prevented any effective control by either managements or unions of work-group based fractional bargaining. As Fox and Flanders (1969: 162) put it: 'Those groups with sufficient power break through and impose their own norms. Insofar as they serve as reference points for other groups, either in the same system or in others, their example is followed. Extreme frustration builds up among those groups who come under the same tensions but who lack power. Meanwhile, each normative system becomes either replaced or supplemented by a number of smaller systems.' When the Donovan Commission (1968) evaluated the industrial relations system it based its recommendations on the need to decentralize bargaining to the company or plant level in the private sector in order to provide for a closer relationship between collective bargaining and the company's economic performance, thus acknowledging the need to make industrial relations decisions at the level of the basic economic unit. In the public sector, where the employer unit is largely co-extensive with the industry, a centralized structure remained appropriate; indeed, the public sector was largely exempted from analysis or criticism by the Commission. This relative complacency is now no longer the case; concern about industrial relations structures in the public sector has overtaken that about private sector structures, especially over wage inter-relationships.

Differences in modes of decision-making

Table 14.3 indicates some dimensions of decision-making in the private sector and the two public sub-sectors. Major decisions in the private sector are generally taken by boards of directors, but lower-level managers are also expected to contribute with initiatives at their own levels. The great majority of firms in Britain are small, whether measured by sales turnover or number of employees, and this enables lines of communication to be short. Others are of course large, complex and bureaucratic in operation, but even here since company markets and production processes are often segmented by specialization in the goods produced, there is frequently a need to decentralize a good deal of power to the operating units, leaving the headquarters primarily concerned with coordination and capital allocation functions. Decentralization can have weaknesses, as in the industrial relations field, where it was largely the abstention of boards of directors from policy-making which led to the rapid expansion of fractional bargaining and the exploitation of a managerial (and union) power vacuum at plant level by small work groups. Marsh (1971), for instance, found that some two-thirds of multi-plant companies in engineering did not have a member of the board responsible for industrial relations, and Winkler (1974) has argued that even when such directors do exist, they are too remote from the shopfloor to respond effectively. Even so, although the Donovan Commission's strong recommendation that all boards of directors should develop their own industrial relations policies may not have been achieved to the extent hoped for, it does provide a model of decision-making which offers to improve efficiency in the longer term. Moreover, the organizational climate in the private sector is more responsive to managerially induced change, since managers at all levels are expected to think in terms of initiatives, risk, and potential personal rewards.

In contrast, in the public sector, and especially the non-market part of it, decision-making takes place in a very different atmosphere. In general the function is one of administration rather than management, with actual decisions often not being clearly made by single individuals or groups short of the Cabinet. For the most part policy is formulated on the basis of long-term rules rather than spontaneous *ad hoc* decisions, since the rules must be both general, in that they apply across a range of situations, and specific, to give detailed guidance. For this reason also decisions must generally be made quite high up the organization and are merely interpreted lower down. In considerable part this is a function of the scale of operations in the public sector but it also has to do with the need for consistency and continuity. As the head of the Civil Service, Sir Douglas Allen (1977: 6), has put it: 'The scale requires large numbers of people who have to be organised in many units across the country in order to carry out the policies. The desire for uniformity of treatment, coupled with accountability for decisions, require elaborate codes and rules so that a multiplicity of decision-makers can produce acceptably similar results in similar cases. Inevitably this limits the extent of delegation.' A further factor is the diffusion of goals in the public sector. Whereas the private sector manager can often easily appreciate what will advance the goal of profit or sales or output to which he works, goals in the public sector are more difficult to determine and evaluate. To quote Sir Douglas Allen again: 'in the public sector there is a vast range of policies with aims which are complex and frequently difficult to establish. Performance in achieving them is usually a matter of judgment and is rarely measurable.' Moreover, most goals are set through political means rather than any internal process, and to permit too much flexibility would be to substitute executive for political judgment. There are frequent assertions from politicians that this is what happens anyway (House of Commons Expenditure Committee, 1977: lxxviii), and the threat of political reaction, combined with the possibility that wrong decisions will be exposed in the media, combine to reduce autonomous decision-making compared to the private sector. The tendency is therefore to play safe at both a personal

Table 14.3. *The private, public non-market and public market sectors: selected dimensions of modes of decision-making*

Dimension	Private sector	Public non-market sector	Public market sector
1. Nature of decision-making process			
a. Policy decisions	Boards of directors	Primarily political but based on Civil Service advice	Jointly between politicians, Civil Service and corporation boards of directors
b. Lower-level decisions	Relatively autonomous, decentralized management	Bureaucratic following rules set higher up	Limited managerial discretion
2. Delegation of decision-making	Usually high	Low	Relatively low
3. Decision criteria for management	Market and profit-oriented	Diffused across a range of objectives	Maintenance of industry position
4. Visibility of policy decisions	Usually taken in private	Relatively public, often subject to review by media	Relatively public, often subject to review by media
5. Approaches to risk and change	Emphasis placed on rewards for risk in progressive companies. Acceptance of inevitability of uncertainty in economic climate	Tendency to play safe. Superiors less interested in success than the avoidance of mistakes. Little acceptance of need for change	Some limited willingness to innovate, especially in area of technology
6. Extent of personal responsibility of managers	High	Sheltered by bureaucratic system	Relatively sheltered

7. Personnel goals	Basically the use of labour as a factor of production	To be a 'good' employer	To be a 'good' employer
8. Nature of personnel function	Coordinating and bargaining; often short-run in perspective, although recognition of need for forward planning in progressive companies	Administrative	Mainly administrative, but recognition of need for forward planning

and organizational level because avoidance of error is more important than initiatives for the individual manager. In total, the system is one of bureaucracy, in which rules are paramount, individual decision-making plays a relatively small role, and the primary objective is consistency.

The managerial environment noted above nevertheless had advantages in providing good administration of industrial relations by comparison to much of the private sector, and this helped to create a harmonious relationship for most of the century. This, however, is no longer the case, as group after group of public service employees has moved towards more militant action. In effect, there has arguably been a breakdown in the tacit agreement whereby public sector employees (including, although to a somewhat more limited extent, the nationalized industries) did not use their full bargaining power in exchange for the acceptance by public sector employers of 'good employer' obligations. In considerable part this breakdown has been the result of what has been felt to be discrimination by governments in the operation of incomes policies. Whatever the truth of this, every public sector group now feels itself to be a special case. A further aspect has been the increasing tendency to centralize financial decision-making within the public sector, and especially in the role of the Treasury. The Treasury always has played an important part in collective bargaining, but one largely behind the formal machinery. In recent years, however, its role has been more overt, especially of course through the system of cash limits, but also even before this. Cash limits constitute an even greater threat to any real latitude for collective bargaining within the public sector if operated on the opinion of the House of Commons Expenditure Committee (1977: iii) that: 'Effective cash limits should be fixed before pay negotiations are entered into . . . the principle of cash limits would fall to the ground if they merely incorporated existing staff levels and the results of pay bargaining automatically.'

The three contexts we have examined all tend to limit the industrial relations decision-making role at least of middle and lower-level management in the public sector by creating centralized structures, sometimes to the point where there is no capacity for managerial motivation of workers. Even senior managers increasingly find that they too have little freedom in respect of industrial relations issues such as pay or jobs, not only because of governmental pressures, but because unions can and frequently do go over the heads of public sector managers on these latter issues. The recent past has seen the exacerbation of these

144

contextual constraints as the public sector has come under pressure in terms of financing, employment and wage levels and governments have felt obliged to treat the sector as a whole as far as possible.

Various reports have recognized the tendency to reduce the role of public sector managers to a purely administrative rather than a managerial one; the House of Commons Expenditure Committee (1977: lx) has perhaps gone further than most in arguing for a higher degree of personal responsibility, with commensurate rewards, for civil servants, as opposed to mere changes in machinery or policy. Yet most such attempts have foundered on the political pressures to obtain accountability, to react to lobby groups, and to impose the wider national interest, as in the case of pay policy. It is difficult to see that these latter pressures will diminish, or therefore that the managerial roles or behaviour will be greatly modified.

15

Personnel management in its organizational context

SHAUN TYSON

'The old Chairman instilled his own doctrine towards people – management by intimidation – didn't like too much independence amongst his staff.'

– Staff controller of large retail store

'Nowadays, Personnel staff are being brought into departments too frequently without experience on the shop floor – they don't know what it's like to be bored, to work long hours on routine jobs, filling cartons all day long. I don't believe that social theory or psychology have a place, except to support commonsense opinions.'

– Company personnel manager in a process industry

'I was successful because the Chairman was always behind me. I was often invited to put my case before the Board.'

– Personnel manager, consumer durables factory

The personnel function

The history of personnel management in the United Kingdom can be used to demonstrate that the way specialist personnel and industrial relations activities in management have developed, and the kinds of policies that have been pursued, are largely a consequence of reactions to a range of contextual variables which often seem, to those trying to cope with them, to be 'out there' in society (Watson, 1977; Legge, 1978). The market size for particular products and services, State intervention via laws and agencies, the level of unemployment in specific labour markets and 'custom and practice' in collective bargaining in the industry in question are clearly relevant for many business decisions. However, these factors are interpreted by managers in the enterprise in accordance with their marketing objectives and investment policy, their

assumptions on managerial prerogatives and authority and their decision-making habits. In addition, perceptions of the relative power and
influence of personnel and industrial relations department specialists held
by employees, shop stewards and line and functional managerial staff
tend to condition the creation of new personnel policies. Such policies
and the customs and practices they sustain are themselves significant
factors which underpin management ideologies and agreed methods of
decision-making.

The place of the personnel department in the organization and the
reason for its emergence has often been explained without recourse to
any discussion of managerial beliefs and perceptions, but simply by
reference to changes in market size and market share, or factors such as
new technology and investment policies. An example here would be the
emergence of personnel departments in such expanding industries as
chemicals, synthetic fibres and multiple retail stores in the inter-war
period. Reader (1975: 60 *et seq.*) points out that in 1926, ICI's centralized labour department helped to create a corporate identity, to produce
order at a time of major changes, and to control the expanding divisional organization in matters such as management development and
industrial relations strategy.

Similarly, it has been argued that it was expansion at Pilkingtons and
the new markets for their products at Courtaulds which led to the reorganization of their management hierarchies, and to the genesis of their
personnel departments (Barker, 1977; Coleman, 1969). New investment created the need for personnel departments to cope with recruitment and training problems, and mergers which required the rationalization of different conditions of service acted as a stimulus in this area.
The two world wars themselves created an expansion in market size and
production on unprecedented scales. The consequent demand for new
labour provided an urgent need for specialist employment management
and associated welfare work (Niven, 1967; McGivering, 1970). The
existence of the need, however, does not explain the development without taking into account why managers respond to the need in a particular
way. One obvious factor here is the influence of the thinking of politicians, government officials, journalists and academic writers on reforms
required in employment and industrial relations policies. Although such
approaches as Whitleyism, advocated in the 1920s and 1930s, may have
had only face validity to the more cynical manager, there was a residual
effect. Clegg (1972) points to the importance of ideas on joint consultation in the training of personnel managers. The State had a major

impact on conditions of service in civilian establishments during both world wars, and increasingly through legislation the State has tried to create a climate where certain industrial relations policies are likely to be approved, the 1960s seeing the development of so called 'property rights' of employees over their jobs.

In the inter-war period, the scientific management movement emphasizing the notion of 'efficiency' as a rationale for managerial legitimacy produced personnel techniques in the fields of selection testing, job evaluation, ergonomics, time study, and new training methods, often seeded in organizations by consultants, such as those from the National Institute of Industrial Psychology (NIIP). Considerable variation between companies should be noted in terms of their overall managerial style. Overt paternalism was still accepted in some companies whilst in others such a style provoked disputes. For example, one may contrast the strike at Courtaulds caused by the outdated paternalism of their managing director, Harry Johnson, in the 1930s (Coleman, 1969: 443) with the avuncular view of employees which was accepted by the employees of the small firm of Thomas Walker and Son Ltd in the same period (Wilmott, 1951).

Decision-making habits also changed frequently as a consequence of new approaches to collective bargaining. The withering away of employers' associations and the emergence of a stronger shop steward movement reinforced company-level bargaining. Although the extension of the public sector and post-war incomes policies produced a counter-trend local strategies on both sides have been pursued. One consequence for the industrial relations specialist is the extension of negotiation into new areas on such issues as appraisal and training, reinforced by the expansion of white-collar unionism. The practice and experience of negotiation may have considerable effects on the beliefs and objectives of personnel specialists.

The basis of personnel specialists' orientations and belief systems

If, as argued, it is necessary to understand the actual criteria used by personnel decision-makers and their orientations in order to explain the development of personnel management and the industrial relations policies used in organizations, it is also necessary to study the basis of these beliefs. One school of sociologists tries to use the concept of an 'occupational ideology' in order to explain such beliefs. However, studies of personnel management as a discrete occupation and profession seem inconclusive and unsatisfactory (Timperley and Osbaldeston, 1975; Watson, 1977: 116), since the claim to professional status appears to be only a strategy (Legge, 1978), rather than valid in itself. In particular, no client relationship or clearly defined exclusive body of knowledge has been discerned. As personnel managers are part of management they will themselves contribute to the beliefs about society, power and authority which form the enterprise's management ideology. The question then arises of how far there are conflicts between their own values and those prevailing amongst other managers. Do personnel specialists bring a particular set of criteria to bear on business decisions or are such specialists absorbed into the particular 'organizational cultures' of each firm?

The evaluative nature of personnel work, which entails trading in personality theories and exchanging views on employees, makes essential an understanding of the phrases describing others (the 'definitions in use') utilized by personnel staff. The saliency of such insights resides in the discovery of the criteria used when making judgements about employees.

The way personnel management is carried out seems frequently more relevant to the outcome than *what* is done, for example, in handling grievances, dealing with redundancy, recruiting, or negotiating a change in the conditions of service. Many of the technical skills used in personnel work are interpersonal skills in interviewing, counselling and negotiation where meanings can be changed and compromises reached. As a 'broker' of different value sets, the personnel manager may act as a socialization agent, conducting the policies through which employees experience authority in their working world.

In order to test the argument that personnel specialists do *not* have a specific occupational culture of their own, four organizations were taken as case studies, the research being arranged so that different contexts could be compared. Two of the cases were groups of companies which operated in unstable environments with diverse marketing interests, and consequently with organic structures (Burns and Stalker, 1961). The other two were bureaucracies, stable and devoted to administrative work on a large scale. Table 15.1 shows details of the contrasting characteristics of the four organizations.

In order to ascertain the actual perceptions and constructs used by personnel and industrial relations specialists, it was necessary to go beyond the normal questionnaire survey approach and attempt to study a number of individuals in depth. Accordingly, the Repertory Grid tech-

Table 15.1. *The four organizations studied*

	A	B	C	D
Industry	Engineering chemicals manufacture	Engineering chemicals manufacture	Commercial dept of petro-chemical conglomerate	Public sector administration dept
Ownership	British	American	British International	British
Type/range of products	Valves, seals, paints, chemicals	Chemicals, engineering metals	Services/trade	Administration
Structure of personnel dept	Divisional HQ and individual enterprise personnel depts	Divisional HQ and individual enterprise personnel depts	HQ personnel dept	HQ and local depts
No. of employees	3,300 (various locations)	5,000 (various locations)	5,000 (one location, mostly white-collar)	9,000 (various locations, mostly white-collar)
Unionization	Few white-collar members. Higher % of blue-collar membership	Few white-collar members. Strong blue-collar membership	Company-based staff assoc.	Total unionization within Civil Service union
Investment process	By acquisition of mostly small companies	Through development & application of advanced technology		
Organization	Decentralized, small, flexible organic structures responding to market conditions	Decentralized, small, flexible units within each division working on organic lines	Centralized, hierarchical structure, large concentration of employees covered by procedures	Centralized, hierarchical structure, employees following procedures in a rule-governed environment

nique was used to investigate the 'interpretations' or constructs of twenty subjects in all. Personal 'constructs' are the 'interpretations' or representations of their world by each subject (Kelly, 1955). Constructs are thus the ways of understanding in which the values and beliefs of the subject can be seen. The subjects chosen were mostly in the age group thirty to forty-five, both men and women, who were performing middle-ranking personnel jobs. All of them were experienced in personnel work with upwards of eighteen months' service with their companies. The technique adopted was similar to the original method devised by Kelly (Slater, 1977; Fransella and Bannister, 1977). The subjects were presented with twelve typical 'roles' encountered in their work, each representing what was thought to be a significant role relationship for the specialist in question. These roles were:

       'A Successful Colleague'
       'Happy Person'
       'Typical Line Manager'
       'Disruptive Person'
       'Hard Worker'
       'Threatening Person'
       'Typical Trade Unionist'
       'The Subject's Manager'
       'The Managing Director or Senior Manager'
       'Pitied Person'
       'Ethical Person'
       'Self'

Usually between ten and twelve constructs describing perceived characteristics of these roles were elicited from each personnel manager, the roles being rated on all the constructs, with equal ratings permitted.

The core constructs

There is not space here for a comprehensive account of the results but, for the purposes of this discussion, one of the most pertinent areas was in relation to the 'core constructs' of personnel managers. These may be defined as those constructs which help the subject to maintain his identity.

The most important results of the study were the similarities which emerged between the core constructs of the five personnel managers in each organization.

In case A, the core constructs of the managers interviewed emphasize calmness, high interpersonal skills and those values which are often associated with the upper middle class – individualism, competition, and the survival of the fittest. In organization B, the core constructs relate to a belief in technical competence and professionalism, this being interpreted as a positive, practical approach to problem-solving by the use of social skills. The organic organization structures in A and B, where survival depends on mutual support amongst managers – in A by superior interpersonal skills and a belief in shared values, in B by showing that practical results stem from personnel management expertise – may in part account for this result.

In organization C most of the core constructs stressed the belief that the personnel managers were successful in personal relationships and possessed the ability to see what was good for the organization as a whole. In D, personnel managers identified themselves as being firm, with their personal life well under control, and with a capacity to take a mature, comprehensive view of the world. Again, one interpretation of these core constructs is that they derive from the bureaucratic organization structure and management ideologies in which such a view of oneself is necessarily compatible with how one is defined by others. The ideologies current in both C and D were based on the belief that those in more senior positions possess special merits, and that one must support the system which has brought the reward of office.

It was hoped that the way personnel managers cope with divergent values would become apparent by the inclusion of those elements (roles) which they regarded as disruptive or threatening. In some cases, constructs which were related to success and economic efficiency were placed in strong antithesis to constructs relating to equity and to ethical considerations. Although one might expect some self selection into organizations where the sense of identity will best be satisfied (Ingham, 1970), personnel managers may be assumed to adjust their values at least to some extent when entering a specific place of employment. From examining the constructs in each instance an 'adaptive response' was discovered; either this was a construct which was strongly related to their core constructs and was common throughout the five subjects in each organization, or it indicated that the subject was distancing himself from his actual role. The 'adaptive response' was perhaps a way that the subject could prove to himself that if perceived in a different way, threatening constructs could be accepted.

The differences between individuals in the same organization were far less marked and could be explained by differences in personal circumstances and life career. These circumstances included their individual work situations, their feelings about senior managers, and their current pressures of work. The beliefs and values of these twenty personnel managers demonstrate that management ideologies are in reality personal sets of interpretations, which can have organizational significance because of the ways that they are moulded and adapted over time, especially through the structures and constraints perceived by those working within such organizations.

Industrial relations and appraisal systems

In looking at how personnel managers construe the role of 'typical trade unionist', there is an area of unanimity to the extent that the element evoked less intensity of response than, for example, the subjects' 'own managers'. Trade unions were not construed as threatening in A, B and D, although they seemed to be equated with 'disruptive' characteristics. In C, the role of 'typical trade unionist' was particularly associated with those who were either threatening or disruptive. Collective bargaining procedures and practice meant personnel managers in A and B have little need in their current jobs to contact white-collar union representatives, most of their negotiating being with craft unions. They also meet the latter on joint consultative committees. The unions in D are Civil Service unions, some of whom are extremely active, but they were given responses in the Repertory Grid Study which accords them only a nuisance value. In C, there are no recognized unions but attitudes to unions may reflect frustration from the effects of disputes elsewhere in the group. As a relatively unknown quantity to personnel managers in organization C, unions may have seemed potentially threatening.

It has been argued that management ideologies are significant in the creation of industrial relations and personnel policies. An examination of appraisal systems brings us into touch with their ideologies. In looking at how personnel managers construed 'successful colleagues', 'hard worker', 'disruptive' and 'threatening' persons, the construct 'ambition' appears as a superordinate construct to fourteen of the subjects. Two views of ambition emerge: *normal* ambition, which is defined by the subjects as wanting to be reasonably successful, being tough when necessary, but also being fair in the pursuit of advancement; and secondly, a *self-assertive* form of ambition, this being egoistic, self-seeking ambition. Personnel managers in all of the cases seemed to regard the first form as the more legitimate, but differences between organizations also emerged.

'Hard workers' in A and B are those who get on quietly with their jobs, whereas in C and D to be classified as 'hard workers' they need to be more pushing and assertive. One reason may be that ambitious people present 'problems' for personnel departments. They tend to demand opportunities that are out of the ordinary and may represent a real threat to the personnel department. Organizations C and D had much more highly developed formalized career management policies. Perhaps one of the objectives of such policies is to control ambition, until it becomes what one subject described as 'normal'. Smaller organizations such as A and B, with limited opportunities for transfer and a policy of recruiting and promoting to specific jobs, also clearly have to constrain self-assertive ambition.

Management ideologies and decision-making practice may be said to converge in the area of management development. Individual values and beliefs about the qualities needed to be successful, and the sorts of activities that should be rewarded can be compared with the criteria used in formal appraisal systems. A principal components analysis of all the constructs in each organization produced the first three principal components in each case. These bi-polar constructs represent the consensus constructs of personnel managers in the organization, and are the criteria used in making judgements about others and in evaluating evidence.

From Table 15.2, it is clear that in each organization there is a relationship between the 'consensus' constructs and the criteria against which people were evaluated when being appraised by their managers. In A, the importance of achieving performance targets is underscored; in B, 'professionalism'; in C, the combination of personal drive and independence; and in D, the use of personalized intellectual criteria with implications of stereotyping.

Appraisal systems were operated with varying degrees of formality. The appraisal reports were not the only determinants of action on the career development of employees, and even where they were consulted, investigation showed that it was naive to assume that the descriptive phrases used in the reports had an unequivocal meaning. There were various formal and covert procedures for reviewing managers' performance in which personnel staff were involved. Part of the personnel role was to reinterpret information to facilitate management action, and

Table 15.2. Personnel management in the organizational climate

Organization	Consensus construct		Criteria stated on appraisal documents
A	i. Easy, relaxed, undemonstrative, unsophisticated	↔ Anxious, voluble, sophisticated	Importance of achieving targets also of the way objectives achieved
	ii. Not self-seeking by devious means	↔ Ambition at all costs	
	iii. Alienation, resentment, hopelessness	↔ Involved, satisfied, individually successful	
B	i. Good social relationships, honest, flexible	↔ Poor relationships, dishonest	Technical competence evidenced by results plus high interpersonal skills
	ii. Untrained, unprofessional approach	↔ Trained, committed, professional	
	iii. High moral standards	↔ Low moral standards	
C	i. Inflexible, slow, insensitive	↔ Flexible, good relations, quick on uptake	'Helicopter' concept, can stand back with broad vision and see relevance of work
	ii. Inoffensive, dependent	↔ Independent, abrasive	
	iii. Decisive, potentially able, instrumentally attached	↔ Altruistic, softer, not very able	
D	i. Quiet, reliable, organization man	↔ Vociferous, unreliable, disinterested	Personalized intellectual criteria – e.g. 'Judgement', 'Penetration', Personal relationships
	ii. Strict, ambitious, old-fashioned	↔ Easy going, modern compromiser	
	iii. Undemonstrative, weak, low status	↔ High status, strong, influential	

the personnel specialists concerned drew on what they thought senior managers would accept as appropriate, depending for example on what was understood to be a 'normal ambition'.

Conclusions

From these brief examples of the results of the research a number of conclusions may be drawn. Problems facing personnel management do not lead to action unless interpreted by the managers themselves. Their sense of structure is part of their personal constructs, resulting from their role as socialization agents.

This role makes such specialists particularly sensitive to the specific 'culture' of a particular enterprise, as this is central to any attempt to encourage identification with the enterprise. Paradoxically, the organizational orientation of personnel managers is part of their occupational orientation. It is only through his or her specific role situation that personnel specialists are able to interpret their working world. Values which are common in organizations are pervasive, and because of the need to demonstrate openly that he or she represents authority, such values *have* to be seen in the actions of the personnel manager. The process by which individuals come to adapt to these values seems like a form of cognitive dissonance (Festinger, 1957) and, depending on prior orientations, may give rise to feelings of ambivalence and stress. It is also possible, however, for personnel specialists to influence at least some aspects of the overall managerial ideology and this leads to a partial accommodation process. The interpretation of who ought to be regarded as 'successful' illustrated one activity in which both senior line managers and personnel specialists can engage and in which such an accommodation process may take place.

The real specialism of personnel management could be described as the capacity to survive, to be adaptable, and to facilitate senior management actions. The ability to change in accordance with the organization's culture, and the latest dictum from the board of directors does not result in the personnel manager being a chameleon, because the interactive character of his work constantly provides the possibility of changing meanings. This may prove satisfying, for it permits the solution of problems by redefining them, for example, by changing rules. In this sense, personnel managers could be described as specialists in ambiguity. Such a role, however, clearly limits the possibility of developing a capacity to contribute to managerial strategic thinking.

16
Organizational survival as an act of faith: the case of the BBC

PETER SEGLOW

'An important thing to know about the BBC is that it resembles the Catholic Church not only by being greatly improved by a little persecution. Just as the Church's paramount objective, to which all other subordinate, is the preservation of the faith, in the BBC the object is at all costs to preserve the BBC.'

(Peter Black: *Mirror in the Corner,* Hutchinson, 1972, p. 211)

Introduction

This paper is based on a study of the BBC. Its aim is to demonstrate the link between organizational objectives and industrial relations strategy. The dimensions of this link will be made explicit by showing how industrial relations strategies change in an attempt to accommodate re-definitions of organizational goals.

Corporate objectives

The objectives of the BBC as set out in its Charter are to provide a broadcasting service as a means of information, education, and entertainment. Yet, as Burns (1970: 135) has pointed out, this definition is so wide that it could equally be claimed for the commercial television companies. Clearly what distinguished the BBC from its commercial competitors is that whereas the latter rely on the sale of advertising time for their revenue, the existence of the BBC depends on its appropriation of the licence fee. This suggests that a more realistic definition of the objectives of the Corporation would include a continuation of a system whereby the BBC's income derives from some form of public funding. This is important because it also suggests a second objective, namely the maintenance of a sufficiently large share of the broadcasting audi-

157

ence. As Hood (1972: 411) has written: 'If, it is argued, the ratio of BBC : ITV ratings were consistently 30 : 70 or lower (which is roughly what it was when the full impact of ITV's competition first made itself felt), then the BBC's enemies in the House of Commons . . . would be able to urge that a broadcasting organisation which was unable to attract a larger share of the audience should not be given any more funds.' It follows that if the BBC is to continue its claim to the appropriation of the licence fee, it must project itself as being The British Broadcasting Corporation. For the BBC, however, public funding has never meant governmental intervention in the Corporation's programme policy or in programme content. The BBC is proud of its independence and a powerful argument for a continuation of the licence fee system (as opposed to any more direct form of government finance) is precisely based on the view that the system safeguards the Corporation's autonomy and ensures its impartiality, particularly on issues of political controversy.

This brief analysis suggests that a more realistic statement of the BBC's objectives would include the provision of a broadcasting service to inform, educate, and entertain the public but to do this whilst:

1. maintaining the Corporation's role as *The* British Broadcasting Corporation;
2. ensuring the Corporation's independence from government and the pursuance of a non-partisan policy in matters of programme policy and content;
3. ensuring, equally, that the Corporation should have no formal accountability to any outside interest or pressure group, particularly one representing commercial interests.

Historical background

From its foundation until about 1940, the pursuit of these objectives posed few problems for the BBC. However, the outbreak of the Second World War saw a broadening of the role of broadcasting. It was to play a vital part in the war effort. Its contribution in sustaining morale amongst both civilians and troops is well known. In addition, the outbreak of war meant the development of foreign services and the coming of the so-called 'War of Words'. Between September 1939 and May 1941, the BBC began broadcasting in twenty-five different languages from Albanian to Urdu. A consequence of this expansion of services was a substantial increase in staff numbers. From employing under five thousand people when the war broke out, by the end of 1941 this figure had increased to over ten thousand. It was during this period that the BBC acquired its reputation as the voice of democracy and of maintaining a high standard of accuracy and truth in its reporting. The BBC has sought to retain this reputation ever since.

Despite widespread acclaim for the Corporation during the war, by the late 1940s and early 1950s a view emerged that the monopoly position of the BBC in British broadcasting was harmful. This view became increasingly influential after the publication of the Report of the Beveridge Committee in 1951. The Report noted that 'when a sense of mission such as animates the BBC is combined with security of office it may grow into a sense of Divine Right, as it did in the case of Charles I. The dangers of monopoly are not imaginary.'[1] Beveridge also contained a minority Report written by Selwyn Lloyd, MP calling for the introduction of commercial broadcasting as a service to co-exist with the BBC. With the election of a Conservative government in 1951 and the success of a cleverly orchestrated public relations campaign by the so-called Popular Television Association supported behind the scenes by important advertising interests, the campaign for the introduction of commercial television was mounted. It proved successful and a new body, the Independent Television Authority (as it was then still called), with powers to license programme companies that would rely on advertising for their revenue, became law with the passing onto the Statute Book of the Television Act of 1954.

In essence, the reaction of the BBC to the advent of unprecedented competition was to pretend it did not exist. As the BBC's Director General remarked at the time, 'The coming into existence of ITV in no way changes our responsibilities'.[2] He and others assumed the BBC could continue in its old ways, confident that its continued exclusive claim to virtue in broadcasting remained unaffected. However, within the space of about a year, the BBC had retained only about a quarter of the total television audience. Whilst the extent of ITV's advantage did diminish, it was not until the mid-1960s that the Corporation were successful in restoring the balance of audience figures to nearer 50 : 50.

Perhaps the most important reason for the BBC's renewed ascendancy resulted from the Report of the Pilkington Committee which was published in mid-1962. The Pilkington Committee roundly condemned ITV. The commercial companies were criticized for being preoccupied with maintaining their lead in audience figures. The BBC were, however, applauded, and the Report recommended that a third television channel should be created and allocated to the Corporation. BBC2 duly went on the air in April 1964. This implied a fundamental change in the structure of competition between the two sectors of the industry. With two channels available to them, the BBC could designate programmes intended to appeal to minority audiences to BBC2. This left BBC1 in a position to show the more popular programmes and therefore able to compete with ITV on its own terms.

For the BBC's personnel policy the creation of a second television channel had two important consequences. First, it confirmed the position of television within the Corporation and the declining importance of radio. Secondly, it necessitated the recruitment of more staff for the new channel. Between 1963 and 1965 the number of staff directly employed in the Corporation's television service increased by 30 per cent, making the television service the largest single employer within the BBC. Whereas in 1956, the year after ITV started, only 15 per cent of the BBC's staff were directly employed in its television service, by 1970 this had increased to over 33 per cent. In short, television became the Corporation's dominant 'product division'. To accommodate this new development, the BBC built the Television Centre at White City. Although the building had been started in the late 1950s, it was not until the 1960s that the scattered parts of the television service came together under one roof.

Trade unionism at the BBC

In pre-war days the approach of the BBC towards its staff was essentially autocratic, an autocracy interspersed with occasional bouts of paternalism. Reith, the BBC's first Director General, was concerned above all to inspire an attitude of loyalty among BBC employees towards the Corporation. Unionism was discouraged, and the BBC did not recognize any trade union. Indeed, the BBC's attitude towards unions came in for much criticism. Attlee, for example, wrote that in order to counter autocracy and paternalism, 'the BBC should definitely recognise the right of every employee to join an appropriate union and that a proper system of consultation and collective agreement should be instituted'.[3]

Nevertheless, it was not until the outbreak of the war that staff associations were formed within the BBC and were granted a limited form of recognition. Reith had left the Corporation in 1938, and some seven months after the outbreak of the war Frederick Ogilvie, his successor, accepted the newly formed BBC (Wartime) Staff Association agreeing that it was an appropriate body for consultation on staff matters.[4] A

The case of the BBC

year later a similar form of recognition was accorded to the newly formed Association of BBC Engineers. Of course, neither of these bodies was an established union with members outside the Corporation. Indeed, one of the two original objectives of the BBC (Wartime) Staff Association was 'to promote the Welfare of BBC Staff as a contribution to the efficiency of the broadcasting system'. Few unions have defined their objectives with quite such concern for the well-being of the employer. But then the Staff Association was scarcely an independent union. For some years its offices were on BBC premises, its staff were seconded from the Corporation and facilities, including stationery, office furniture, and telephones, were provided by the BBC. In these circumstances it is hardly surprising that the Staff Association came in for considerable criticism from older-established unions, particularly those who were claiming recognition from the BBC. Indeed, at its tenth anniversary dinner in 1950, Lord Simon, then Chairman of the BBC Board of Governors, suggested that the Association might change its name to the National Union of Broadcasters, a name, which, he told his audience, 'might take the edge off some of the criticism you receive from outside unions'.[5]

However, during the late 1950s and early 1960s the Staff Association slowly began to change its character. Its name was changed to the Association of Broadcasting Staff (ABS) in early 1956. The ABS affiliated to the TUC in 1963 (though they are still not affiliated to the Labour Party), and more articles reflecting traditional trade union concerns appeared in their journal. However, it was not really till the late 1960s that the ABS finally succeeded in shedding its image of a weak and compliant organization, more like an internal pressure group of the BBC than an independent trade union. Not that there was much in the way of industrial trouble at the BBC. Compared to ITV, industrial relations in the BBC were, during that time, still a model of peace and tranquillity.

It is not difficult to explain why. Before the 1960s the BBC's staff were mainly middle class and had widely disparate skills. They were engaged in tasks as different as painting and constructing scenery to monitoring Albanian language broadcasts. Furthermore, they were physically dispersed. The monopoly position of the BBC in the labour market before 1955 helped the Corporation to secure continuing loyalty from its staff. In these circumstances the attitude of staff in the BBC was characterized by their deference to a paternal and benevolent, yet immensely powerful, employer. The fact that the BBC paid reasonable salaries with annual increments, and that job security was as steadfast

161

as in the Civil Service implied that industrial relations presented few problems for the Corporation's management. But in 1969 the ABS for the first time in its history called its members in the BBC out on strike. Since that date the BBC has had to contend with several other serious industrial disputes, many of them involving the ABS. Comparing the years before 1969 with the period since, it is clear that industrial relations in the Corporation have fundamentally changed.

The changing pattern of industrial relations in the BBC

The paradox of the situation was that the very success of the Corporation was responsible for the dissatisfaction amongst its staff, and for galvanizing the traditionally passive ABS into unprecedented industrial action. Strangely enough, in the short term at least, it was the growing popularity of ITV which had helped to keep the BBC out of industrial trouble. Commercial television was largely responsible for the growth of television ownership in Britain. Whilst in 1954, the last full year before commercial television went on the air, less than three and a quarter million licences had been issued, by the end of the 1960s this figure had increased to over ten million. Because the BBC's income relies on the payment of a licence fee which, of course, has to be paid on all televisions this growth of set ownership meant that the BBC's income also increased. Between 1960 and 1963 alone, the income of the Corporation went up by 22 per cent even though the licence fee remained constant.

However, by the mid 1960s saturation point had virtually been reached in terms of audience penetration. Colour television did not start on BBC1 till the end of 1969 and, with the vast majority of viewers owning monochrome sets, it was clear that it would take several years before the ownership of colour sets, commanding the higher licence fee, would make any significant contribution to the Corporation revenue position. Yet costs were rising rapidly. Between 1966–7 and 1970–1, operating costs for domestic radio and TV rose by 51 per cent. The licence fee had been increased to five pounds in August 1965, and this was the period of the prices and incomes policy of the newly elected Labour government. Productivity bargaining was becoming fashionable, and the Prices and Incomes Board were promoting it as a central chapter in the new testament of economic policy. To meet the situation of rising costs with a nearly static income, the BBC embarked on an economy campaign. As part of this, McKinsey and Co., the well-known firm of management consultants, were engaged to examine the Corporation's organization and finances. Whilst their report did not suggest that the BBC was particularly extravagant in the use of its resources, it did recommend important internal reorganizations with new values implicit in them. Programme production and costing were brought closer together. Considerations of cost effectiveness were to become of important concern to those whose interests had been restricted (*sic*) to the quality of programme output. To many in the BBC the new ideology did little other than provoke anger and resentment.

Moreover, as the television service grew in both size and importance a sizeable group of employees with more homogeneous skills came into existence, and with the gradual completion of the Television Centre they now worked in closer proximity to each other. And in the second half of the 1960s, the BBC needed to embark on an economy campaign. The result was an end of expansion and a blockage of accustomed opportunities for promotion. As the Report of the Annan Committee, writing of the time when expansion proceeded apace, noted, 'Promotion became easy, young directors leapt into places of responsibility . . . The hangover came later.'[6] The economy campaign also resulted in an attempt to trim culturally defined expectations to new, budgetary standards. In consequence, senior staff became more remote, whilst a new and growing group of professional administrators emerged and consequently increased the social and physical distance between those responsible for taking the more important decisions and those who were to carry them out. In combination, these factors led to increasingly more complex and cumbersome administrative procedures. With the increasing size and promotion blockages and the attempt to inculcate the Corporation with an alien, cost-conscious ideology, it was perhaps inevitable that discontent should take root, and collective action as a method of redressing grievances now became a structurally based, realistic objective.

As Burns shows, in essence it was the growing clash between a traditional commitment to providing a public service of broadcasting and the emergence of careerism with developing notions of collective self-interest. Decisive was the increasing strain between the realities of management structure and a more traditionally defined organizational purpose. As one of Burns's informants in the Corporation said in a very revealing remark, 'The BBC is full of people who care more for the job than for getting on. The trouble is that they see other people round them getting on faster' (1977: 106).

The union response

It was, perhaps, inevitable that the unions' reaction to the increasing bureaucratization of their members' conditions of employment should be the emergence of issues which might be seen as justifying industrial action. In this, of course, the experience of the BBC is merely one case in the well documented general growth of white-collar unionism and developing white-collar militancy (Seglow, 1978; Bain, 1970; Lumley, 1973).

In 1969 the ABS embarked on its first strike against the Corporation. The following year there was a strike called by the National Association of Theatrical, Television and Kine Employees (NATTKE), involving members of both these unions. More serious was the strike by production assistants in the Corporation's drama and light entertainment departments who were organized by the ABS and which continued on and off from June to August of 1974. Since then, there has been a threatened strike by BBC film editors, as well as a series of separate disputes between the BBC and the National Union of Journalists (NUJ) during late 1975 and early 1976. In late 1977, the ABS were again taking industrial action in support of their pay claim well in excess of the government's guidelines. The first target was the blacking of the Queen's opening of Parliament in November. The important thing to note is that this outbreak of union activity in the BBC contrasts with the absence of almost any industrial action in the previous forty years of the Corporation's history.

The evolution of industrial relations strategy

This brief history of industrial relations in the BBC can now be put in the context of the organizational objectives of the BBC outlined at the beginning of this paper. As was noted, the BBC's stated objectives had to be placed within the context of maintaining the Corporation's role as *The* British Broadcasting Corporation and ensuring its independence from both government and other outside interests by maintaining the licence fee system.

Before the war, the pursuit of these objectives posed few problems for the Corporation's staff relations. However, as we have seen, even at that time there was criticism that the most 'audible' part of the public sector, an organization whose activities are daily brought into almost every home in the country, did not recognize trade unions. On the other hand, its independence from direct government control meant that the Corporation was never simply a mouthpiece of government and this helped the Corporation to develop its role as the voice of democracy. It was inevitable that this should lead to some form of recognition of trade unionism in the BBC. A public sector, yet independent organization, broadcasting values of freedom and democracy loudly and with pride, could not ultimately deny the right of its own employees for a measure of representation. It was precisely the denial of these rights in war-time enemy countries and in occupied Europe that the BBC was attacking. Thus unions came to be formed and recognized though they made very little impact in those early days. An important reason for this was the particularly powerful position of the BBC which, with its monopoly position in the labour market upto the advent of commercial television, commanded exclusive jurisdiction over job opportunities for broadcasters. The position of the BBC as a part of the public sector, and its objective in maintaining its independence from direct government intervention, clearly has influenced the response of the Corporation in its industrial relations strategy. Largely because of its traditional, but unusual, position as an independent part of the public sector, the activities of the BBC have come under periodic review through a now well entrenched mechanism of Committees of Inquiry into broadcasting. Thus there have been the Committees chaired by Sykes (1923), Crawford (1926), Ullswater (1935), Beveridge (1949), Pilkington (1962), and Annan which reported in the spring of 1977. Since Ullswater, all of these Committees have commented on staff relations within the BBC. During the hearings of the Beveridge Committee, the TUC and twelve affiliated unions, particularly the Association of Cinematograph Television and Allied Technicians (ACTT), made representations claiming recognition from the Corporation. The Beveridge Committee (1949) recommended that the BBC should recognize any union which could meet three conditions: first, that it should declare its willingness to work with other unions; secondly, that it should not have a closed shop policy; and last, that it could demonstrate that it had a membership of not less than 40 per cent of the total group seeking recognition. The BBC accepted this recommendation, but then used it to withhold recognition from the ACTT (with its reputation for militancy) and instead extended it to the then much more weak and compliant BBC Staff Association. The BBC justified this by maintaining that the 40 per cent clause had to be interpreted within the framework of the Corporation's grading structure. This cuts across occupational boundaries so that employees in radically different occupations find themselves placed in a common grade. The ACTT being more of an occupational union would have had little difficulty in satisfying the 40 per cent clause for those occupations which it had traditionally organized such as cameramen. However, the grading structure places cameramen within a range of occupations whose work has nothing even to do with television. Thus the ACTT has not been able to claim that it has met the criterion.

Two examples

It is worth commenting further on the Corporation's grading structure for it illustrates the relationship between the corporate goal of survival and industrial relations strategy. The strike by production assistants employed in the BBC's drama and light entertainment departments in 1974 concerned their claim to be re-graded. The grade to which they had been allocated did not entitle them to payment for overtime, but instead to time off in lieu. The production assistants maintained that they were working between fifty and fifty-seven hours most weeks, but that they never received the time off in lieu to which they were entitled. Their claim was to be placed in a new grade which would entitle them to payment for overtime. In reply, the BBC argued that half the production assistants were working a forty-two-hour week and that it would therefore be wrong to re-grade them all. But what was really at stake was the whole of the Corporation's grading structure which cuts across occupational boundaries. This is vitally important because the maintenance of common conditions of service and a grading structure applicable to all the Corporation's employees is one of the important features which gives the BBC its corporate identity. The strike, therefore, involved more than the relatively small numbers of staff concerned. Had the BBC given way it would have created a precedent with potentially an incalculable number of consequential claims. It would have made an impressive dent in the Corporation's personnel policy as it would have demonstrated the sectional differences of interest within the BBC. If the grading system and the accompanying salary structures were to break up, with the television service, sound radio, and other departments all evolving systems to suit their particular circumstances, it would be arguable whether or not there was one BBC. This, of course, would have provided useful ammunition to those who wished to break up the BBC. Small wonder the Corporation were anxious to resist, and the strike failed.

A second example concerns the ABS strike of 1969. This, like the dispute affecting the Corporation during the winter of 1977, was in support of an ABS claim for a pay increase. However, both of these disputes have to be seen within the context of the financing of the Corporation through the licence fee system which tries to ensure freedom from direct government intervention. The maintenance of financial independence is one of the most important objectives of the Corporation, and this was strongly supported by the Reports of the Pilkington Committee and the Annan Committee. However, the licence fee system still means the Corporation is to some extent dependent on the government, as it is the government which decides on the size of the licence fee: in consequence the BBC has no control over its revenue. Whilst in commercial television, the companies can pass on increasing costs by raising their advertising rates, the BBC has no similar jurisdiction over the price charged for its services. However, for the government, the size of the licence fee is not simply a matter of the economics of the BBC. To raise the licence fee in an inflationary period would lead to criticisms that the government was, itself, increasing prices in one of the few areas where it exercised direct control over their level.

Until the late 1960s, this financial dependence of the Corporation could be used by the BBC as an argument in pay negotiations. However, during the 1969 strike, the Grint Court of Inquiry, convened to examine the dispute, rejected the view that the BBC's financial position – a function of the size of the licence fee – should prevent them from paying salaries which were fair and reasonable. The paradox of the situation for the BBC is that set ownership was still increasing rapidly up until the mid-1960s and, therefore the BBC hardly needed to use the argument until it was taken away from them.

Conclusions

It is precisely the inconsistency between maintaining the ultimate corporate objective of survival, and the development of a viable industrial relations strategy, which is at the heart of the problem for the BBC's management. The BBC's objective of maintaining its independence from commercial pressures necessarily places the Corporation in the public sector. This in turn leads to a vicious circle arising from the BBC's requirement for revenue. Whilst the objective of independence from government control led to the Corporation being financed through the licence fee system, this very system perpetuates the financial dependence of the BBC on governments. Moreover, it has meant that in order to justify its continuing appropriation of the licence fee, it has had to expand its services; whilst this very expansion, occurring only shortly before a period of increasing financial stringency, was responsible for creating just those personnel problems which the Corporation was ill-equipped to meet with its traditional industrial relations strategy.

This analysis illustrates the interdependence of organizational goals and industrial relations strategy. It also demonstrates the unstable and, therefore, changing nature of this relationship: for even the objective of survival has different policy implications at different times. Neither organizational goals nor industrial relations strategies are static. Each continually redefines the other, whilst both are, of course, subject to external pressures.

To the extent that this argument is accepted it also suggests the need for some reorientation in industrial relations research, where all too often an artificial distinction is drawn between institutions and processes. As a result, in the traditional academic study of industrial relations, managements and unions are treated as essentially static entities. Only really in the inter-action between them, for instance in the process of collective bargaining, is the process of change recognized. Yet institutions, be they managements or unions, do not exist independently from the process of change, nor does the process of change have a momentum unique unto itself existing independently from institutions.

The conclusion then is that whereas typically managements and unions are conceptualized as institutions, they need at the same time to be considered as processes. It follows that if progress into the study of the functions of management in industrial relations is to be made, it needs to take as its starting point the fact that management structures have a history. In the same way as one cannot understand the history of management without a knowledge of its structure, it is also hard to understand the dynamics of managerial structures, functions, and objectives without an excursion into history.

As this paper has shown, even the most obvious and enduring of managerial objectives, ensuring its own survival, can have very different meanings depending on the circumstances prevailing at a particular point in time. The study of management therefore, like that of unions, needs to proceed within a dynamic framework which stresses its kinetic nature as a social, economic and political process.

17

Centralism versus federalism: corporate models in industrial relations *

RAY LOVERIDGE

Introduction

The current dismantling of national co-ordinating machinery is merely the latest setback for indicative planning in Britain in a succession of attempts by post-war governments to move towards a more centrally focussed decision-making arena. The failure of such a concordat in Britain has been ascribed to both a lack of motivation among the principal actors and the lack of a suitable institutional framework (Crouch, 1979; Currie, 1979). The fragmented and fractionated manner in which influence is exercised in labour unions has been described frequently as a major obstacle in the development of a corporate apparatus in Britain (Flanders, 1965; Donovan, 1968). The failure of British entrepreneurs to adopt long-term horizons and their preference for disjointed incrementalism in decision-making has been noted by a number of critics (Loveridge, 1973; Department of Prices, 1978). Their inability to adapt their analysis to that required in the planning mode of strategy formulation has often been ascribed to lack of suitable vocational education in the United Kingdom (Mant, 1969).

Relatively little attention has been paid to the manner in which business strategy in the large corporation is related to the exercise of corporate control over employment and the climate of industrial relations. Evidence of the nature of this relationship discovered in four engineering companies located in the West Midlands will be presented here and briefly compared with that found in other manufacturing and service concerns. An alternative explanation to that of the historical evolution of corporatism is offered in terms of the choices made by entrepreneurs towards dispersing or absorbing the risks contained in their operations.

*The data included in this chapter were gathered in a project financed by the Department of Employment and conducted with the help of Geoffrey Broad and Paul Lloyd.

Centralism versus federalism

The options are most clearly articulated in the polar types of corporate centralism and corporate federalism.

Theory and practice in British business administration

For the economist the entrepreneurs' motive for growth is usually seen to be the attainment of supernormal profit through increased efficiency combined with increased control over resources (including knowledge) and control over the product market (Chamberlain, 1933; Robinson, 1933; Schumpeter, 1939). The organizational theorist more often elevates the entrepreneurs' desire for control to primary significance and links it with a complementary desire to reduce environmental uncertainty, both in pursuit of greater organizational efficiency (Blau, 1955; March and Simon, 1958). The routinization of the labour process and standardization of the firm's inputs and outputs are seen by both groups of theorists to be an important means to the achievement of the economies of scale deriving from merger and acquisition. The rationalization of managerial control systems is given more significance in the work of behaviouralists and often, in the tradition of Weber and Michels, is causally associated with changes in company regime at the level of policy and strategy formulation rather than with the mode of production as such (Child and Kieser, 1977).

Complementary historical trends towards centralization of capital control and the rationalization of the labour process are seen by many scholars such as Schumpeter (1939) and Mandel (1975, 1980) to be related to a sequence of long-term business cycles. Thus, the peaks of merger and acquisition that can be discerned to have occurred in the 1880s and 1890s, the early 1930s and the late 1960s, are often related to so-called 'climaterics' in economic activity during which increasing costs were matched by decreased confidence among investors. These climaterics are seen by Kondratiev (1935) to have contributed to situations triggering technological innovation in capital goods, that is to say in labour-saving process innovation.

Both the precise historical relationship of process innovation to business activity and whether, this far, it has resulted in the greater centralization of knowledge and skills are a matter for continuing debate. Periodic 'waves' of merger and acquisition, following periods of protracted growth, were experienced in most industrial countries. Steel, chemicals, pharmaceuticals, foods, brewing and tobacco were all prominent in the early phase of mergers in the nineteenth-century take-overs, and mergers in metal goods, ship-building, engineering and printing were to come in the twentieth century. It was a movement complemented by a decline in the number of small independent manufacturers in Britain to the point where the total number of small independent British firms is now below those of Germany and France (Supple, 1974).

However, what distinguishes Britain from the latter countries is the tendency for merged or acquired companies to retain their former market identity and separate trading base after the marriage is consummated. 'Even mergers taking place in the 1960s appear to have resulted initially in companies operating a holding company structure in situations which by American standards would have been judged appropriate for divisionalization. British Leyland is one well-known example' (Child and Francis, 1981: 11–73).

The failure of marriages of interest in British industry to lead to modifications in the mode of operations employed has been the basis for much of the criticism directed at them (Pratten, 1976; Meeks, 1977). Neither is the synergy of managerial philosophy and structure postulated by prescriptive theory apparently being achieved (Miller, 1963; Kitching, 1967; Newbould, 1970). By the mid-1970s, Prais (1976) suggests the number of plants owned by the typical large British enterprise had almost tripled in the previous fourteen years (since 1956) while the average number of employees in those plants had fallen by nearly a half. 'The size of the average plant owned by the hundred largest [manufacturing] enterprises can be described as moderate, with hardly more than some 400 employees' (Prais, 1976: 61). For example, Guest, Keen and Nettlefold (GKN Ltd), ranked sixth among the Western world's metal-using companies, was at that time made up of 247 operating units many of which had more than one establishment and most of which were of only moderate size. Often these establishments continued, and continue, to trade under the family name of the original founder/former owner or the original trade name. Much the same may be said of the many British companies (for example, General Electric, Unilever), some among the largest in the world in terms of the resources owned by a single corporate body.

Child and Francis (1981) present a historical account of the manner in which, through standardization of administrative procedures and specialization of management tasks, centralized control is achieved incrementally and indirectly. The general pattern observed in the development of most large capitalist enterprises is through the extension of head office control by means of increased intervention in conflicts within and between subsidiaries. In this manner, procedures become more standardized across the company's holdings on the basis of precedent. From *ad hoc* interventions, head office moves into the design and co-ordination of policy, its authority deriving from the advice and assistance offered by its functional specialists. Ultimately, strategy in each subsidiary comes to be determined in relation to an overall company plan and regulated in a uniform manner across all units of the owning group.

In arriving at this state, the company has, however, moved through at least three phases of decentralization followed by a return to centralized control which finally converges on the classical model of functional lines of command stretching from the point of production to product or regional divisional executives. In describing this sequence, we shall refer to the first phase of decentralization as a holding federation (or confederation depending upon whether the group was formed by acquisition or merger). The second will be labelled a financial federation and the last a consultative federation. The intervening periods of centralized control will be referred to as entrepreneurial, executive, and the final state of corporate development, as professional.

The importance of the Child/Francis model is in its recognition of the historical process by which power is accrued to the centre of the organizations rather than passed down to the periphery. The assumption that is often found in the static analysis of formal organization structure is that control is *delegated* as a consequence of internal or organic growth and of its associated problems of managerial co-ordination across multiplying specialisms (Hall *et al.*, 1967; Pugh *et al.*, 1969; Child, 1973a). Though several stages of this evolution are described by Child and Francis as representing a decentralization of control, until companies acquire executive or professional regimes their employees have generally not experienced centrally exercised authority except in the early years of owner-proprietorship. Unless all subsequent growth is self-generated each new acquisition involves a metabolic change in the nature of the acquired company, an essentially political adjustment.

These political strategies provide some explanation for the early stages of corporate development in a federal mode. They do not explain why many British procurers prefer to remain in a federal mode of administration in which former entrepreneurs are allowed to retain operational control over their establishments and little is done to modify the customary modes of administration.

Theory and practice in the management of the labour process

For radical writers, for example Edwards (1979), as for consensus theorists such as Dahrendorf (1959), employers in the new process-control industries, for example chemicals, food and cigarette manufacture, are seen as the epitome of a new, and apparently more benign, managerialism. High earnings and assured levels of work serve to ensure the continuity of employment for a stable core of workers. However, this stability combined with the specificity of aspirations which may develop among these employees can become a source of frustration. Size of establishment was found to be the most likely predictor of industrial strife in a recent Department of Employment study of strikes (1978) as was the concomitant existence of formalized systems of administration (Turner *et al.*, 1977). In 'progressive' companies these alienating effects of large size, routinization and isolationism are combated with techniques designed by neo-human relations theorists. Employers are seen to exercise control over the labour process through the discovery and satisfaction of a range of intrinsic needs displayed by subordinates within the workplace.

Yet limits to the willingness of both employers and employees to accept a restructuring of workplace relationships in a way that would modify the conflictful by-products of scientific management have been evident in many recent studies. Nichols and Beynon (1977) offer a cynical perspective on the operation of neo-human relations techniques in a chemical company and Blackler and Brown (1980) are uncommonly frank about the largely cosmetic nature of managerial attempts to redistribute authority in line control in Shell Oil. More aggregative approaches such as those of the Aston School provide evidence of the continued importance of the formalized instruments of line control in manufacturing industry, as against the greater importance attributed to selection and career development procedures in public service and financial sector employment (Pugh *et al.*, 1969).

Clearly the unilinear development of management philosophy and of workplace organization sometimes typified in chronicles of social change is over-simplified (Bendix, 1956; Child, 1969; Salaman, 1979). At any given moment in history a variety of forms may exist. Piecework payments in British industry were reported by the National Board for Prices and Incomes (NBPI) in 1968 to have shown considerable variations in form and in formality of application over the previous century (NBPI,

1968a: 7). In the same year the Board reported somewhat scathingly on the operation of job evaluation systems in Britain as compared to those in the USA (NBPI, 1968b). The establishment of the NBPI in itself might be regarded as recognition of a perceived loss of managerial control over the labour process and over workplace earnings by the then Labour administration.

The legitimacy of the 'scientific' standards of work measurement were seen to have been widely challenged and subverted by workgroup representatives over the post-war period. A Royal Commission appointed in 1966 concluded that

> by far the most important part in remedying the problem of unofficial strikes and other forms of unofficial action . . . be played by reforming the institutions of whose defects they are a symptom. Unofficial strikes are above all the result of the inadequate conduct of industrial relations at company and plant level. They will persist so long as companies pay inadequate attention to their pay structures and personnel policies, and the methods of negotiation adopted at the workplace remain in their present chaotic state. (Donovan, 1968: 120–1)

Ramsay (1977) sees this apparent crisis in line management control as part of a series of oscillations in operational modes associated with long-term movements in the market environment. On the upturn of the business cycle employers have been willing to concede more control over the manner in which tasks are allocated to the operatives responsible for carrying them out. But reduced profit margins signal oncoming crises and lead to attempts to reduce labour services and to rationalize production. As a result confrontations may occur between management and labour. Alternatively, and with increasing persistence, employers have attempted to co-opt labour into managing this rationalization of their tasks through a process of joint consultation or productivity bargaining. But employer efforts at normative involvement wane as the recession deepens and their authority can be seen to rest on their superior market position in relation to labour. Economic revival comes at a time when the employers' belief in the management prerogative is at its greatest. Thus employer attitudes and the techniques of control they deploy are seen to follow a cycle of lagged responses to environmental conditions.

Business strategy and industrial relations in the firm

The industry upon which Donovan (1968) focussed his principal attention was the sprawling collection of metal-using manufacturers in what is loosely termed the Engineering Sector. Its boundaries are most clearly delineated by membership of one of the thirty-nine district associations making up the Engineering Employers' Federation (EEF). Though one of the oldest and potentially most powerful of national employer coalitions, this Federation has consistently refused to set up a permanent national forum for negotiation with the unions since its formation:

> though such Boards had been tried in engineering in some parts of the country there was a general fear among trade unionists that employers might seek negotiations on the restrictive rules and regulations upon which craft security was based, and that agreements might limit their field of manoeuvre. Employees felt that their primary interest lay in preserving for themselves as much freedom as possible from trade union craft control in the rapidly changing market and technical circumstances of the industry. The focus of their thinking was 'on the right of managements to run their establishments as they thought best'. (Marsh, 1965: 16)

While a precise statistical relationship between ownership and employment cannot be made on the basis of existing data, a crude comparison between EEF membership records and Moody's Index suggests that by the late 1960s well over half of those employed in Federated (EEF) firms were ultimately responsible to no more than a dozen or so holding companies whose interests were not all confined to metal-using industries. The subsidiary units of these groups were generally not only registered as independent limited liability companies but also independently federated to the industrial employers' association, often on a plant by plant basis. The ultimate ownership of these firms was not identified in any of the analyses of industrial relations of the period in which they were simply described either as 'single establishment or multi-establishment' concerns, or by reference to their indirect membership of the EEF.

In general the study of business strategy has proceeded in isolation from the analysis of line management or labour relations. This dichotomy represents a distinction in scholastic frames of analyses; it also reflects the distinctive operational models used by the actors themselves. It is hardly surprising that analysis of the labour process usually takes entrepreneurial goals and strategies as given, while studies of business strategy often assume goals to emerge from a unitary source variously described as the 'entrepreneur', the 'organization' or the 'dominant coalition'. The influence that labour practices have on strategy formulation and vice versa has historically been made most evident in confrontations between engineering masters and men in 1851, 1897 and 1922 and more recently in the BL motor vehicle company in 1981.

With this research and operational problem in mind the present author with other colleagues at Aston gained access to four Midland companies in order to monitor managements' expressed intention to involve employees in the process of strategic decision-making over a two-year period from 1977 to 1979 (the companies are here given fictitious names). One, Alloyco, was a specialist foundry employing 2,400 workers in the production of castings for a range of industries including motor vehicles. Its structure came closest to that of the 'consultative federation' in the adapted Child/Francis typology but in the economic recession that was deepening over the period of the study Head Office interventionism was moving the process of strategic formulation towards that previously described as a 'professional mode'. The second was an electrical components manufacturer, Electrico, serving the motor vehicle industry, which employed 6,250 workers and was part of a wider product division within an international electronics manufacturer. It was clearly run in a 'professional mode'. A third, Engco, assembled motor vehicle transmission systems and employed 1,500 workers. The group to which it belonged was organized as a 'financial federation'. The study began in a furniture making company, Woodco, employing 700 workers and controlled by a metal manufacturing group operating in an 'entrepreneurial mode'. Other data were drawn from plants elsewhere in the groups to which these companies belonged and in a body press plant employing 1,500 people belonging to a major motor car assembler then organized in a 'centralized professional' corporate structure.

Exact categorization becomes difficult not only through lack of data but also because of the problems of operationalizing and measuring the amount of influence used by one part of management over another in anything other than the comparative–static dimensions of formal structure used by Child and Francis. Information on procedural forms was elicited through structured interviews at all levels of management, up to group (divisional) managing director and with shop stewards and shopfloor workers in each company. These were supplemented by recorded observations of meetings within management and between management and stewards, and with post-coded diaries kept over a five-week period by most local managers and stewards.

In each case the most permanent formal link between the parent group and the subsidiary was through the office of divisional director held by the chairman of the latter's board. The most regulated area of head office 'monitoring' was that of financial management and capital expenditure: in all cases regular reports were made to divisional office. Budgeting procedures were standardized and incorporated the forward projections of the subsidiaries' capital expenditure, though these were never taken as anything more than a crude indication of present intentions. The exchanges were largely one way only and it was never clear that the directors of the two smaller subsidiaries, Engco and Woodco, knew the place that their company held in the overall strategy of the group. Only in the electrical components company were decisions taken by a closely interlinked divisional executive and company management board. Functional managers in Electrico reported to specialists in divisional headquarters who were housed on the same site. The foundry, Alloyco, was the head office of the European division of the parent and its staff were occasionally used to act on its behalf in such matters as, for example, the recently negotiated acquisition of two competing outlets for their products (mineral ores).

In the two smaller firms in the sample the company chairman provided the main link with the group and often appeared to be treated by the managing director as his merchant banker. There was indeed evidence that at least one group board saw the activities of its subsidiaries as generating cash flows that provided the group with low interest funds. At the same time their various autonomous activities allowed the movement of capital and semi-manufactures in a manner which maximized returns from government subsidies and rebates accruing to the group as a whole.

Three companies had come into existence as a result of vertical expansion on the part of metal manufacturing groups, at which time they had represented a link between the owners and their ultimate consumer. The fourth, Electrico, was the original base from which its now diversified activities had developed. Across companies the extent of the group's dependency varied from the importance of the foundry, Alloyco, as the major European outlet for the mineral products of the parent group to the almost negligible use by the furniture manufacturer, Woodco, of the metal components produced by the parent. Both the component firms, Engco and the larger Electrico, sold directly to vehicle assemblers and were subject to the short- and long-term variations in demand created by the nature of their shared product market and the vertically interdependent nature of manufacturing processes in the industry. Electrico had responded to this uncertainty by marketing its products world-wide on the basis of product innovation and used the group's resources and facilities in order to do so. Engco, the transmissions firm, was more entrepreneurial in its own right, as indeed was Woodco, and each had developed its own products and negotiated its own sales contracts on a somewhat less ambitious (but still international) basis.

One of the remarkable characteristics of the motor vehicle industry and of West Midlands engineering generally (see Sargent Florence, 1948) has been the degree of horizontal specialization across firms in regard to each stage of manufacture. Furthermore, it is traditional practice for the costs of interrupted or discontinuous production to have been almost immediately passed on through the operation of suspension or cancellation clauses which could operate within as little as three days on contracts that might otherwise last for a year and be renewed several times over the life of any single vehicle model. Production in very large batches or continuous operations is therefore rare in component manufacture since this would effectively destroy the employers' ability to close or suspend batches of work in response to such abrupt changes in demand. This was so even in Electrico: indeed the flexibility of the small batch methods used in Engco was proven during the period of our study when the latter obtained American orders to provide components for which their Detroit competitors could not retool in the lead-time available to them.

Both Alloyco and Woodco were engaged in the extensive automation of production over the period of our study. In both cases, but more especially in the latter, this change in technology became viable only by virtue of a change in marketing outlets, to supermarkets and departmental stores and away from small dealers or bespoke customers. By contrast, the motor component firms generally served a small number of known customers in the vehicle assembly industry. These latter have encouraged competition in the supply of components to the point of sponsoring new entrants where necessary. They have pursued a policy of double-sourcing for many purchases, especially since fear of labour disturbances has replaced their pre-war fear of supplier monopoly (Turner, 1973). Faced with customers who prefer to spread their orders, component firms such as the group to which Engco belonged adopt a dispersed market identity. In this way, they are able to offer a number of alternative sources of supply to potential customers. In the face of a declining traditional market Engco and other companies in that group were encouraged to take individual initiatives and even to compete with one another in pursuit of new markets.

But neither form of dispersed market identity would have been sustainable without an underlying complementarity in employee loyalties and commitments. This was much better achieved in Engco and Woodco than in the other two companies. In both of these small firms management felt their careers to be conterminous with the fortunes of the firm; with the exception of the chief executive appointments, career movement within both groups was by way of open competition within localized markets for junior managers. As important for non-managerial employees was the fact that redress of grievance was by way of a procedure that previously had ended at an industrial level (by way of the district employers' association) but, since the early 1970s, grievance procedures terminated within the company, that is, with the board and district official of the trade union. At no stage was the group's involvement in the settlement of industrial relations conflict made overt. While this was also true at Alloyco, 'the company' in this case was synonymous with the divisional head office; at Electrico the grievance procedure, like the negotiating machinery, was focussed on the division and, to a surprising degree, almost all employees were aware of the ultimate authority of the owning group board.

Work study was used at Alloyco, though not at Woodco, and in neither case did it form the direct basis for remuneration. Electrico was one of the first employers in the region to introduce Taylorist methods in a totally committed way to the extent of setting up institutions in several British universities devoted to the study of production engineering. Before World War Two its Works Study Department trained all new management entrants to the company and its graduates formed a cadre of now ageing managers in other companies across the region. The work of the department had been reduced in importance after the war as a result of shopfloor bargaining and the broadening of management education. The concentration on its largest site of multiple new product lines employing a range of modes of organization and equipment has of itself produced an enormously more complex system than existed pre-war. For the most part, the work is of a sub-assembly nature, but components, many of which are common across products, are machined and prepared at different sites within the company. To the multiplying complexity of internal organization is added the stress of meeting short-term contractual obligations to customers whose own market and organizational strategies had to be adapted to the so-called 'stop–go' cycles of business activity throughout the 1950s and 1960s.

Before the war, Electrico had federated with the employers' association on a plant basis and basic shopfloor earnings had followed those determined at national level for the engineering industry. During World War Two and the period of full employment that followed, grievance procedure had been used by stewards to advance localized pay claims and to dispute time measurement on 'jobs' (pieces of work). Until the late 1960s management resisted attempts by the unions to negotiate at company or divisional level, preferring to handle grievances at plant level before passing them out to the 'local conference' of the Engineering Employers' Federation. Company recognition had been conceded first to toolmakers, then to skilled operatives before being given to operatives and finally to foremen and clerks. By this time the underlying structure of shopfloor bargaining was well established. Earnings levels had thus gained a dual momentum from the comparisons made in intersectional bargaining between groups involved in different processes and different product lines and from the differentials in basic rates earned by different occupations across the company at large.

Throughout our period of observation Electrico management were involved in periodic confrontations at both company and shop level. The long-term result of these negotiations may or may not have affected the company's market position but in the short run the uncertainty created by both fragmented bargaining and by restrictions on the deployment of labour completely undermined the interdependent costing and scheduling of the Taylorist system of management. Management's response varied from 'flight' to 'fight'; sometimes product designs were changed without notification of the stewards in the hope that if the customer received at least some of their order before production stopped the contact could be maintained and production to meet it could be resumed after the strike had been settled. At other times special jobs had been partially sub-contracted out to small suppliers in spite of union agreements forbidding sub-contracting of all work which even included floor cleaning.

The influence exercised by any single group of production workers was in part related to the shortage of labour services of all kinds then experienced in the West Midlands. But in circumstances in which individual operators cannot be easily hired and fired the very interdependency within the mode of production created by the operation of a Taylorist system served to enhance the bargaining leverage exercised by even the most lowly regarded group of operatives. When linked to the interdependencies existing between sequential processes within the industry the potential impact of the actions of any centrally placed groups was far reaching.

By way of contrast the negotiation of a new procedural agreement in the much smaller transmissions company in 1971 (the year after the national trade unions abandoned the grievance procedure for the engineering industry) was based on a management commitment to respect the structure of internal organization established by custom and practice. In other words, permanent changes to the batch production system were entirely dependent on the retention of the informally established job territories and their concomitant rewards. Together these constituted a structure of induction through which line employees passed from the job of work-mover or labourer by promotion to semi-skilled operative and to a ladder which eventually could lead to a setter's post or more usually that of a machine-minder. Earnings levels had been achieved at a degree of stability as a result of the internal consensus that existed around work and job allocation. The only recent job confrontations had been with toolmakers and clerks whose qualifications lay outside those determined by the internal labour market.

In two companies, Woodco and Alloyco, the introduction of employee participation was clearly geared to technological innovation. In the former company a new, group-appointed, managing director had negotiated a profit-sharing (value-added) scheme with the district officer of the union and in the face of fierce opposition from the machinist tradesmen. The high earnings stemming from the productivity-related bonuses were sufficient to gain employee compliance, though by no means commitment, to subsequent work reorganization and deskilling. The investment of one million pounds in a new powder reduction furnace by Alloyco had been accompanied by the introduction of a comprehensive job-evaluation system closely followed by the imposition of a profit-sharing scheme on a similar value-added basis to that used by the furniture manufacturer. (As in the latter case the stewards were largely circumvented, this time by the use of a company-wide plebiscite.) As a result of these changes in grading and remuneration the focus of collective negotiations with the shopfloor had shifted to company level where the forge management had negotiated a unique (for Britain) union contract some years previously.

The issue of employee participation within all four companies was currently articulated in the context of the government-initiated debate surrounding the appointment of the Bullock Committee and the passing of the Industry Act (1975) in which it was envisaged that financial subsidies to industry might be contingent upon union involvement in company planning procedures. The group to which the Woodco company belonged did little by way of response. Indeed, it continued to regard the latter's value-added scheme and its involvement of works representatives in production management with intense suspicion. The group to which the Engco company belonged contributed to the national debate through the CBI evidence to Bullock. The then managing director issued an obscurely worded guide to the managements of subsidiaries. As far as we are aware Engco was the only member of this group to subsequently set up a strategically oriented employee council as a result of the managing director's circular. By contrast, the managing director of the electrical group pursued two channels of communication. He initiated informal talks with trade union officials and senior stewards (separately) on the likely nature of a new consultative structure. He then appointed a divisional-level working party which presented a brief to a sequence of meetings of managers down to line level across all establishments within his division.

Over the two-year period of our observations the only significant change to take place in the institutional arrangements of Electrico was the formation of a management association registered as an independent trade union. A similar outcome was observed in Alloyco where managers, on the advice of the personnel director, brought their spontaneously formed association under the wing of ASTMS. The major difference between the two centrally administered companies was that the forge management again used a plebiscite of all company employees to introduce a consultative council related to the workings of the new profit-sharing scheme – without prior consultation with any group outside of the board. Along the various attitudinal dimensions by which employee involvement and satisfaction were measured in our study, the schemes introduced in the two small companies might be considered the more successful as indeed they might in interactional terms as well (Loveridge, 1980).

Contingency and culture

In the analysis of these companies a contrast may be drawn between the unitary structure of strategic authority represented in Alloyco and Electrico and the fragmented or federal structures of which Engco and Woodco form a part. The four companies might be categorized in terms of the administrative structures derived from these contrasting approaches to strategy formulation. We may also attempt to categorize task or line management in terms of the degree of autonomy allowed either to first line supervisors or to operatives in handling uncertainties deriving from the labour process. Combining these two dimensions in the manner shown in Figure 17.1 the four companies might be placed against each dimension in a way that positions them somewhere in the quadrants formed by an intersection of these measures.

In general, organizational theorists have considered movement along the horizontal dimension to be related to the production technology used by the operatives. While a number of organizational theorists such as Thompson (1967) and Perrow (1970) have put forward more general propositions relating the design of control structures to the entrepreneur's perceived state of uncertainty, most attribute causal significance to the mode of production. Perrow, for instance, places causality with the knowledge input required of the operative in the performance of his or her task and the range and scope of variability in inputs and outputs (that is, in relations between the workflow and its environment). These impose constraints on the level of discretion allowed to line operatives as well as indicating the degree and form of interdependence within the administrative structure and locus of organization power (Perrow, 1970; see also Figure 17.1).

Within all such deterministic theories there is an assumption of a shared rationale and logic between the actors derived from the realization of similar market and technical constraints on their actions. Even where, as in Stinchcombe (1959), Thompson (1967), and more recently in Reeves and Woodward (1970), conflict and compromise are recognized to exist there remains an assumption of the acceptance of 'objective' constraints. The disregard of cognitive and even behavioural structures of activities in explaining economic performance in contrast to the concern shown for formal rules and regulations by both organizational and industrial relations scholars has been remarked in a number of recent critiques (Silverman, 1970; Clegg, 1975). The constraints that were observed to exist in the case studies described earlier arose out of shared

Centralism versus federalism

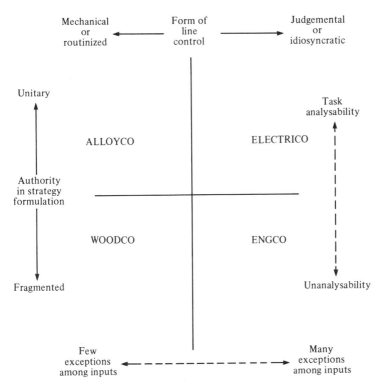

Figure 17.1 The control systems of four companies categorized by the mode of strategy formulation and line control compared with the contingency terminology of Perrow (1970). Adapted from Reeves and Woodward (1970)

experiences and mutually imposed sanctions rather than from the technical requirements of the company operations. Both managers and operatives perceived the social and market arenas within which they interacted to have extremely stable boundaries. But within these boundaries there was a high degree of variability and complexity of pattern caused, indirectly and often unwittingly, by the nature of their own interactions. For example, the variability of demand within a long-standing market for motor vehicles is translated into costs involved in the short-term nature of contracts between different sections of the vertically differentiated industry. This strategy of uncertainty transference or externalization of risk has been complemented by the short-term basis upon which employment has been offered.

The context of management strategies

In recent times the West Midlands craftsmen with formal qualifications who worked in factories and contributed directly to the production process seem to have remained higher than in other regions. But it was not the imposition of formal craft restrictions on entry to the trade that was predominantly responsible for most constraints on the employers' control of the line. Of far greater importance was the long tradition of task-autonomy in job traditions which has emerged from workshop practices that are up to two centuries old. These have been described by Allen (1929) to be dependent upon the intricate web of sub-contractors which existed across the nascent metal processing and manufacturing trades of Birmingham and the Black Country. To a large extent these networks were substantially responsible for shaping the development of each small enterprise. By the end of the nineteenth century local engineering firms and union branches, whose members' skills were specific to narrow local trades, had become highly interdependent. Given the specificity of skills the union branch provided a pool of labour which insulated the entrepreneur from the costs of short-term lay-offs and long-term training (Fox, 1955).

The mode of strategy formulation emerging from this mutual interdependency has been described by Lindblom (1959) as 'the science of muddling through'. This author suggests that short-term incrementalism in decision-making enables greater flexibility at the lowest risk for the decision-taker. Cyert and March (1963) see this form of 'disjointed incrementalism' as emerging from the uncertainty of negotiated outcomes in conflictful situations. Thompson (1967) describes the outcome as compromise; but in a high risk environment, or one in which both parties are reluctant to take risks, the present author has suggested that the use of open-ended agreements and reliance on informal understandings may become a further conscious or unconscious means by which both parties seek to avoid risks of mutual dependency (Loveridge, 1973).

The conduct of industrial relations at plant/enterprise level was traditionally based on informally agreed norms of procedure and working practice. By the 1950s this practice amounted to the avoidance of standardization of earnings levels above or beyond the nationally or company-negotiated basic rates and to the designation of tasks through localized and often highly informal negotiations. The result was a fragmentation of skills rather than the routinization of tasks. Even where, as in Alloyco, a foreign-owned foundry, a centrally controlled produc-

186

tion system is accompanied by a formal job evaluation scheme, manning of new equipment has to be negotiated department by department and in the light of the hierarchy of seniority among manual workers within these departments. A hierarchy of line tasks established in the incremental evolution of a mode of production has become attached to a structure of expected earnings levels and to differentials, which work groups seek to maintain or to improve over the course of short-term market cycles.

The regulation of the line was to a greater or lesser extent shared between first line supervisor and the steward or worker representative, a situation which depended heavily on mutually shared understandings of their respective roles rather than on formally prescribed rules and conditions. In all four firms transactions between line management and operatives began from the basis of a shared paradigm of the workplace system. This does not in any way imply a moral commitment to prevailing controls and sanctions but rather to the *de facto* manner in which they emerge. Such a position could be maintained indefinitely providing local (subsidiary) managers continued to work to short-term horizons and were still able to maintain the viability of their enterprise in the face of external exigencies in a manner demonstrated by a succession of outstanding executives at Engco (all of whom were subjects of local legend).

More usually operations management shaped their actions in relation to known boundaries of influence and the anticipated reactions of customers, clients and subordinates. Paradoxically the embeddedness of habitual recipes among local management was demonstrated by Woodco's success in routinizing and deskilling the labour process in that company. After completing the change to flow line production the marketing strategies of management remained geared to supplying small batch orders. Their consequent failure to use the automated plant effectively led to a loss of confidence in the senior executives, all of whom had been recruited from local engineering firms, and to their subsequent resignation. It was left to their successors to reorient production to new outlets requiring long runs of standardized products – and to centralize production control within the local company.

By contrast Alloyco management seems to have anticipated the change in operational paradigm required for successful innovation. Prior to the imposition of the present unitary authority structure in the foundry and the current attempts to further routinize the production process, the main plant was moved from Birmingham to its present location in a rural market town. That this move was undertaken shortly after its acquisition by an American group might be taken as evidence of a new frame of reference being applied to the contingencies facing the organization and a break with the values underlying the previous organizational structure. Its present labour forces have almost entirely been recruited from among a population with no previous experience in the industry. The manner in which the employees in this company regard their employment appears to be a product of the 'benign professionalism' displayed by the management in socializing their new labour force.

Control contingency and risk

In many ways, the four group boards contained in the survey might be said to have been facing broadly similar contingencies in shaping their long-term strategies of control. Such contingencies can be briefly defined as the evident sources of risk facing the entrepreneur – or the probable costs associated with any chosen course of potentially profitable action. However, it appears difficult to establish a *direct* relationship between such sources of risky dependency and a generalizable taxonomy of the company structure in the manner suggested by contingency theorists such as Stinchcombe (1959) and Perrow (1970). Both situational risk and dependency in any given circumstance are assessed by the decision-taker against a personalized frame of reference and are subjected to 'an essentially political process in which constraints and opportunities are functions of the power exercised by decision makers in the light of their ideological values' (Child, 1972: 21).

Explanations of structural form should, therefore, account for these mediating values and the situationally related strategies that emerge from them. But within these four companies the means used to deploy and utilize capital can be seen to be based on distinctive managerial attitudes towards uncertainty and risk. In the first, authority is centralized and, through the routinization of work, knowledge and risk absorption is confined to an élite. If we follow the development sequence suggested by the Child/Francis typology the authority of this group may be entrepreneurial and personalized in the first instance but can develop into the formal power of a general executive board which later still can be composed of specialized professional members. Throughout this process the progressive routinization of tasks within the central workflow of the company and of the standardization of administrative procedures is designed to ensure the universal dominance of central government.

The second paradigm of management is one in which power is exercised in a less overt manner and risk is, wherever possible, laid off or externalized. This, by default, also means an increased dependency on external agencies. Risks can be minimized, however, through the choice of contractual terms upon which goods and resources are exchanged. Entrepreneurs can choose from a range of techniques including the employment of part-time labour, the employment of labour on short-term contracts, or of hourly paid labour, or payment by the piece. Their control can be less direct but equally effective through the licensing out of production rights on a product or the franchising of product outlets to self-employed retailers.

Each of these contractual means to externalizing risk (and responsibility) may of course be used to supplement a centralized mode of strategy formulation. There is for example considerable evidence that many central executives and professional boards maintain a buffer of sub-contracted and part-time work to protect their own employees from short-term variations in the product markets in the manner suggested by radical economists. Licensing, or in retailing the granting of sales concessions, can also be used in this way to maintain a stable core of production services (Cosyns *et al.*, 1981). Furthermore in times of prolonged recession it is evident from present evidence that many central boards divest themselves of all but essential functions in order to maximize liquidity for income and transactional purposes (Keynes, 1936: 207).

This is a different usage from that of the 'federal' firm where no such core activity need exist and there is no concern for direct control over the mode of production. Organized as a financial or consultative group (see previous definitions), its strategy is to deploy capital in a manner which minimizes and diffuses risk while ensuring an acceptable rate of return. Such groups appear generally to accept their acquisitions as 'going concerns' and as a means of buying into an existing network of customers and labour skills. In doing so they also appear to accept the constraints imposed by the structure of the local and internal labour markets. While the need for operational effectiveness may push groups into the provision of consultancy services to their subsidiaries there seems no necessary reason for these head office specialists to acquire executive responsibility or for this control to be exercised in an overt manner. This then is not the externalization or laying-off of risk so much as its *diffusion*.

The context of management strategies

There seems no impelling structural imperative towards the absorption of uncertainty at the centre of large organizations given this view of risk and responsibility. In the analysis of contractual relationships some recent economic theory, like that of behavioural analysis, sees the establishment of hierarchy as inevitable. This view extends beyond the historical analysis of the Marxist to modern utilitarians like Coase (1937) and Williamson (1975).

Yet the externalization of risk in the manner of the owners of Engco and Woodco ensures the survival of the firm through a number of localized crises such as those facing metal manufacture at the present time. In an industry such as engineering in which self-finance has been the norm and in which product specialization has been so intense it is hardly surprising that entrepreneurs have continued the practice of diffusing risk along networks provided by the communities in which they are nested. The result has been to perpetuate the environmental uncertainty in a manner which goes far beyond the firm. The group itself, however, retains an ability to transfer its commitments to other, more profitable areas of activity, in a manner not open to the overt corporate bureaucracy.

In engineering the strategy of risk-spreading evolved as a natural supplement of the ideology of 'management prerogatives' and self-help individualism among small entrepreneurs which had already led them to their unwitting alliances with line operatives in the creation of internal labour markets. Open-ended agreements and reliance on custom and practice provide an appearance of autonomy and shopfloor influence which, given the group's ability to shift resources and dependencies elsewhere, must be considered to be extremely localized. The manner in which this strategy and its attendant power was realized and utilized by corporate groups appeared to vary. The group to which Engco belonged accepted the constraints placed upon its operations by the strategies adopted by its subsidiaries but it had little compunction about divesting itself of local subsidiaries or even a whole division over the period of our study. The board was reported in the *Sunday Times* (8 November 1981) as being consciously committed to 'getting out of Britain as fast as possible'. The location of its headquarters was described to us by divisional staff as having moved up and down the M1 from London to Birmingham and back in relation to the residence and interests of a succession of group chief executives. The group to which Woodco belonged had retained its headquarters in the Black Country.

As a consequence, its metal manufacturing interests had declined in fortune in line with those of the surrounding region.

Corporatism and culture

The research question to which this paper was addressed was that of explaining the existence of a corporate federalism in the United Kingdom. For that reason, if for no other, we should briefly consider the extent of corporate centralism in other major industrial nations. Of these the comparisons most frequently made are with America, Germany, France and Japan. On the basis of the crudest of comparisons it would appear that forms of organizational control do not vary greatly in aggregate across the five countries (including Britain). Similar proportions of companies adopt functional, holding or divisional (centralized) structures in each country (Chandler and Daems, 1974). However, the longevity of the holding or federal corporate structure in Britain appears to give this type of framework a stability that it does not possess in other economies where it acts as no more than a stage in the company's growth path.

In more specific inter-country comparisons Child and Kieser (1977) have demonstrated the greater tendency towards centralized control in a sample of German firms when compared with a similar British sample, having controlled for size of organization. Other comparisons, most notably that of Dore (1973) with Japanese firms, and Maurice, Sorge and Warner (1980) with German and French firms, demonstrate a higher degree of vertical differentiation in the administration of companies in these countries when compared to British counterparts of similar size, technology and product market.

More processually the importance of 'cultural context as a contingency', to use Child's (1979) terms, is reflected in the comparatively deferential attitudes of German managers towards superordinates when compared with British managers and with the concentration of strategic decision-making at board level (Child and Kieser, 1977). The work of Dore, Abegglen (1958) and others reflects similar attitudes among Japanese managers and, of course, more importantly the effect of 'nemawashi', or participative decision-making, which complements the sharply differentiated hierarchy of formal authority (Howard and Teramoto, 1981). French attitudes to authority, as described by Crozier (1964),

Gallie (1978) and others appear to create a far greater dichotomy between situations appropriate to the exercise of bureaucratic authority and those in which individual choice is paramount. Both French and American employees, for entirely different reasons, appear to accept authority more readily within areas concerning their careers and livelihoods than their British counterparts.

While explanations for these differences in behaviours and values may be found in accounts of the political and social history of each society, it is business activities that serve to reinforce and perpetuate their underlying ideology (Chandler and Daems, 1974; Cole, 1979; Littler, 1981a). Within each of these countries the large firm has grown up in the context of a legal–rational system of rules quite foreign to British common law traditions. New occupations, brought into existence by technological and social changes, have quickly obtained official recognition and acknowledgment. In Germany, for instance, the Central Institute for Occupational Structure records and co-ordinates the demand for new types of skill and knowledge training in all parts of the economy and has done so since 1929. Conflict over task control at line level is handled formally within the Works Council and only rarely leads to fractional bargaining within departments or workshops. This is not to say that grievances do not exist in German industry or in that of America, France or Japan, simply that the structure of rules makes it more costly for the individual or group to express it in the spontaneous fashion of much of British industrial behaviour. Given this general acceptance of the system of law within the former societies, most protest is accordingly channelled through formally provided procedures.

Given also the provision of a statutorily endorsed structure of recruitment and employee control, corporate centralism is more likely to be the chosen method of development in newly industrializing countries. The risks attendant upon trade by 'free market spot bargaining' to use Williamson's (1975) terminology, are translated into known boundaries formed by the legal–rational hierarchies within the key institutions in society and by a basic acceptance of the long-term validity of formal contract. The reasons for this acceptance may be as Dore (1973) suggests the effect of institutional 'learning' from the experiences of industrialization in Britain. But this learning actually takes place within the context of specific cultures which provide bases for the acceptance of legitimate authority unique to each country – not simply as the inevitable consequence of capitalist development (Kumar, 1978).

Conclusions

This paper has set out to describe the underlying structure of control in one industrial sector, and the reasons why it should have emerged and why it continued to exist. Possible explanations have been found in the concept of nested contingencies in which strategy in the external environment impacts upon strategy in the internal concerns of the enterprise and so shapes and constrains managerial action in both areas. The major explanations for choice of strategic mode were found in the view of risk taken by senior management and their adoption of a federal structure as a means of laying-off risks, or uncertainty transference.

Such explanations provide a basis for understanding the prevalence of observed modes of capital control across different sectors and countries. This is not to say federal corporations in Britain may not become standardized towards a centrally determined model or that, perhaps as a result of even greater climateric economic change, centralized authority may not be drastically modified towards greater delegation to outlying units (Brusco, 1981). Rather, it is to suggest that the outcomes of ongoing social events in which the transition from one 'epoch' to another, or one 'stage' to another, is by no means as predictable as most worldview theorists suggest. For this reason ideal-type models which become transmuted into analytical distinctions should be subjected to constant analysis and updating. The danger of such distinctions is that they often appear to convince politicians that legislation designed to hasten the 'inevitable' movement towards a given model may bring about its more rapid achievement. The inevitable thus becomes the intended.

PART III

Business strategy and industrial relations

18

Business strategy and industrial relations strategy

KEITH THURLEY and STEPHEN WOOD

Definitions

Many writers dealing with managerial and business decision-making have used the term 'strategy' to describe a particular set of choices taken over a period of time for a given objective. In an organizational setting, this implies that there is a hierarchy of decision choices, so that one decision will result in memoranda or guide-lines laying down 'policy' to steer the more specific decisions taken by operational managers who have to deal with a myriad of short-term problems and issues. A 'strategy' therefore means *a consistent approach over time which is intended to yield results in the medium and long term for a specific problem.* A strategic approach assumes it is possible to review the overall situation facing decision-makers in the way that a general reviews a battle situation before actual hostilities break out. When they do break out, tactical decisions will have to be made for temporary advantage, but it is hoped that the decision on overall strategy will help to prevent short-term decisions, taken in the heat of battle, from cancelling each other out.

It follows that the term 'strategy' can be applied to any set of business decisions regardless of content. Industrial relations is no different in principle from any other decision area. However, there is a problem of the relationship of industrial relations decisions to other business decisions and, more particularly, of the relationship of any industrial relations strategy to overall corporate strategy, decided by a business for pursuing its long-term business objectives.

Business strategy, in Ansoff's eyes, is mainly concerned with *the choice of the product-market portfolio of a firm* (Ansoff, 1969). This, he argues, should depend on how far the environment of a firm is seen as unstable and turbulent. If there is a 'gap between the objectives and

197

the future potential of the firm's present strategic position', or there is great instability of the firm's present product market environment, then a 'strategic change' or 'a shift in the product or service mix produced by the firm and/or the markets to which it is offered' is necessary (Ansoff, 1969: 21). The determination of corporate objectives is therefore a crucial part of determining a business strategy. Such objectives, as Simon (1957) argues, are neither simple nor autonomous; decisions should be seen as discovering courses of action which satisfy a whole set of constraints. Such constraints in an organization arise from the logic of the roles occupied by the decision-makers. The approach of Ansoff and colleagues underlines the importance of having organizational resources which allow the firm to review its situation and decide on a basic business strategy, rather than allow one to develop simply through managers dealing with individual problems.

Industrial relations strategies refer to *long-term policies which are developed by the management of an organization in order to preserve or change the procedures, practice or results of industrial relations activities over time.* They are discussed here from a managerial viewpoint and may include *any* objective in industrial relations; they may, for example, be aimed at strengthening union or steward organization or perhaps at reaching specific agreements on the joint regulation of work rules. Alternatively there may be an objective to limit or prevent unionization. Such a strategy might be a highly centralized one which tries to push all industrial relations decisions to the enterprise level or it might be a very decentralized approach, leaving such questions to be settled by foremen at the shop floor level. It could extend to reliance on an employers' association. It could include backing one union against another, allowing unionization for one level of staff and preventing it for others. It might include a highly paternalistic or human relations approach by management or it could mean a highly coercive one.

The debate so far: the nature of industrial relations strategy

The concept of an industrial relations strategy has been a key idea for a number of industrial relations specialists who have been concerned with managerial policy, but this is not always as explicit as the view of the Commission on Industrial Relations (CIR):

> A company's industrial relations policy should form an integral part of the total strategy with which it pursues its busi-

> ness objectives. In this way it will not only define the company's course of action with regard to particular industrial relations issues; it will also reflect the interaction of industrial relations with policies in other areas, such as production, marketing or finance. (CIR, 1973: 4)

This CIR statement, which introduced the main analysis and argument of the 1973 report on 'The role of management in industrial relations', raises a number of important issues. It showed very clearly that the CIR believed that industrial relations could easily be neglected by top management concentration on purely 'business' objectives. Clearly defined industrial relations policies would promote consistency in business decisions and develop security and good-will among employees and union representatives, viz: 'A total corporate strategy needs to include a policy defining the company's industrial relations objectives and the principles which should guide management in its every-day pursuit of them' (CIR, 1973: 5). Such a policy is most necessary, it was argued, when companies are faced with problems of change. It should lead to a clarification of the respective roles of the personnel manager and of the operational manager, involving the latter in the formulation of industrial relations policy and the former in being part of the management team taking major decisions.

The assumptions which lie behind this argument can be taken to include the following:

(a) that firms normally have corporate strategies to determine their approach for achieving business objectives;

(b) that strategic thinking is required for corporate success, and that businessmen, left to themselves, will tend to allow industrial relations to be played by ear on an *ad hoc* workshop basis;

(c) that businessmen have some choice in the matter;

(d) that in choosing their industrial relations policies rationality implies they be linked to other objectives and policies;

(e) that the introduction of 'more' strategic thinking into management is simply a matter of will, there are no obstacles to or pressures against its development.

In this book, the closest argument to that of the CIR is followed by John Purcell. He spells out the type of industrial relations policy and strategy which he perceives to be most feasible. The implication is again that top management need to be persuaded of the advantages to be gained by developing a coherent industrial relations strategy.

A more pessimistic flavour dominates the approach of empirical researchers such as Marsh and Gillies. They approach the question by studying what line managers actually do in industrial relations issues, showing that whilst they are not reluctant to be involved in industrial relations negotiations and consultation, they are in fact frequently uncertain about the objectives and policies that their firm is actually following. Whatever else the firm is pursuing, it hardly seems to be following a coherent industrial relations strategy.

Other papers in this book can be used to illustrate a contrary approach to industrial relations strategy. Here the existence of such strategies is taken for granted and the issue explored is the nature of the strategy and the reasons for the managerial decisions to pursue certain objectives. For some (Gospel, Henley) this is a question of the broad context or level of social economic and technological development in the society in question and the influence of the particular élite governing the State and its agencies. Clearly a 'macro-level' explanation of managerial actions questions the nature and existence of real choice for individual managements. A Marxist argument such as that of Braverman (1974) tends to explain the thrust, say, of scientific management policies as due to the increasing need to extend control over the labour process or system of production, given competition and the pressures to maximize profit. Of course, such pressures on management to extend control may still leave room for *some* choice in how this is achieved. In a recently published study of management strategy and worker response, for example, in a large chemical factory, Nichols and Beynon (1977: 121) comment:

> Chemco plant managers don't thrust their power in workers'
> faces. They try *not* to let the iron fist behind the velvet glove
> show and they certainly don't tell workers that 'a man with a
> good manager doesn't need a union'. Riverside managers
> play it 'firm but fair'. They push and jostle workers and stew-
> ards, they 'jump on them' – but their overall strategy is to
> seek to enmesh workers, to bring about a situation where they
> don't have to be driven.

The reason for such a strategy is still the need for management to 'sub-ject the labour force to a degree of order, regulation and control' (ibid.: 129) and 'to prevent the system from running out of control' (ibid.: 130). The question thus arises as to how far the forces operating on capital in its advanced monopolistic phase allow some choice as to how

Table 18.1. *The nature of managerial industrial relations policy*

View of management		Empirical questions and issues
(a) Management as a social/ political élite	→	What are the actual beliefs and objectives of management in a particular society?
(b) Managers as collective bargainers	→	Who bargains with unions and for what objectives?
(c) Managers as agents of capital	→	What choices exist for managers in controlling labour?
(d) Management as an entrepreneurial/economic function	→	How far do managers derive industrial relations policy from market objectives?
(e) Management as an organizational function	→	What organizational conditions determine IR policy?

workers are managed and controlled. The degree of choice is clearly of the greatest importance in the analysis of the reasons at the enterprise level for taking a particular approach.

The organizational context of industrial relations strategy is the focus of the final group of researchers illustrated in the papers in Part II. For Tyson, this is largely a question of tracing the adaption of the beliefs and values of personnel managers and industrial relations managers to particular organization cultures. For others, it implies an analysis of economic objectives for the enterprise in question (Thomson, Gospel) or the specific historical evolution of the organization and its objectives (Seglow, Loveridge) in terms of an internal and external socio-political analysis. For these writers, the issue is the contrast in industrial relations policies and strategies between organizations.

Not surprisingly, therefore, it can be said that discussion of managerial industrial relations strategies reflects the fact that different writers have taken *different* problems as the focus of their argument. In a real sense there has been no debate, only a set of competing and somewhat ill-defined arguments about management, making quite different assumptions in their explanations of managerial actions. Table 18.1 illustrates the basis of some of the main issues which have tended to be conflated in discussion. The question of how far industrial relations decisions of managers can be described as a 'strategy', clearly differs according to

Table 18.2. *Disaggregating the problem of industrial relations strategies: the main issues for research*

	The relationship of business strategy and industrial relations strategy	The development of a 'strategic' approach
Theoretical questions	How far can the actual choices of business strategy be explained in terms of the 'rational' choice of managers given certain structures and conditions? What links can be deduced between business strategy and industrial relations?	What are the organizational conditions which allow and encourage 'strategic thinking' among managers?
Empirical questions	Which structural constraints on management and which structured conditions in any society are more important in shaping managerial thinking and action?	Is there evidence to show the development of 'strategic thinking' in industrial relations in large organizations, e.g. MNCs?
Normative questions	How far should managerial industrial relations strategies be directly based on business strategies and policies?	Is a formalized pre-planned strategy in industrial relations more likely to achieve results than 'muddling through' or the use of 'crisis management'?

each approach. In (a) and (b) it may or may not exist; in (c), (d) and (e) it tends to be assumed by *a priori* reasoning.

Table 18.2 sets out the major questions which need to be explored.

Defining the issues afresh: business strategy and strategic thinking

This paper attempts to develop this debate by considering the question of 'business strategy' as formulated not by industrial relations specialists, but by those in the field of business policy and so-called 'corporate strategy'. How far is it useful to analyse organizational behaviour in 'strategic' terms?

Business strategy and industrial relations strategy

The business policy literature aimed at a business school audience is both analytical and normative or prescriptive in its thinking. Part of the argument lays heavy emphasis on the need to study how and why strategies are developed by managers in particular circumstances. A second part lays equally heavy emphasis on the need to develop a 'strategic' approach rather than tackling problems in an isolated fashion.

When dealing with industrial relations strategies therefore we should distinguish the question of the *analysis* of the factors influencing industrial relations strategies (or preventing them from existing) from the discussion of the *usefulness* of 'strategic' industrial relations thinking. We also need to distinguish the question of industrial relations strategy as an issue in its own right, from the more complex issues of relating corporate business strategy to industrial relations strategies and studying the implications for industrial relations of a shift to 'strategic' thinking.

The relationship of business strategy and industrial relations strategy: theory

Clearly there is a continuum of organizational situations in any society from that of conscious strategic planning which is acted upon, to the other extreme of managers who are reacting minute by minute to pressures upon them with the sole goal of personal survival. How far a policy of 'muddling through' is in reality a strategy, depends on the capacity of managers to evolve a consistent approach to medium- and long-term goals out of their reactions to the issues selected and thrust upon them.

This possibility is largely ignored in the corporate strategy literature which tends to imply strategy must be largely autonomously determined 'from above', possibly with specialist strategists (Wood, 1980). This work has been founded on the assumption that at least in the past, such strategic management was not prevalent, and that environments are now changing at such a rate that this is no longer viable. As Steiner and Miner (1977) imply, an organization's success 'to a large extent . . . will depend upon how well it formulates its policy/strategy in light of its evolving environment, how well it defines and articulates its policy/strategy and how well it issues its implementation'. The success of 'strategic management' depends, according to this kind of view, on getting management to lay emphasis on strategic planning, or management by structured foresight, that is, the laying out in a clear way the nature of the strategy framework and relating decisions to the results of surveys of the future.

Those who appeal for such a strategic management tend not to treat its occurrence as problematic, but instead imply that its very necessity should guarantee its eventual implementation. They thus do not raise the question of whether there are different approaches to strategy formulation as Mintzberg has, and whether in fact in some situations, at least for some functions, strategic management may not be necessary or possible. Certainly, the model of strategic management utilized by corporate strategists seems limited in its existing application in the main to the giant conglomerate.

Whilst we would not necessarily accept the positivist version of contingency theory (managers do 'fit' their organizations to meet contingent factors) or the normative version (that managers should fit their organizations thus) we could utilize it as a means of generating ideal types, against which we might judge the rationality and reality of managerial life.

Business strategy can be said to be rationally connected to:
(a) product market objectives;
(b) the market position of the enterprise in question;
(c) the organizational conditions of the enterprise (size, etc.);
(d) political, social and economic conditions of the community where the operations of the enterprise are carried out (expressed in government policy and legislation and interest group pressures).

Clearly there are many possible relations between these factors. However, it is useful to depict seven types of organizational situation (see Table 18.3) as a starting point and define the overall business objectives which might be typically expressed in such situations and the conditions which are appropriate for a successful execution of a business strategy to carry out these conditions.

Industrial relations strategies similarly can be defined as connected to:
(a) union strength and type of unionization;
(b) the relative need to institutionalize conflict;
(c) labour/capital cost ratios and price competitiveness of products;
(d) the relative supply of available labour and the effectiveness of labour markets;
(e) political and social objectives of the labour movement;
(f) the types of technology (production systems) employed and their human requirements.

Any industrial relations strategy also has appropriate conditions necessary for its success.

Table 18.3 is therefore a matrix which sets out a number of hypothetical relations between the two types of strategy in different organizational conditions. These we would hope may serve as a basis for empirical research on actual relationships (that is, measuring the deviance from the ideal type).

The industrial relations strategies in Table 18.3 are linked to the business strategies, but it becomes obvious from reading the table that the relationship is different in different cases. In 'A' and 'E', for example, both strategies are decided by top management and are directly related. In 'B', there may be little choice for management on their industrial relations policy as they are directly affected by government policy on for example recognition. 'C' and 'D' are cases where much depends on union strength, objectives and tactics. There are, of course, many cases of multi-national corporations deciding to accept a highly unionized structure as part of the cost of operating in a given society. 'F' is a case where unionization might depend on the occupational norm of the industry in question, rather than the business strategy. 'G' is interesting as the industrial relations strategy might be a basic condition of a new business strategy rather than being derived from it. The table therefore demonstrates that the two types of strategy are only linked through their place in the overall organizational situation and climate. Purely logical links depend on this situation for any validity.

Business strategies and industrial relations strategies: empirical evidence

We can start by examining the question of what 'structural conditions' in a society appear to be most important in hindering or encouraging the development of business strategies. The most useful step is to take the extreme case of the large multi-national conglomerate, which may be thought to be most likely to develop a clear long-term business strategy based on top management decisions taken on the advice of a central planning and intelligence unit. How far is this hypothesis borne out in practice in different societies?

Granick (1972) argues that there are major differences in the objectives, roles, institutions and practice of management in large industrial concerns in advanced industrial societies. He sees the planning process, the types of rewards and the systems of control used as varying accord-

Table 18.3. *Various types of strategy and situation*

Example	Business strategy	Appropriate conditions	Industrial relations	Appropriate conditions
A				
Department store (e.g. Harrods, John Lewis), banks, insurance	*Economic mission based* Rational long-term pursuit of objectives given by founders, e.g. service or provision of products for profit	Stable single market environment with established market share. Low level of technological innovation. Hegemony of top management established	Recognition/non-recognition decided by top management beliefs. Selection of employees according to this criteria. (Non-union or closed shop possible.) Narrow scope for collective bargaining	Labour market allows selection to be severe and dismissal a real possibility. Tight managerial controls over work operations
B				
Public sector service organization (Civil Service, local authority, public corporations, educational and cultural organizations)	*Public service based* Provision of effective service to clients and/or public at lowest cost. (Satisficing solutions sought for problems)	Monopolistic market environment, public accountability and governed by formal rules	Recognition for different strata/occupations with own unions. Occupational semi-autonomy and important role for professions. Wide scope for collective bargaining and industrial democracy likely	Public recognition of monopoly and occupational rights. Growth needed to avoid severe zero sum conflict. Loose management control over work operations
C				
Key private and public companies	*Based on government industrial policy*	Existence of govt. industrial policy	Recognition normal for different occupations	Strong personnel/IR dept, also union and

e.g. steel, aircraft, ship-building, airlines, cars	effective production of certain products; innovation in products for own sake	large-scale investment. Large resources for research and development and provision of qualified manpower. Existence of major export markets	term industrial peace, so investment in joint decision-making, disclosure of information, involvement of stewards in management	needed to avoid internal conflict over operations
D Multi-national conglomerate	*Based on long-term and regular market intelligence* Exploitation of full profit from product life and development of new products	Effective market intelligence on world basis; formalized divisional product organization and powerful central organization for strategic decisions. Large resources for research and development and investment	Decentralized IR policy, at factory level, if possible. Resistance to multinational bargaining. Recognition to blue-collar and lower white-collar acceptable, not top management. Collective bargaining of wages and conditions, not industrial democracy. Emphasis on high rewards to give motivation for key staff	Localized personnel/IR dept. Job rotation and careers available for key managers and specialists who are geographically mobile. Deskilling of operational jobs and automation very desirable (to avoid sectional bargaining)
E Small firms and subcontractors for C & D	*Based on economic survival* Short-term profitability and maintenance of sales to other firms and customers	Flexibility in production organization. Good relations with major customers. Dependable source of finance	Avoidance of shop steward control; limited recognition to certain trades. Use of personal IR style to avoid union power	Line management control with limited IR/personnel function. Availability of low-cost labour (women, immigrants, etc.)

Table 18.3. (cont.)

Example	Business strategy	Appropriate conditions	Industrial relations	Appropriate conditions
F New firm trying to create market or break into market	*Based on product innovation* Development of new product and marketing of product	Staff with technical and business problem-solving capacity. Links with possible customers. Financial support for investment	Avoid trade union recognition, if possible. Emphasis on occupational and professional skills	Highly skilled staff, adaptable and innovative. Willing to work long hours for low rewards, initially
G Established firm in economic decline	*Based on crisis resolution* Development of new markets, improvement of product availability and reduction of price and costs	Crisis due to inefficient production control, overmanning, poor plant design, plant breakdowns, industrial conflict, communication problems, etc.	Productivity bargaining and technical and organizational innovations, achieved through shop steward/management committees at every level	Union or closed shop. Strong steward organization and good personnel management/IR/line management collaboration. Possibilities for redeploying staff in or out of company. Third-party help (consultants) likely to be necessary

ing to the importance of qualifications achieved through higher education, the influence of the state over planning objectives and the types of status attached to managerial roles in society, together with cultural assumptions about work, power and responsibility. These clearly affect the objectives and motivation behind the formulation of business strategy. In particular, compared with the United States, France and the Soviet Union, British managers of large enterprises have special difficulties in developing long-term strategies. These difficulties stem from a number of special characteristics of British management, and include the following:

(a) 'the extreme form of British decentralization . . . To the extent that British executives attempt to establish small and relatively independent management, economies of scale at the establishment as well as at the corporate level are lost' (Granick, 1972: 360).

(b) 'The British is the extreme form of an ''open promotion'' system while the French have a ''closed promotion system''. In Britain, there is little pre-selection before entrance into the firm of those who will reach management positions' (ibid.: 362).

'Precisely because industrial management is not a prestigious career in Britain as it is elsewhere, less vigor, inventiveness and risk taking is shown by British managers' (ibid.: 364).

(c) 'The narrowly functional career lines followed in Britain and the Soviet Union lead to a rich degree of differentiation of roles among managers. Managers are quite specialized in experience and in their attitude. But co-operation among functions suffers badly as a result' (ibid.: 386).

The implication of these characteristics of management in Britain is that strong strategic management policies are unlikely to develop; power is too diffused and sectional interests are open in their pursuit of shorter-term goals. It would also be true that individual managers are often biased by their experience towards taking a problem-solving 'tactical' role and consequently they are unable to take a strategic view (Marples, 1967).

The problem clearly is to relate these hypotheses and insights, which have considerable face validity, to empirical evidence of the actual behaviour of managers and firms and to the structural constraints of managerial decision-making. Many of the most famous studies of industrial structure, for example Sargent Florence (1961), are based on data which are considerably out of date. The most pertinent data can be found in the recent study of George and Ward (1975) of the structure of industry in the EEC. The authors emphasize the relatively high level of concentration in British industry compared with other EEC countries. It is also true that 'the size of firms in terms of multiples of the average size of the four largest plants, is greater in the United Kingdom than in either Germany or France' (George and Ward, 1975: 36). However, 'the proportion of the work-force engaged in large plants has *not* shown a great deal of change in either country' (ibid.: 39). Table 18.4 shows the distribution of the 100 largest EEC companies in 1962 and 1972 (by size of employees).

The domination of the UK in food, drink and tobacco, textiles, paper and printing contrasts with the decline shown in vehicles, aircraft and metals and metal products. George and Ward (1975: 58) comment that 'the UK strength in terms of large firms is biased towards those sectors which have on the whole been least affected by international competitive forces'. The implication here is perhaps that oligopolistic positions in a semi-protected market may have been achieved by mergers, but that growth based on successful product market innovation is less common. However, such evidence is purely circumstantial and direct information about business strategies is really required (Channon, 1973).

Some direct evidence about the effect of strategic planning is provided by Grinyer and Norburn (1974) who argue that formal procedures among companies for receiving market and other intelligence are also associated with a greater use of such information, although informal talking to customers and competitors is also important. This seems to show that formal strategic planning *is* beginning to be important in large UK companies as in other societies.

The UK economy in fact shows widely diverse business and industrial relations strategies between industries and indeed companies. Clearly there are some examples of 'strategic management' type firms in certain industries, but the reality of many large industrial companies, particularly in engineering, is very far from this state.

The comparison of Britain and Japan is perhaps most pertinent here. The Japanese situation apparently contrasts strongly with that of Britain. As is well known, an extraordinary period of rapid economic growth over the last twenty years has been achieved by large corporations with a very high investment rate, aggressive export policies and a coherent industrial relations strategy of supporting enterprise union bargaining of basic wage rates through annual wage negotiation. Japan appears, therefore, first, to differ sharply from the United States in that a coherent set of business strategies, aided and supported by government, is *directly*

Table 18.4. *Industrial composition of 100 largest EEC companies, 1962 and 1972*

	1962				1972			
	UK	WG	France	Total	UK	WG	France	Total
Food, drink, tobacco	9½	—	—	10	13½	1	—	15
Textiles	2	—	—	4	2	—	—	3
Paper and printing	3	—	1	4	2	—	—	2
Rubber	1	—	1	3	½	—	1	2
Mining	1	2	—	3	2	1	2	5
Vehicles and aircraft	7	3	5	16	4	4	4	13
Electrical engineering	5	3	1	11	5	3	2	12
Oil	1½	1	1	6	2½	1	2	8
Chemicals	1	6	2	10	3	3½	1	12
Metals, metal products	10	11	6	31	5	7	6	22
Other	1	—	1	2	2	1	3	6
Total	42	26	18	100	41½	21½	21	100

Source: Fortune Directory (George and Ward, 1975: 57)

related to a particular type of industrial relations strategy, at least since 1955. Secondly, this industrial relations strategy is fundamental for the basis of employee loyalty to the firm and is widely seen in Japan as expression of 'managerialism'; that is, corporation growth undertaken *not* for shareholders' profits, but for the welfare and promotion prospects of employees in general and managerial employees in particular. Thirdly, the growth of large organizations is frequently viewed as an aspect of monopolistic capitalism in which smaller sub-contractors are 'exploited' for the benefit of employees of the larger parent company. Such a system implies that the industrial relations strategy is not a pragmatic adaption to environmental factors, but is deliberately chosen to support top management growth policies.

This popular view of Japanese industrial organization, however, can be questioned on a number of counts. In the first place, according to the recent Brookings Institute study, the degree of concentration in Japanese industry in terms of the relative dominance of large firms is not strikingly different from that common in the USA. The emphasis by many writers on the special nature of oligopoly in Japan with its 'dual structure' of large modernized firms and more traditional small and medium sized firms may have been somewhat exaggerated (Patrick and Rosovosky, 1976). Competition between firms in Japan, in fact, has been gravely under-estimated by foreign observers (see Magaziner and Hout, 1980).

A second point is that 'managerialism' in Japan is perhaps also exaggerated.

> Thus the divorce of control from ownership has not proceeded as far in Japan as in the United States. On the contrary, recent data shows a rapid shift of shareholding towards companies and financial intermediaries that may be restoring cohesive minority-owner control over some Japanese firms.
> (Caves and Vekusa in Patrick and Rosovosky, 1976: 467)

In the third place, it can be argued that 'enterprise unionism' is *not* derived from the basic business strategy followed, but reflects a compromise solution between managerial wishes to control left-wing power and the strong demand of Japanese employees for a corporated representative system to guard their interests. There *is* little doubt that the special decision-making processes in Japanese management are based on institutionalized forms of traditional methods of handling interpersonnel relations (Yoshino, 1975). Such methods reflect very different values to those of American management. They also reflect different reward systems, promotion systems and so on. The relationship with industrial relations strategy is built not only on a capacity for taking management decisions, but also on the acceptance by management of the need to sponsor the welfare of all permanent employees, that is, on the relatively new egalitarian aspects of mass society in Japan. The example of Japan, therefore, indicates the importance of general social and cultural factors in influencing the thrust and direction of strategic managerial thinking.

The development of a 'strategic' approach: theory

We are now in a position to consider the industrial relations implications of the argument of Ansoff (1969) and others for the development of a conscious strategy. As we have seen, the argument is that the success of strategic management depends, according to such writers, on persuading management itself to lay emphasis on strategic planning. This is described as 'management by structured foresight' (Steiner and Miner, 1977: 33), that is, defining clearly the nature of the policy/strategy framework and relating decisions to predicted scenarios. This is necessary because of the rapid pace of changes of all types, technological, economic, political and social. Steiner and Miner (1977: 33) outline the components of corporate strategy as in Figure 18.1.

The model reflects a view of strategy which requires a centralized intelligence and planning unit. It is clear that the survival of the organization and the extension of its powers are assumed as given and strategy is seen as a way of rationally building in the modifications of policy required for survival and growth. Such an approach fits the giant conglomerate corporations perfectly; it justifies being prepared to change everything (policies, products, employees) in order to allow survival and growth. Clearly industrial relations strategies are necessary within such an overall master strategy. Such strategies will be likely to limit commitments to unions, employees and governments, however, because of the need to preserve freedom of action for the future.

Granick (1972) provides a useful examination of the process of strategic planning inside large American corporations and compares it with Gosplan and the Soviet system of planning. American planning is described as 'satisficing' not for the meaning attached to this term by Simon (1957) but because it takes into account intangible investments at divisional level. He argues that profits are planned at a 'satisficing'

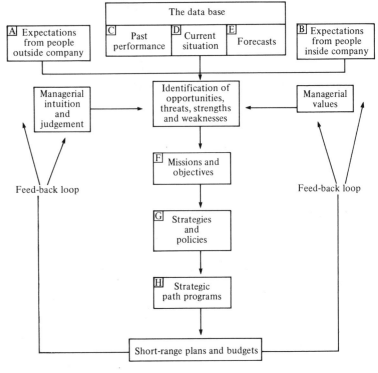

Figure 18.1 Conceptual model of strategic management

level for divisions and corporate management and that 'over-fulfilment of plans' is *not* encouraged, unlike the Soviet system which emphasizes maximization of output at all cost.

> One way of interpreting this difference between the American and Soviet model systems of planning is to say that the Russians place their stress on a 'logical' organization, in which the maximization process is devoted to the priority criterion, while the Americans are much more intent on developing a system that is less tidy but functions better in terms of human reactions to it. The Russian system follows an engineer's concept of rationality, and attempts to mold human beings to it. *American company top managers are much more concerned with human relations problems and with shaping a structure that is adapted to the managers who actually exist.* Thus the

Russians 'maximize' the priority criterion, while the Americans 'satisfice' with regard to it. (Granick, 1972: 39) (our italics)

This is, of course, a hypothesis which, as yet, has had no rigorous testing; it also clearly fits with the ideology prevalent in American business schools. It is therefore prudent to reserve judgement on whether the Granick model of large corporation behaviour has validity. This does not, however, detract from the issue raised by his argument. 'Strategic management', he is saying, can imply for large corporations a capacity to build flexibility into local organizations, so that managerial initiative and talent can be utilized. This clearly suggests that personnel and industrial relations policies need not be centralized, but might be deliberately allowed to reflect local pressures and beliefs. This decentralization is likely to be still not at the workshop level, but rather at the divisional or possibly enterprise level.

In any society there are likely to be variations in the business strategy used according to organization size, type of product market and the influence of the government. Nevertheless, there are many grounds for supposing that the American economy is dominated by large conglomerate corporations and for believing that 'strategic management' does dominate the approach of top management in those companies. To say this is *not* to fall back on the old argument about 'managerialism' and the effect of the separation of management and shareholders. As Child (1969a) argues, the evidence supports the *overlap* of interest between top management and large shareholders, for example, in relatively low distributed profits.

The argument of Ansoff, Steiner and Miner and Granick goes beyond this controversy into the rationale of decision-making at the corporate level and its dependence on a centralized corporate planning function. Given the existence of such functions, there is at least the opportunity that decision-making will proceed in the way indicated in Figure 18.1. The extent to which this opportunity is taken depends on the cohesiveness and independence shown by top management and on both their objectives, and capacity for judgement. These factors, in turn, ultimately depend on: (a) the type of strata from which managers are recruited; (b) the type of higher educational experience of top managers; (c) promotion systems typically used for managers in a given society. Figure 18.2 sketches out these relationships in a diagrammatic representation of the basic factors hypothesized to lead to 'strategic' manage-

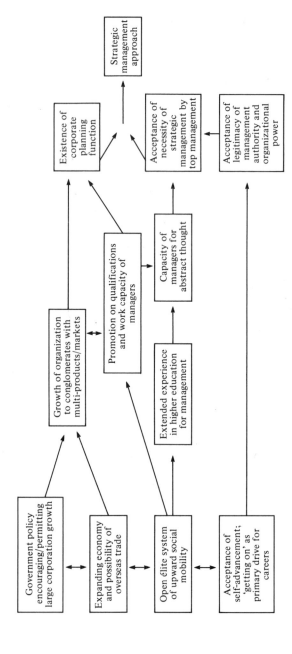

Figure 18.2 Sociological model of determination of 'strategic management' approach in large organizations

ment. There are four basic conditions covering political, economic, social structural and cultural factors – and the intermediate factors are, as Granick argues, concerned with the type of organization structure and capacity and the values of managers. On this argument, then, the development of 'strategic management' depends ultimately on a special mix of characteristics making up fundamental aspects of a particular society. It should be noted that the model is an 'industrial society' model and might be relevant for capitalist, socialist or mixed economics. It should also be clear that there is nothing inevitable about these causal links; there is no support here for Galbraithian notions of technocracy. On the contrary, the emphasis is on the range of possibilities which are open in an industrial society.

Given the growth and predominance in a society of organizations practising 'strategic management', can one predict the implications for industrial relations strategies? In the USA, the growth of large corporations practising such an approach has not been accompanied by a shift in managerial views towards supporting unions and unionization. On the contrary, the emphasis on personnel policies of human relations, organizational development and job enrichment have all been at least, latently or partly, anti-union. Industrial relations institutions and collective bargaining exist, of course, in a large number of American corporations, but most evidence suggests that this is a fact of life which has to be tolerated for blue-collar workers, rather than a deliberate objective of managerial industrial relations strategy. Strategic management, in its American context, will undoubtedly allow a tough anti-union line of management to be modified if it proves desirable; but it does not provide any positive motivation to sponsor unionization.

Industrial relations and personnel management strategies of multi-national companies: empirical evidence

The crucial aspect of industrial relations strategies in a large multi-national conglomerate is the capacity to separate out the overall business strategy from the situation in either a plant or office, or in any single society. The benefit of 'strategic management' is the possibility of national long-term planning combined with pragmatism and localized industrial relations policies. Two recent studies provide an empirical test of this reasoning. A study of personnel and industrial relations policies and practices in more than 200 Japanese subsidiary companies, branch enterprises and joint enterprises in the United Kingdom (Thurley *et al.,* 1980) showed that there was a large variety of practices in this respect. Although all enterprises had a dual system of personnel management for Japanese and local staff, there were, however, rather few cases in which Japanese companies seemed to be trying to extend their traditional systems of paternalism and human relations to their local UK staff. In general it was accepted, especially among manufacturing establishments and the direct sales offices of Japanese manufacturers, that local personnel management practices should be encouraged in dealing with local staff. Several Japanese companies reported they had undertaken local labour market studies before establishing a factory, in order to avoid excessive competition for labour with nearby British manufacturers. Where local labour was strongly unionized, Japanese manufacturers have decided to accept a post-entry closed shop provided only one union is recognized and, in one case, provided full flexibility of transfer of labour between grades is accepted by the union. Where the level of unionization of local labour is weaker, sometimes companies have tried to avoid unionization. In one case, the famous YKK zip fastener factory at Runcorn, this decision was reversed after three ballots of staff and constant pressure from the TGWU for recognition. Pragmatic acceptance of local feelings about labour relations has been strongly evident, although this has been combined, where appropriate, with attempts to build up a workforce largely recruited from school leavers and trained to accept fairly strict discipline over absenteeism and behaviour in the factory.

The situation of the banks, insurance, security and trading companies, operating largely in the City of London, contrasts starkly with the factories, sales and distribution offices established by Japanese manufacturers. In these establishments, there has been a need to operate Japanese-style commercial systems relying on telex communication from local offices to the centralized intelligence and decision-making systems of head offices in Tokyo, Osaka and Kobe. Local personnel practice common in the City of London has again been followed for the clerks and ancillary staff employed. It is of interest, however, that local management is substantially operated by Japanese nationals sent from the parent company, and there is some latent conflict between them and locally appointed British managerial staff. The contrast between manufacturing, where Japanese nationals are used mainly in a start-up situation and then withdrawn except for specialist advisers and key personnel, and the commercial and financial establishments can be used to substantiate the view that 'strategic management' on the lines of Steiner and Miners's model *does* characterize the operations of Japanese companies abroad. In the first case, the special aspects of employee management, for example the training in quality control and the use of flexibility agreements, are enforced on 'Japanese' lines, where these are regarded as critical for factory performance. Other aspects of personnel management can be settled according to local wishes. The basic strategy of Japanese TV manufacturers operating in Britain has been well summarized in a letter to the *Financial Times* (15 July 1980):

> We have learnt that we can build to much higher quality levels than previously with the same personnel and the basic reasons are: prove the design before you start mass production; get the co-operation of your suppliers and make sure they understand precisely what you want and if necessary school them in quality control methods; have the best tools for the job; and don't let turnover pressure cause you to use substandard material – work towards a situation where your operators care about what they do – this is far more efficient than employing masses of inspection and rectification on line.
>
> This does not sound like 'Japanese magic' to me, it's more like British common-sense – and not forgetting hard work.
> (A. C. Shirley)

In the second case, it is clearly regarded in Tokyo that the operation of a world-wide commercial and financial system requires Japanese nationals to monitor operations, collect information and act following decisions made at head office. Again this shows the predominance of a strategic approach. Until now there has been little unionization of white-collar staff in the City of London institutions and the cost of training British nationals to perform in a similar way and to similar standards of those of the Japanese staff is a very heavy one. The industrial relations/personnel management strategy therefore differs from manufacturing, but on entirely 'rational' and predictable lines.

A second study (Lyons, Thurley and Wirdenius, 1982) also throws light on the validity of the 'strategic management' thesis applied to multinational companies. This is a project carried out in Ireland in the spring of 1980 by an international team of specialists in supervisory development organized by the Irish Training Authority (ANCO) and the European Institute for Vocational Training. Seven factories were analysed and compared in terms of their personnel policies and their need for development of their supervisory and production management. These factories had been recently established, six by foreign companies (German, French, Swedish, Japanese and American) and one by an Irish co-operative company. The major personnel question was the problem of training largely rural workforces to adapt to operating new technology at a high performance level. The foreign companies had all designed their production systems from overseas and there was little evidence of any special study of the training problem in the Irish context, except perhaps in one case of a giant American multi-national. Only one company had any serious friction between expatriate managers and local Irish staff, and relations with unions – except in this case – were reasonably cordial. The response of four of the companies to problems of low skill performance by operatives was to plan further automation and reduce skill levels further.

In general terms, then, the factories had been planned as technical production units in their own right, with relatively little investment in studies of the special training and adaption problems involved for the workforce in spite of fairly lavish government assistance in this field. Even the most sophisticated of the companies with a great deal of personnel expertise in other countries were tending to use standardized training programmes and procedure. Was this 'strategic management', in line with the experience of the Japanese companies in the UK? There was some evidence to suggest that foreign companies were following quite clear business strategies, but that the build-up of reasonably satisfactory human and industrial relations had been taken rather for granted, given intelligent and sensitive handling of the situation at the factory level by the plant managers. The project raised the question as to whether this would be sufficient in the medium-term future, in view of the effectiveness of the supervisory systems studied. It may be that the personnel planners at corporate level in these companies had underestimated the need to develop specific personnel policies in the Irish context.

Conclusions: how far is a 'strategic' approach to industrial relations justified?

Turning now to an evaluation of the usefulness of the idea of 'industrial relations strategy' for practitioners, researchers and those concerned with the academic study of industrial relations, it is possible to draw the following conclusions.

Strategy as a theoretical concept

As an approach for the analysis and explanation of managerial actions in industrial relations it is clearly fruitful and seems superior to other approaches, such as explaining managerial decisions in terms of collective bargaining theory, organizational contingency theory, or a macro-level theory of managerial values, roles or assumed objectives. Its use lies in the possibility of comparing the likely results of different strategies in different situations and in the awareness that only selected aspects of industrial relations may be judged as an important condition for the success of a given business strategy. In short, we can start to build a relatively sensitive and sophisticated comparative method in industrial relations for study at the enterprise and establishment levels.

The first limitation of the approach lies in the tendency, shown in the examples given, to impute rationality and intention to managerial actions, which may be taken for entirely different reasons and are possibly responses to pressures and problems rather than pro-active decisions. Rationality is always relative to the cognitive model of the actor and the information he perceives as important. It is often easy to perceive a motive and intention from an act which would surprise the actor. The remedy for this problem is to study the organizational, political and economic context of the decision-maker, but too often in industrial relations this is impossible as the information is too sensitive.

A second limitation, which is a severe one, is the problem of 'political' opposition to a strategy which results in it being modified. Does this mean that there is no strategy, but only a set of political deals? It is easy to depict managerial strategy when they have power to carry it out, but what of the situation when this power is frustrated? When compromise rules the day and management/union agreement is reached, is this a really flexible and sophisticated 'strategy' or opportunism? The answer to this problem can only lie with understanding the detailed justification of a set of business decisions. If a particular business strategy requires a given product price and therefore a certain labour cost ratio, it is clearly *not* a sophisticated industrial relations strategy if this ratio is ignored in any settlement. On the other hand, many aspects of personnel policy and industrial relations policy may be 'neutral' in relation to the precise business strategy followed and compromise over such policies does not necessarily compromise the strategy itself.

A third problem in using the concept of strategy, is what theory of organizational behaviour is in fact being used (Wood, 1980). Is this a term which assumes a dominant managerial élite, integrated in its view and 'rational' in its decision-making about production and marketing problems? Much of the corporate strategy literature certainly seems to assume an organizational rationality which most industrial relations practitioners and theorists would instinctively reject. The assumption here is that this type of model of organizations need not be accepted. On the contrary, it is assumed that organizations are political entities, formed of groups with competing policies and interests, each struggling to have their way. This means that a decision on a certain business strategy is a decision against alternative strategies. What *is* also assumed is that a political control system exists which will allow a particular strategic decision to be carried out – otherwise there can be no meaning to a decision on strategy. Managerial control is, however, again a relative concept; not all strategies are acceptable and the study of strategy decision and implementation is a study of a political process by which a predominant coalition may be formed to make sure the decision goes through. Strategy implementation is therefore always problematic, it can never be assumed *per se*.

'Strategic thinking' as a policy in industrial relations in the UK

For practitioners, the attraction of the idea of strategy is the belief that industrial relations questions are best solved with a long-term rational approach. A good example here is the much discussed new industrial relations strategy at British Leyland since Sir Michael Edwardes became managing director. In an interview, Pat Lowry, then personnel director, argued:

> It is a sad reflection that only when a company is pushed almost to the point of extinction that managements think seriously about how to change attitudes and workers respond . . . When we started down this road we knew we had to go out and tell people more than the unions did – more, perhaps, than the unions were capable of doing. Every employee knew our side of the story at every stage. Before any ballot there were works meetings addressed by the managing director, video tape interviews with senior figures, very intensive campaigns on the shop floor and a barrage of leaflets and letters to workers' homes . . . But the important thing is always to work to plan, always know your objectives. You have to plan

your way out of the industrial relations mire. Then you have to accept that the unions are in business for their own ends. They are not necessarily yours . . .

Finally, you are not going to get anywhere without taking some tough stands. And remember; you do not back off when the going gets rough. Otherwise you destroy your credibility.
(J. Torode, *Guardian:* 10 July 1980)

The appeal of 'strategic thinking' is precisely that it offers the possibility of taking a clear cut route 'out of the mire'. Our evidence here is that this is only credible:
 (i) if the industrial relations strategy is justifiable by its relationship to a clear and acceptable business strategy;
 (ii) if there exists an effective organizational capacity for study and analysis of conditions, monitoring of effects of actions and explaining the rationality of the strategy in question;
(iii) if there is considerable acceptance of the legitimacy of management and its control systems by employees;
(iv) if top managers have the educational training to allow them to attack problems in a systematic, detached, 'rational' fashion.

We saw that there were a number of basic characteristics about the structure of large organizations in Great Britain which make it difficult to develop a strategic approach. Nevertheless the evidence from the Japanese survey and even the quotation from Pat Lowry above seem to indicate that these macro-level characteristics of the social structure *could* be overcome. Most problems arise from the unanticipated consequences of organizational structures and reward systems developed to solve specific tasks and problems or to meet 'informal' political pressures. A 'strategic approach' is much easier to envisage in a 'green-field site' situation.

The Irish study reminds us, however, that 'rationality' is not enough in designing an adequate human/industrial relations strategy. Strategies there on the whole did not seem to be adequately concerned with the training issue. This could be interpreted as a 'tough' stance on an area of policy which could be neglected without any real penalties; it could also be foolishness based on lack of intelligence and foresight. On balance, it would seem to indicate defective 'strategic thinking' as there was little evidence that the whole problem had been adequately considered by top management (although this could not be proved by the research which was at factory level).

Business strategy and industrial relations

We can conclude that a 'strategic approach' to industrial relations must proceed far beyond the simple proposal of formalizing industrial relations policy at board level before it can really yield results. All the major problems – wage inflation, job inflexibility and over-manning, lack of job security and consequent defensive attitudes, inter-union conflict at the steward level, inadequate reward systems and career routes, lack of internal qualification systems – are rooted in organization of production and the processes of recruitment to management, its lack of training, the conflict between functional and line staff and the way that top management takes decisions. Reform of industrial relations does require a new strategic approach from management, but this inevitably goes far beyond industrial relations itself. There has to be a corporate managerial capacity and the will to formulate strategies and carry them through. Only major organizational changes in structure, recruitment and development could provide such a capacity and only major political changes at least within the large company sector could provide the will for this. It remains to be seen whether Lowry is correct in thinking that the pressures of near bankruptcy brought on by the recession can push management to the point of making such changes.

Notes

3 Management and managerial unionism

1 The EPEA became the founding section of the Engineers' and Managers' Association (EMA) in 1977. The great majority of EMA members still come from the electricity supply industry.
2 After several years' flirtation with the major manual workers' union in the steel industry, the Iron and Steel Trades Confederation, SIMA, decided in 1980 to merge with the EESA, the white-collar section of the Electrical, Electronic, Telecommunications and Plumbing Union (EETPU).

8 Management control through collective bargaining: a future strategy

1 For example, some companies pay union members to attend branch meetings or hold them during company time (*Industrial Relations Review and Report,* March 1977, No. 147: 8).
2 Such a situation occurred in the British Airways maintenance men's dispute in 1977 and International Harvester in 1975 (ACAS, 1975).
3 Flanders, Pomeranz and Woodward (1968: 183) give an illustration of how this is achieved in the John Lewis Partnership, albeit a non union firm. 'Above all freedom of criticism pervades the organisation, and the general ethos is such as to encourage managers to be constantly and genuinely concerned with the interests of those who are subject to their authority . . . [a] major effect of the system [of industrial democracy] on management is paradoxically to reinforce its authority so that it is stronger and commands greater power than is usual, and often possible, in the normally run private and public enterprise today.'
4 For an example in the London docks see Social Policy Research (1975: 20).
5 The trenchant opposition of British Leyland to the 1977 tool makers' strike for separate bargaining rights is a good illustration.

10 Management decision-making and shop floor participation

1 See, for example, the submissions by the CBI and the BIM (British Institute of Management). Also this point was noted by Brannen *et al.* (1976: 37).
2 For work relating to the propensity to participate, reference should be made to Ramsay (1977), for example. Investigation of management's acceptance of workers' participation has been dealt with in a separate paper by the authors (Marchington and Loveridge, 1979) and an in-depth investigation of participation has been published in Marchington (1980).
3 In this analysis, we could also have included a variable relating to owner-ship. However, it was not particularly relevant in this case, since both firms operated in the private sector, and were subsidiaries of larger organizations.
4 A number of diary and observation studies of managers have noted the large number of issues handled during any one day. See, for example, Marples (1967) and Mintzberg (1973).

13 Corporate strategy and employment relations in multinational corporations: some evidence from Kenya and Malaysia

1 Minister of Labour, *Legislative Council Proceedings*, 23 April 1959, cols 6763–4.
2 For example, when the Malaysian government's Pioneer Industries Scheme was inaugurated in 1957, the authorities declared that they expected the trade unions to act according to the 'truth' that overseas investment 'will need a higher rate of reward than would be appropriate in the case of conventional ventures' (*Legislative Council Proceedings*, 13 December 1957, col. 4250).
3 Tom Mboya, formerly leader of the Kenya Federation of Labour and then a Cabinet Minister, stated: 'The new Government is not prepared to allow any obstruction in the economic development of Kenya either from trade unions or any other groups of persons' (*The Challenge of Nationhood*, London, Heinemann, 1970, p. 66).
4 In fact, the expansion of membership is even more impressive if only industrial and commercial workers are considered. Between 1965 and 1972 membership density increased from 29 per cent to 50 per cent, representing an increase in membership from 56,000 to 118,000. There are thirty national unions in Kenya today but one is not permitted by law to affiliate with COTU – the teachers' union. Source: *Registrar of Trade Unions Annual Returns* (Government of Kenya, 1965–76, Nairobi).
5 Communalism refers to the tendency of multi-ethnic states to segment into district and socially isolated population groups with relatively little cross-cutting communication. It is typically a response to the dynamics of the political struggle for the scarce resources of a nation state.
6 The only exception to this rule encountered is one particular transnational

corporation which uses a standardized system of work studied output incentives in all its factories world-wide. It is so much part of the corporate culture that no amount of protest by local management against its inappropriateness is listened to at headquarters.

7 The Confucian classic *The Great Learning* outlines the connection between personal responsibility and sound administration as follows: 'To cultivate oneself, *hsiu shen*, then to govern one's family, *ch'i chia*, then to govern one's nation, *chih kuo*, then to bring peace (through administration) to the world, *p'ing t'ien hsia'*. There are obvious parallels with Japanese employment practices but we would argue that Malaysian practices represent a different synthesis of traditional and modern values; in particular they include certain British influences. Muslim influence is increasing and is most noticeable in the provision of separate dining facilities for Malays and non-Muslims and an extended lunch break for prayer on Friday, but this is more an expression of external political power and the key role assigned to religion in defining Malay identity.

8 The most striking evidence of this lack of resistance was the introduction by the Ministry of Finance of an incomes policy administered by the Industrial Court which is, at the same time, charged with arbitrating between employers and trade unions. Apparently the arrangement works to all parties' satisfaction.

16 Organizational survival as an act of faith: the case of the BBC

1 *Report of the Broadcasting Committee 1949*. Cmd. 8117, 19.1, para. 185.

2 Sir Ian Jacob (the BBC's Director General) in *Ariel* (the BBC house journal).

3 *Report of the Broadcasting Committee 1935*, Note of Reservation by C. R. Attlee.

4 Memorandum of Evidence of the BBC Staff Association to the Committee on Broadcasting 1949, Appendix 'H', op. cit.

5 Quoted in BBC Staff Association *Bulletin*, Vol. II, No. 25, July–August 1950.

6 *Report of the Committee on the Future of Broadcasting 1977*. Cmd. 6753, para. 9.3.

Bibliography

Abegglen, J. (1958), *The Japanese Factory*, New York, Free Press.

Advisory, Conciliation and Arbitration Service (1975), Report to the Company Joint Negotiating Committee, *International Harvester Company of Great Britain Limited: Payments Systems and Structures*, July.

Allen, Sir Douglas (1977), 'The Problems of Civil Service Management', *Management Services in Government*, February, pp. 5–8.

Allen, G. C. (1929), *The Industrial Development of Birmingham and the Black Country*, London, Allen and Unwin.

Alpander, G. G. (1973), 'The Drift of Authoritarianism. The Changing Management Styles of the US "Executives Overseas" ', *Journal of International Business Studies*, Vol. 4, No. 2, pp. 1–14.

Amsden, A. H. (1971), *International Firms and Labour in Kenya, 1945–70*, London, Frank Cass.

Ansoff, H. I. (1969), *Business Strategy*, Harmondsworth, Penguin.

Arrighi, G. (1970), 'International Corporations, Labour Aristocracies and Economic Development in Africa' in R. I. Rhodes (ed.), *Imperialism and Underdevelopment: A Reader*, New York, Monthly Review Press, pp. 220–67.

Arrighi, G. and Saul, J. S. (1969), 'Socialism and Economic Development in Tropical Africa', *Journal of Modern African Studies*, Vol. 6, pp. 141–69.

Bain, G. S. (1970), *The Growth of White-Collar Unionism*, Oxford, Oxford University Press.

Bain, G. S. and Clegg, H. A. (1974), 'A Strategy for Industrial Relations Research in Great Britain', *British Journal of Industrial Relations*, Vol. XII, No. 1, pp. 91–113.

Barker, T. C. (1977), *The Glassmakers, Pilkingtons 1826–1976*, London, Weidenfeld and Nicolson.

Batstone, E., Boraston, I. and Frenkel, S. (1977), *Shop Stewards in Action – The Organization of Workplace Conflict and Accommodation*, Oxford, Blackwell.

Bibliography

Bendix, R. (1956), *Work and Authority in Industry*, New York, Harper and Row.

Beynon, H. (1973), *Working for Ford*, Harmondsworth, Penguin.

Blackler, F. H. M. and Brown, C. A. (1980), *Whatever Happened to Shell's New Philosophy of Management?*, Farnborough (Hants), Saxon House.

Blau, P. (1955), *The Dynamics of Bureaucracy*, Chicago, University of Chicago Press.

Brannen, P., Batstone, E., Fatchett, D. and White, P. (1976), *The Worker Directors: A Sociology of Participation*, London, Hutchinson.

Braverman, H. (1974), *Labor and Monopoly Capital*, New York, Monthly Review Press.

Brewster, C. and Connock, S. (1978), 'Industrial Relations Training: A Focus on Policy', *Personnel Management*, Vol. 10, No. 8, pp. 28–9, 35.

Brown, W. (1965), *Exploration in Management*, Harmondsworth, Pelican.

Brusco, S. (1981), 'Labor Market Structure, Company Policies and Technological Progress', presented to the Research Seminar, European Economic Community, Pont à Mousson, September.

Bullock, Lord (1977), *Report of the Committee of Inquiry on Industrial Democracy*, London, HMSO, Cmnd. 6706.

Burns, T. (1970), 'Public Service and Private World' in J. Tunstall (ed.), *Media Sociology*, London, Constable, pp. 135–57.

Burns, T. (1977), *The BBC*, London, Macmillan.

Burns, T. and Stalker, G. M. (1961), *The Management of Innovation*, London, Tavistock.

Carr, J. C. and Taplin, W. (1962), *History of the British Steel Industry*, Oxford, Blackwell.

Carr-Saunders, A. M. and Wilson, P. A. (1933), *The Professions*, Oxford, Oxford University Press.

Chamberlain, G. (1933), *Theory of Monopolistic Competition*, Cambridge (Mass.), Harvard University Press.

Chandler, A. D. (1962), *Strategy and Structure*, Cambridge (Mass.), MIT Press.

Chandler, A. D. (1977), *The Visible Hand: The Management Revolution in American Business*, Cambridge (Mass.), Harvard University Press.

Chandler, A. D. and Daems, H. (1974), 'The Rise of Managerial Capitalism and Its Impact on Investment Strategy in the Western World and Japan' in H. Daems and H. van der Wee (eds), *The Rise of Managerial Capitalism*, The Hague: Martinus Nijhoff, pp. 1–34.

Channon, D. (1973), *The Strategy and Structure of British Enterprise*, London, Macmillan.

Child, J. (1969), *The Business Enterprise in Modern Industrial Society*, London, Collier Macmillan.

Child, J. (1972), 'Organizational Structure, Environmental Performance: The Role of Strategic Choice', *Sociology*, Vol. 6, No. 1, January, pp. 1–22.

229

Bibliography

Child, J. (1973a), 'Organization: A Choice for a Man' in J. Child (ed.), *Man and Organization*, London, Hutchinson, pp. 234–57.

Child, J. (1973b), 'Predicting and Understanding Organization Structure', *Administrative Science Quarterly*, Vol. 18, No. 2, pp. 168–85.

Child, J. (1979), 'Culture Contingency and Capitalism in the Cross-National Study of Organizations' in L. L. Cummings and B. M. Shaw (eds), *Research in Organizational Behaviour*, Vol. 3, New York, JAI Press.

Child, J. and Francis, A. (1981), 'Strategy Formulation as a Structured Process', *International Studies of Management and Organisation*, Summer, Vol. VII, No. 2, pp. 110–26.

Child, J. and Kieser, A. (1977), 'The Development of Organizations over Time' in P. C. Nystrom and W. H. Starbuck (eds), *Handbook of Organizational Design*, Vol. I, Oxford, Oxford University Press, pp. 28–64.

Clayton, A. and Savage, D. C. (1974), *Government and Labour in Kenya, 1895–1963*, London, Frank Cass.

Clegg, H. A. (1972), *The System of Industrial Relations in Great Britain*, Oxford, Clarendon Press.

Clegg, H. A., Fox, A. and Thompson, A. F. (1964), *A History of British Trade Unions since 1889*, Oxford, Oxford University Press.

Clegg, S. (1975), *Power, Rule and Domination*, London, Routledge and Kegan Paul.

Coase, R. H. (1937), 'The Nature of the Firms', *Economica*, Vol. X, No. 3, pp. 534–70.

Cole, R. G. (1979), *Work, Mobility and Participation: A Comparative Study of American and Japanese Industry*, Berkeley, University of California Press.

Coleman, D. C. (1969), *Courtaulds: An Economic and Social History*, Oxford, The Clarendon Press.

Coleman, T. (1965), *The Railway Navvies*, London, Penguin.

Commission on Industrial Relations (1973), *The Role of Management in Industrial Relations* (Report 34), London, HMSO.

Commission on Industrial Relations (1974), *Industrial Relations in Multi-plant Undertakings* (Report 85), London, HMSO.

Confederation of British Industry (1976), *The Road to Recovery*, London, CBI.

Coser, L. (1956), *The Functions of Social Conflict*, London, Routledge and Kegan Paul.

Cosyns, J., Loveridge, R. and Child, J. (1981), 'Microelectronics, Organization and the Structuring of Employment in Retailing', in the *International Colloquium on Organization Innovations in the 1980s*, European Group on Organization Studies, University of Strathclyde, March.

Crichton, A. (1968), *Personnel Management in Context*, London, Batsford.

Crouch, C. J. (1979), *The Politics of Industrial Relations*, London, Fontana.

Crozier, M. (1964), *The Bureaucratic Phenomenon*, London, Tavistock.

Bibliography

Currie, R. (1979), *Industrial Politics*, Oxford, Clarendon Press.

Cyert, R. M. and March, J. G. (1963), *A Behavioural Theory of the Firm*, Englewood Cliffs, NJ, Prentice Hall.

Daems, H. and van der Wee, H. (eds) (1974), *The Rise of Managerial Capitalism*, The Hague, Martinus Nijhoff.

Dahrendorf, R. (1959), *Class and Class Conflict in Industrial Society*, London, Routledge and Kegan Paul.

Danaraj, N. (1976), *The Law on the Right to Strike and the Case of South East Asia Firebricks*, Kuala Lumpur, Malaysian Trade Union Congress.

Department of Employment (1978), Manpower Paper No. 15, *Strikes in Britain*, compiled by C. T. B. Smith, R. Clifton, P. Makeham, S. W. Creigh and R. V. Brien, London, HMSO.

Department of Prices and Consumer Protection (1978), *A Review of Monopolies and Mergers Policy*, London, HMSO, May.

Donovan, Lord (Chairman) (1968), *The Report of the Royal Commission on Trade Unions and Employers' Associations, 1965–1968*, Cmnd. 3623, London, HMSO.

Dore, R. (1973), *British Factory – Japanese Factory: The Origins of National Diversity in Industrial Relations*, London, Allen and Unwin.

Dore, R. (1975), *The Diploma Disease*, Hemel Hempstead, Allen and Unwin.

Downs, A. (1957), *An Economic Theory of Democracy*, New York, Harper and Row.

Edwards, R. (1979), *Contested Terrain: The Transformation of the Workplace in the Twentieth Century*, New York, Basic Books, and London, Heinemann.

Festinger, L. (1957), *A Theory of Cognitive Dissonance*, Stanford, Stanford University Press.

Flanders, A. (1965), 'Industrial Relations: What is Wrong with the System', reported in A. Flanders, *Management and Unions*, London, Faber and Faber.

Flanders, A., Pomeranz, R. and Woodward, J. (1968), *Experiment in Industrial Democracy: A Study of the John Lewis Partnership*, London, Faber and Faber.

Fox, A. (1955), 'Industrial Relations in Nineteenth-Century Birmingham', *Oxford Economic Papers*, Vol. 7, Part 1, pp. 57–70.

Fox, A. (1974), *Beyond Contract: Work, Power and Trust Relations*, London, Faber and Faber.

Fox, A. and Flanders, A. (1969), 'The Reform of Collective Bargaining from Donovan to Durkheim', *British Journal of Industrial Relations*, Vol. VII, No. 2, pp. 151–80.

Fransella, F. and Bannister, D. (1977), *A Manual for Repertory Grid Technique*, London, Academic Press.

Friedman, A. L. (1977), *Industry and Labour*, London, Macmillan.

Bibliography

Gallie, D. (1978), *In Search of the New Working Class*, Cambridge, Cambridge University Press.

George, K. D. and Ward, T. S. (1975), *The Structure of Industry in the EEC*, Cambridge, Cambridge University Press.

Gill, C. G. (1974), 'Industrial Relations in a Multi-Plant Organization: Some Considerations', *Industrial Relations Journal*, Vol. 5, No. 4, pp. 22–35.

Godfrey, M. (1977), 'Education, Training and Productivity: A Kenyan Case', *Comparative Education Review*, Vol. 21, No. 1, pp. 29–36.

Goffee, R. E. (1977), 'The Butty System and the Kent Coalfield', *Bulletin of Society for the Study of Labour History*, No. 31, Spring, pp. 41–55.

Goodman, J. *et al.* (1977), 'Focus on Footwear: Formula for Conflict but a Pattern for Peace', *Personnel Management*, Vol. 9, No. 6, June, pp. 23–6.

Gospel, H. F. (1974), 'Employers' Organizations: Their Growth and Function in the British System of Industrial Relations in the Period 1918–1939', University of London, PhD Dissertation.

Granick, D. (1972), *Managerial Comparisons of Four Developed Countries: France, Britain, United States and Russia*, Cambridge (Mass.), MIT Press.

Greaves, M. (1978), *Kenya's Managers*, University of Edinburgh, PhD Dissertation.

Grinyer, P. H. and Norburn, D. (1974), 'Strategic Planning in 21 U.K. Companies', *Long Range Planning*, August, Vol. 7, No. 4, pp. 80–8.

Guest, D. and Fatchett, D. (1974), *Worker Participation: Individual Control and Performance*, London, Institute of Personnel Management.

Hall, R. H., Haas, J. E. and Johnson, N. J. (1967), 'Organizational Size, Complexity and Formalization', *American Sociological Review*, Vol. 32, No. 6, December, pp. 908–12.

Hannah, L. (1980), 'Visible and Invisible Hands in Great Britain', in A. Chandler and H. Daems (eds), *Managerial Hierarchies*, Cambridge (Mass.), Harvard University Press, pp. 41–76.

Hawkins, K. (1971), 'Company Bargaining Problems and Prospects', *British Journal of Industrial Relations*, Vol. IX, No. 2, July, pp. 198–213.

Hebden, J. and Shaw, G. (1977), *Pathways to Participation*, London, Associated Business Programmes.

Hobsbawm, E. J. (1964), *Labouring Men*, London, Weidenfeld and Nicolson.

Hood, S. (1972), 'The Politics of Television' in D. McQuail (ed.), *Sociology of Mass Communication*, Harmondsworth, Penguin.

House of Commons Expenditure Committee (1977), Eleventh Report, Session 1976–7, *The Civil Service*, H.C. 535–1, London, HMSO.

Howard, N. and Teramoto, Y. (1981), 'The Really Important Difference between Japanese and Western Management', *Management International Review*, Vol. 21, No. 3, pp. 19–30.

Hunt, A. (1975), *Management Attitudes and Practices towards Women at Work* (OPCS), London, HMSO.

Bibliography

Hyman, R. (1975), *Industrial Relations: A Marxist Introduction*, London, Macmillan.

Ingham, G. K. (1970), *Size of Industrial Organization and Worker Behaviour*, Cambridge, Cambridge University Press.

Jeffries, R. (1978), *Class, Power and Ideology in Ghana: The Railwaymen of Sekondi*, Cambridge, Cambridge University Press.

Kaplinsky, R. (1978), 'Technical Change and the Multinational Corporation: Some British Multinationals in Kenya', Working Paper No. 228, Nairobi, Institute of Development Studies.

Kelly, G. (1955), *The Psychology of Personal Constructs*, Vols 1 and 2, New York, Norton.

Kerr, C. J., Dunlop, T., Harbinson, F. and Meyers, C. A. (1973), *Industrialism and Industrial Man*, Harmondsworth, Penguin.

Keynes, J. M. (1936) (1961 edn), *The General Theory of Employment, Interest and Money*, London, Macmillan.

King, K. (1977), *The African Artisan*, London, Heinemann Educational Books.

Kitching, J. (1967), 'Why Do Mergers Miscarry?', *Harvard Business Review*, Vol. 45, No. 6, November–December, pp. 84–101.

Kondratiev, N. (1935), 'The Long Waves of Economic Life', *Review of Economic Statistics*, reprinted in *Lloyds Bank Review*, No. 129, July 1968.

Kumar, K. (1978), *Prophecy and Progress: The Sociology of Industrial and Post-Industrial Society*, Harmondsworth, Penguin.

Lawrence, P. R. and Lorsch, J. W. (1967), *Organization and Environment: Managing Differentiation and Integration,* Cambridge (Mass.), Harvard University Press.

Legge, K. (1978), *Power, Innovation and Problem Solving in Personnel Management*, London, McGraw-Hill.

Lindblom, C. (1959), 'The Science of Muddling Through', *Public Administration Review*, Vol. XIX, No. 2, Spring, pp. 79–88.

Littler, C. R. (1981a), 'Deskilling and Changing Structures of Control' in S. Wood (ed.), *The Degradation of Work?*, London, Hutchinson, pp. 122–45.

Littler, C. R. (1981b), *Power and Ideology in Work Organizations: Britain and Japan*, Milton Keynes, Open University, D207, Block 3, Study Section 22.

Loveridge, R. (1973), 'Change and Control in Management Systems', University of Aston in Birmingham, *Inaugural Lecture*, 15 November.

Loveridge, R. (1980), 'What is Participation? A Review of the Literature and Some Methodological Problems', *British Journal of Industrial Relations*, Vol. 18, No. 3, November, pp. 297–317.

Loveridge, R., Lloyd, P. and Broad, G. (1981) *Workplace Control and Codetermination*, London, Report to the Department of Employment.

Loveridge, R. and Mok, A. (1979), *The Theory of Labour Market Segmentation*, The Hague, Martinus Nijhoff.

Bibliography

Lumley, R. (1973), *White-Collar Unionism in Britain*, London, Methuen.

Lupton, T. (1971), *Management and the Social Sciences*, Harmondsworth, Penguin.

Lyons, T., Thurley, K. E. and Wirdenius, H. (1982), 'An International Workshop to Compare Supervisory Systems in Cross Cultural Organization', in *Proceedings of the 10th International Training and Development Conference*, August 1981, Irish Institute of Training and Development, Dublin, April.

McCarthy, W. E. J. and Ellis, N. D. (1973), *Management by Agreement*, London, Hutchinson.

McCormick, B. (1960), 'Managerial Unionism in the Coal Industry', *British Journal of Sociology*, Vol. XI, No. 4, pp. 356–69.

McGivering, I. (1970), 'The Development of Personnel Management', in A. Tillett (ed.), *Management Thinkers*, Harmondsworth, Penguin.

Magaziner, I. C. and Hout, T. M. (1980), *Japanese Industrial Policy*, London, Policy Studies Institute, No. 585.

Mandel, E. (1975), *Late Capitalism*, London, New Left Books.

Mandel, E. (1980), *Long Waves of Capitalist Development*, Cambridge, Cambridge University Press.

Mant, A. (1969), *The Experienced Manager – a Major Resource*, London, British Institute of Management.

March, J. G. and Simon, H. A. (1958), *Organizations*, New York, Wiley.

Marchington, M. (1980), *Responses to Participation at Work*, Farnborough (Hants), Gower.

Marchington, M. and Loveridge, R. (1979), 'Non-Participation: The Management View', *Journal of Management Studies*, Vol. 16, No. 2, pp. 171–84.

Marglin, S. A. (1974), 'What Do Bosses Do? The Origins and Functions of Hierarchy in Capitalist Production', *Review of Radical Political Economics*, Vol. 6, No. 2, pp. 33–60.

Marples, D. (1967), 'Studies of Managers – a Fresh Start', *Journal of Management Studies*, Vol. 4, No. 4, pp. 282–99.

Marris, R. (1964), *The Economics of Management Capitalism*, London, Macmillan.

Marsh, A. I. (1965), *Industrial Relations in Engineering*, Oxford, Pergamon Press.

Marsh, A. I. (1971), 'The Staffing of Industrial Relations Management in Engineering Industry', *Industrial Relations Journal*, Vol. 2, No. 1, Spring, pp. 14–23.

Marsh, A. I., Evans, E. O. and Garcia, P. (1971), *Workplace Industrial Relations in Engineering*, London, Kogan Page Associates.

Marx, K. (1967), *Capital*, Vol. I, New York, International Publishers Co.

Maurice, M., Sorge, A. and Warner, M. (1980), 'Societal Differences in Organizing Manufacturing Units; a Comparison of France, West

Bibliography

Germany and Great Britain', *Organizational Studies,* Vol. 1, No. 1, pp. 59–86.

Meeks, G. (1977), *Disappointing Marriage: A Study of the Gains from Merger,* University of Cambridge, Department of Economics, Occasional Paper No. 51.

Melling, J. (1980), ' "Non-Commissioned Officers": British Employers and Their Supervisory Workers, 1880–1920', *Social History,* Vol. IV, No. 3, pp. 183–221.

Miller, S. S. (1963), *The Management Problems of Diversification,* New York, Wiley.

Mintzberg, H. (1973), *The Nature of Managerial Work,* New York, Harper and Row.

Morgan, M. (1977), 'Britain's Imperial Strategy and the Malayan Labour Movement, 1945–50', *Race and Class,* Vol. 19, No. 1, pp. 29–51.

Muir, J. D. and Brown, J. L. (1974), 'Trade Union Power and the Process of Economic Development', *Relations Industrielles,* Vol. 29, No. 3, pp. 474–95.

National Board for Prices and Incomes (1968a), *Report No. 65,* Cmnd. 3627, London, HMSO.

National Board for Prices and Incomes (1968b), *Report No. 83,* Cmnd. 3772, London, HMSO.

National Economic Development Office (1976), *A Study of U.K. Nationalised Industries,* London, NEDO.

National Economic Development Office (1977), *Engineering Craftsmen: Shortages and Related Problems,* London, HMSO.

Newbould, G. D. (1970), *Management and Merger Activity,* London, Guthstead.

Nichols, T. and Beynon, H. (1977), *Living with Capitalism,* London, Routledge and Kegan Paul.

Niven, M. M. (1967), *Personnel Management 1913–63,* London, IPM.

Njonjo, A. (1971), 'Kenya, The Crisis of Succession and the Issues Behind the Plot', mimeo, Princeton University.

Patrick, H. and Rosovosky, H. (1976), *Asia's New Giant: How the Japanese Economy Works,* Washington, DC, The Brookings Institute.

Peace, A. (1979), *Choice, Class and Conflict: A Study of Southern Nigerian Factory Workers,* Brighton, Harvester Press.

Perrow, C. (1970), *Organizational Analysis: A Sociological View,* London, Tavistock.

Pollard, S. (1968), *The Genesis of Modern Management,* Harmondsworth, Penguin.

Prais, S. J. (1976), *The Evolution of Giant Firms in Britain,* Cambridge, Cambridge University Press.

Pratten, C. F. (1976), *Labour Productivity Differentials within International Companies,* Cambridge, Cambridge University Press.

235

Bibliography

Pratten, C. F. and Dean, R. M. (1965), *The Economies of Large-Scale Production in British Industry*, Cambridge, Cambridge University Press.

Pugh, D. S. and Hickson, D. J. (1968), 'The Comparative Study of Organizations' in D. Pym (ed.), *Industrial Society*, Harmondsworth, Penguin, pp. 374–96.

Pugh, D. S., Hickson, D. J. and Hinings, C. R. (1969), 'An Empirical Taxonomy of Structures of Work Organizations', *Administrative Science Quarterly*, Vol. 14, No. 1, pp. 115–26.

Purcell, J. *et al.* (1978), 'Power from Technology: Computer Staff and Industrial Relations', *Personnel Review*, Vol. 7, No. 1, Winter, pp. 31–9.

Purcell, J. and Smith, R. (eds) (1979), *The Control of Work*, London, Macmillan.

Ramsay, H. (1977), 'Cycles of Control – Workers' Participation in Sociological and Historical Perspective', *Sociology*, Vol. 11, No. 3, pp. 481–506.

Reader, W. J. (1975), *Imperial Chemical Industries*, Vol. 2, London, Oxford University Press.

Reeves, T. K. and Woodward, J. (1970), 'The Study of Managerial Control' in J. Woodward (ed.), *Industrial Organization: Behaviour and Control*, Oxford, Oxford University Press, pp. 31–56.

Renold, C. G. (1950), *Joint Consultation over Thirty Years*, London, Allen and Unwin.

Richbell, S. (1979), 'Participative Design and Organisational Sub-Groups', *Industrial Relations Journal*, Vol. 10, No. 1, pp. 40–50.

Robinson, J. (1933), *The Economics of Imperfect Competition*, Cambridge, Cambridge University Press.

Roll, E. (1930), *An Early Experiment in Industrial Organization: Being a History of the Firm of Boulton and Watt 1775–1805*, London, Longman.

Rudner, M. (1973), 'Malaysian Labour in Transition: Labour Policy and Trade Unionism, 1955–63', *Journal of Modern Asian Studies*, Vol. 7, pp. 21–45.

Salaman, G. (1979), *Work Organizations: Resistance and Control*, London, Longman.

Sandbrook, R. (1975), *Proletarians and African Capitalism: The Kenya Case*, Cambridge, Cambridge University Press.

Sargent Florence, P. (1948; rev. edn 1961), *The Logic of British and American Industry*, London, Routledge and Kegan Paul.

Schloss, D. F. (1892), *Methods of Industrial Remuneration*, London, Williams and Norgate.

Schumpeter, J. A. (1939), *Business Cycles: A Theoretical, Historical and Statistical Analysis of the Capitalist Process*, New York, McGraw-Hill.

Schumpeter, J. A. (1943), *Capitalism, Socialism and Democracy*, New York, Harper.

Seglow, P. (1978), *Trade Unionism in Television – A Case Study in the Development of White-Collar Militancy*, Farnborough (Hants), Saxon House.

236

Bibliography

Silverman, D. (1970), *The Theory of Organizations*, London, Heinemann.

Simon, H. A. (1957), *Administrative Behaviour*, New York, Macmillan.

Simpson, D. H. (1980a), 'How Control Has Shifted', *Journalism Studies Review*, No. 5, July.

Simpson, D. H. (1980b), 'The Industrial Relations of Managers' in M. J. F. Poole and R. Mansfield (eds), *Managerial Roles in Industrial Relations*, Farnborough (Hants), Gower, pp. 102–15.

Simpson, D. H. (1981), *Commercialisation of the Regional Press: The Development of Monopoly, Profit and Control*, Aldershot, Gower.

Slater, P. (ed.) (1977), *Dimensions of Intrapersonal Space*, London, Wiley.

Smith, A. (1776), *An Inquiry into the Nature and Causes of the Wealth of Nations*, London.

Social Policy Research (1975), *Worker Participation in Britain*, London, Financial Times Ltd.

Steiner, G. A. and Miner, J. B. (1977), *Management Policy and Strategy, Text, Readings and Cases*, London, Collier Macmillan.

Stenson, M. R. (1970), *Industrial Conflict in Malaya: Prelude to the Communist Revolt*, London, Oxford University Press.

Stewart, R. (1970), *The Reality of Organizations*, London, Pan.

Stinchcombe, A. L. (1957), 'Bureaucratic and Craft Administration of Production: a Comparative Study', *Administrative Science Quarterly*, Vol. 4, No. 2, pp. 168–87.

Supple, B. (1974), 'Aspects of Private Investment Strategy in Britain' in H. Daems and H. van der Wee (eds), *The Rise of Managerial Capitalism*, The Hague, Martinus Nijhoff, pp. 73–95.

Taylor, A. J. (1960), 'The Subcontract System in the British Coal Industry' in L. S. Pressnell (ed.), *Studies in the Industrial Revolution*, London, Athlone Press, pp. 215–35.

Terry, P. (1977), 'The Organization of Management', *Management Today*, November.

Thompson, J. D. (1967), *Organization in Action*, New York, McGraw-Hill.

Thurley, K. (1975), *The Treatment of Management in Industrial Relations Studies: A New Start?*, London, London School of Economics.

Thurley, K., Reitsperger, W., Trevor, M. and Worm, P. (1980), *The Development of Personnel in Japanese Enterprise in Great Britain*, London, International Centre for Economics and Related Disciplines, London School of Economics.

Tilly, R. (1974), 'The Growth of Large-Scale Enterprise in Germany Since the Middle of the Nineteenth Century' in H. Daems and H. van der Wee (eds), *The Rise of Managerial Capitalism*, The Hague, Martinus Nijhoff, Louven University Press, pp. 145–69.

Timperley, S. R. and Osbaldeston, M. D. (1975), 'The Professionalisation Process: An Aspiring Occupational Organisation', *Sociological Review*, Vol. 23, pp. 607–27.

Bibliography

Tunstall, J. (1971), *Journalists at Work*, London, Constable.

Turner, G. (1973), *The Leyland Papers*, London, Pan.

Turner, H. A., Roberts, G. and Roberts, D. (1977), *Management Characteristics and Labour Conflict*, Cambridge, Cambridge University Press.

Walker, K. F. (1975), 'Workers' Participation in Management: Concepts and Reality' in B. Barrett, E. Rhodes and J. Beishon (eds), *Industrial Relations and the Wider Society: Aspects of Interaction*, London, Collier Macmillan, pp. 434–58.

Walton, R. E. and McKersie, R. B. (1965), *A Behavioral Theory of Labor Negotiations*, New York, McGraw-Hill.

Watson, T. J. (1977), *The Personnel Managers*, London, Routledge and Kegan Paul.

Webb, S. (1917), *The Works Manager Today*, London, Longman.

Williams, A. (1915), *Life in a Railway Factory*, London, Duckworth.

Williamson, O. E. (1975), *Markets and Hierarchies: Analysis and Antitrust Implications*, New York, Free Press.

Williamson, O. E. (1980), 'The Organization of Work: A Comparative International Assessment', *Journal of Economic Behaviour and Organization*, Vol. 1, No. 1, pp. 5–38.

Wilmott, J. E. (1951), *A Short History of the Firm of Thomas Walker and Son Ltd.*, Birmingham (privately printed).

Winkler, J. (1974), 'The Ghost at the Bargaining Table: Directors and Industrial Relations', *British Journal of Industrial Relations*, Vol. XXII, No. 2, July, pp. 191–212.

Wood, S. (1979), 'A Reappraisal of the Contingency Approach to Organization', *Journal of Management Studies*, Vol. 16, No. 3, pp. 334–54.

Wood, S. (1980) 'Corporate Strategy and Organizational Studies' in D. Dunkerley and G. Salaman (eds), *Organizational Studies Yearbook*, London, Routledge and Kegan Paul, pp. 52–71.

Wood, S. (1982), 'The Study of Management in Industrial Relations', *Industrial Relations Journal*, Vol. 13, No. 2, pp. 51–61.

Woodward, J. (1965), *Industrial Organization: Theory and Practice*, Oxford, Oxford University Press.

Woodward, J. (1970), *Industrial Organization: Behaviour and Control*, Oxford, Oxford University Press.

Yoshino, M. Y. (1975), 'Emerging Multi-national Enterprises' in E. F. Vogel (ed.), *Modern Japanese Organization and Decision-Making*, Berkeley, University of California.

Zeira, Y., Harari, E. and Nundi, D. I. (1975), 'Some Structural and Cultural Factors in Ethnocentric Multinational Cooperatives and Employee Morale', *Journal of Management Studies*, Vol. 12, No. 1, pp. 66–82.

Index

Index

Index

Index

European Social Charter

Collected texts (3rd edition)

Council of Europe Publishing

French edition:

Charte sociale européenne – Recueil de textes, 3ᵉ édition

ISBN 92-871-4717-5

Cover design: Graphic Design Workshop of the Council of Europe
Published by: Council of Europe Publishing
Layout: PAO Unit, Council of Europe

ISBN 92-871-4718-3 ✓
© Council of Europe, March 2002,
1997 (1st edition), September 2000 (2nd edition)
F-67075 Strasbourg Cedex
Printed in Germany by Koelblin-Fortuna-Druck